The Defeat
of Rome

The Defeat of Rome

Crassus, Carrhae and the Invasion of the East

Gareth C. Sampson

Pen & Sword
MILITARY

First published in Great Britain in 2008
and reprinted in this format in 2015 by
Pen & Sword Military
an imprint of
Pen & Sword Books Ltd
47 Church Street
Barnsley
South Yorkshire
S70 2AS

Copyright © Gareth C. Sampson 2008, 2015

ISBN 978 1 47382 804 9

Typeset in Ehrhardt by Malcolm Bates, Auldgirth, Dumfriesshire

Printed and bound by CPI Group (Ltd), Croydon, CR0 4YY

Pen & Sword Books Ltd incorporates the imprints of Pen & Sword
Archaeology, Atlas, Aviation, Battleground, Discovery, Family History,
History, Maritime, Military, Naval, Politics, Railways, Select, Social History,
Transport, True Crime, and Claymore Press, Frontline Books, Leo Cooper,
Praetorian Press, Remember When, Seaforth Publishing and Wharncliffe.

For a complete list of Pen & Sword titles please contact
PEN & SWORD BOOKS LIMITED
47 Church Street, Barnsley, South Yorkshire, S70 2AS, England
E-mail: enquiries@pen-and-sword.co.uk
Website: www.pen-and-sword.co.uk

Contents

The Rise of Two Empires

The War

Appendices

To Alex, my wife, with love.

Acknowledgements

This book would not have been possible without Rupert Harding of Pen & Sword Books, whose assistance and comments have been invaluable. Thanks go out to Pen & Sword as a whole for commissioning and assisting with the production of this study.

My membership of the Department of Classics and Ancient History, at the University of Manchester and the John Rylands Library, has given me the time and the facilities to work on this project, so my thanks goes out to them. Everyone at Manchester does a difficult job in increasingly trying circumstances.

I would also like to thank the British School at Athens, for allowing me to stay there for a few weeks of glorious peace and quiet, which allowed me to finish this book. They remain an oasis of calm in a mad academic world.

On a personal note, thanks must go out to my parents, who put up with my bizarre choice of career. Special thanks must be given to my wonderful fiancée Alex, who has had to put up with the project for the last year and has borne the brunt of my obsession with it, as well as the bulk of initial proof reading. Without her I would be lost.

As always thanks go out to the guys in, or from, the Department at Manchester, for keeping me sane and still interested in academia: (in alphabetical order) Arran, Gary, Greg, James, Old Ian, Sam, Young Ian. Also Peter, for his interest in the topic and chats on various aspects, and Carsten for the last-minute info on Augustan monuments. Sincerest thanks must also go out to Liz Diamond-Jones for her excellent artwork depicting the Roman and Parthian warriors.

Finally, as always, my respects to Tim Cornell, without whose supervision I would not be in academia to write this book.

List of Illustrations

Maps

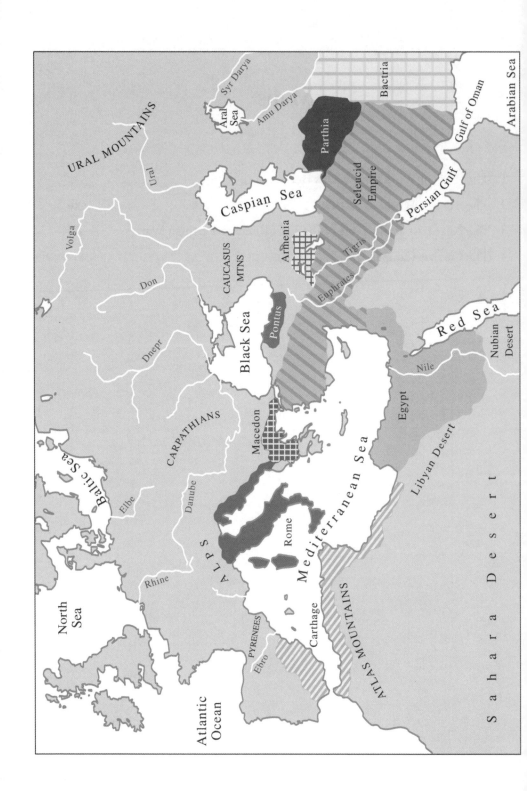

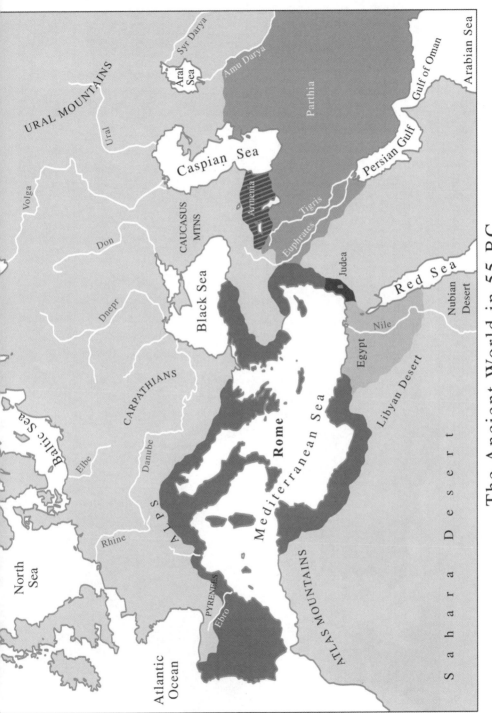

The Ancient World in 55 BC.

The Near East at the time of the First Romano-Parthian War.

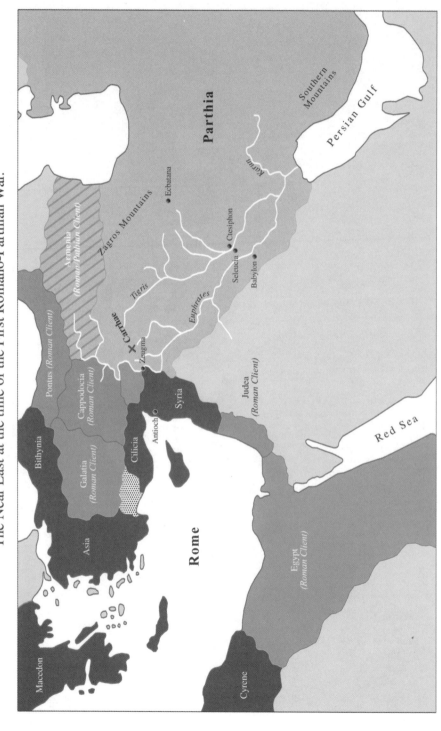

The Carrhae Campaign.

Introduction

In the summer of the year which now equates to the year 53 B.C., two great armies faced each other on the dusty plains of northern Mesopotamia. The battle which followed was not only the first time these two opponents had clashed, but was to set in motion nearly seven hundred years of warfare between these two empires, which dominated the ancient world. On the one side was the army of the Roman Republic, a force of over 40,000 strong, intent on annexing the region to Rome's growing empire. They were led by Marcus Licinius Crassus, one of Rome's most powerful politicians and an experienced general, who was the man who had defeated Spartacus and his slave army. On the other lay a force of no more than 10,000 cavalrymen from the Parthian Empire, led by a Parthian nobleman known only as Surenas.

This battle was no random encounter, but was the culmination of a two hundred year process which had seen both Rome and Parthia carve out mighty empires from the Hellenistic powers which had dominated the ancient world since the time of Alexander the Great. By 53 B.C. these two empires were the ancient world's two great superpowers, which for a generation had been edging closer to each other, both territorially and militarily. The prize they fought for in the short term was domination of the Middle East (modern Syria and Iraq), but in the longer term both strove to achieve the universal empire that had eluded both the Persians and Alexander himself. It was Rome, under the domination of the First Triumvirate, which had made the first move and had invaded Mesopotamia (modern Iraq), intent on annexing the region and humbling Rome's only superpower rival.

Given their seemingly invincible military reputation and massive numerical superiority (over four to one), victory for Rome seemed assured, with the Parthians seemingly destined to join the growing list of states that had already fallen to Rome; Spain, Gaul, Africa, Greece, Asia Minor and Syria and Judea. However, at the dusty plains of Carrhae, after an afternoon's fighting, the near-impossible occurred when the armies of the Roman Republic were comprehensively defeated and slaughtered. Out of 40,000 men barely a quarter made it back to Roman territory, with over 20,000 dead and 10,000 taken prisoner. For Rome, it was one of the worst defeats they had suffered since the time of Hannibal.

In just one afternoon, the myth of Roman invincibility had been shattered and the seemingly inexorable spread of the Roman Empire across the ancient world was brought to a halt. For the next seven hundred years, the world was divided between the two empires of east and west, with the Euphrates and Mesopotamia (Iraq) on the edge of two worlds and two cultures. Furthermore, amongst the dead was Crassus himself, who was one of the three Roman politicians who dominated the late Republic as part of the First Triumvirate. Without him, the other two members (Cnaeus Pompeius Magnus and Caius Iulius Caesar) almost immediately fell out and plunged the Republic into a devastating Civil War; a clash which the destroyed the Republic and ushered in the Roman Empire.

Therefore, it is clear that this battle was and still is of paramount importance to the history of the ancient world. Up until now, this area has been largely neglected, for a number of reasons. This study intends to set this balance right and examine not just the battle itself; analysing just how the Romans were so comprehensively beaten, despite such numerical superiority, but to examine the whole campaign and the First Romano-Parthian War in terms of the clash between these two great empires. Despite defeating the Romans and halting their spread across the eastern world, today the Parthians remains a little known civilisation outside of specialist scholarship. Yet for nearly five hundred years they were one of the two great civilisations of the ancient world and were an equal to Rome, in both territory and culture. Therefore, the Parthian civilisation too needs to be re-examined and brought back into the light in order to see just who they were and how they managed to rival and then humble Rome.

This study comprises of two sections. Firstly, it will examine the background to this momentous clash, by looking at the rise of the Roman and Parthian Empires, as well as that of Marcus Crassus himself. For too long, the Parthians have been seen as nothing more than a one dimensional enemy whom Crassus lost to through his own incompetence; and a defeat which had little wider effect. However, such a view is merely the legacy of wounded Roman pride. The Parthians had an empire comparable to that of Rome and were not merely passive opponents waiting for Roman domination. Likewise, Crassus was no one dimensional, avaricious bungler, whose riches and ambition outstripped his military prowess. The defeat was a shocking one and one that exploited flaws in the Roman military and political systems. Only by understanding this background can we appreciate the battle, and the wider war itself.

The second section will examine the campaign itself, in terms of its details and significance, as well as provide an in-depth analysis of the actual Battle of Carrhae, in terms of formations and tactics used, and the various stages of the fighting. This section will finish with an examination of the subsequent events of the First Romano-Parthian War and examine the considerable implications that this defeat had, not just for Rome, but for the ancient world in general. By the end of this work the reader should have a clearer impression of why this battle was one of the greatest of the ancient world and how modern day civilisations have been shaped and affected by it.

When this book was originally commissioned, the region was in the midst of the aftermath of the American led invasion of Iraq. Seven years later the region that was being fought over 2,000 years ago is again the scene of bloody warfare in both Syria and Iraq. Although today the region is no longer an arena for superpower clashes (between the Roman and Parthian / Persian Empires), the current sectarian warfare traces its roots back to the rise of Islam, which swept away these two mighty ancient empires, whose boundaries were set by events at Carrhae that day. Thus we can see in modern day events the tragic echoes of past conflicts.

Since this work was first published, there has been an increase in the number of books and articles studying both the Parthian Empire in its own right and its conflicts with Rome. The bibliography has been updated to reflect the key recent works. Aside from this, the text remains the same as the original edition, aside from some minor typographical corrections.

Gareth C Sampson
2014

The Rise of
Two Empires

Chapter 1

A New World Order:
The Roman Conquest of the East

In order to fully analyse the nature of the clash that took place at Carrhae in 53 BC, we must understand the seemingly inexorable spread of the Roman Republic from Italy across the whole of the eastern Mediterranean. Although the Roman Republic eventually conquered Spain, Gaul, Eastern Europe, and North Africa, it is the conquest of the eastern civilisations of Greece, Asia Minor and the Middle East that are the most important, as they represented the most advanced of the ancient civilisations. Prior to the rise of Rome, ancient civilisations developed in the east, spreading from Mesopotamia and Egypt, and included such societies as the Egyptians, Babylonians, Assyrians, Hittites, Persians and Greeks. The history of the ancient world prior to Rome had been made by these great peoples. Massive advances made in the fields of politics, warfare, culture, trade, medicine, architecture and exploration had led to the development of societies with a level of sophistication that was comparable to the most recent centuries of the modern world.

This process reached a peak with the campaigns of Alexander the Great, when virtually all the races of the eastern Mediterranean and the Middle East were united in a single kingdom that stretched from Greece to India. Throughout the rise of the civilised east, the western Mediterranean was composed of barbarian tribes, interspersed with Greek colonies on the coastlines. Italy stood at the inter-section of these two differing worlds of the barbarous west and the civilised east, which was reflected in its ethnic composition. There were numerous indigenous tribes, most notably the Latin and Samnite races dwelling in the middle of Italy. Northern Italy was occupied first by Etruscan invaders and later by Gaulish ones, whilst the south was composed of Greek city-states, founded by settlers from mainland Greece. Thus Italy and the races within occupied the periphery of the ancient world.

When looking at the history of Rome, this fact must always been borne in mind. The hub of events and civilisation was Greece and the Near East, with events in Italy of little note. However, whilst the world's attention was focussed on the exploits of Alexander, events were taking place in Italy that were to have serious implications for the rest of the ancient world. For the first few centuries of its existence, Rome was an unremarkable city. Founded in the mid-eighth century (753 BC according to tradition[1]) as a monarchy, Rome spent the first four centuries of her existence engaging in what were the typical activities of an ancient city-state, namely internal squabbles over the system of government and warring with their near neighbours for control of the local lands. Roman conquests from the eighth to the fourth centuries BC had been unremarkable and by the mid-fourth century, Rome was merely the dominant state in the Latin area of Italy; so far an unremarkable fate for an unremarkable city. Yet behind this mediocrity lay a foundation for greatness.

Sources for Roman History

There are numerous surviving sources which detail the history of the period sketched out below. For the early Roman period, we have the histories of Livy[2] and Dionysius of Halicarnassus, though both were written in the late first century BC / first century AD and so are open to question over their accuracy[3]. For the period of eastern expansion we have the histories of Livy[4] and Polybius (who was a Greek fighting against Rome in the second century BC[5]). Plutarch, a first century AD Graeco-Roman writer, has a number of biographies of Roman generals from the period in question.[6] Appian, another Graeco-Roman writer, from the second century AD wrote a number of histories of the Roman wars; in particular, the Syrian wars, the Mithridatic wars and the civil wars. These are our principal histories for this chapter, though there are a number of lesser ones, which will be encountered as we progress. For more detail on these writers and their works, see appendices two and three.

The Roman System of Government and the Military

The city of Rome was ruled by an aristocracy, who in c. 508 BC had overthrown their king and established what is now called a republic.[7] Though that word comes from the Latin *res publica* – the public concern or good – the Romans always referred to their system of government as 'the Senate and People of Rome', or SPQR for short. In theory the two central planks of this system were the aristocracy, whose views were expressed through the Senate, and the people, who were collected together in electoral assemblies. Under the Republic's unwritten constitution, the Senate was merely an advisory council, with all laws being voted into existence by the people's assemblies. In reality the Senate controlled all proposals that were put before the people, who only had limited rights of proposing legislation. The senior magistrates of Rome and the de-facto heads of state were the consuls; two men elected by the people (from the aristocracy) for a period of one year only, who controlled both military and civilian matters (generals and prime ministers rolled into one).

In terms of military organisation this system had both benefits and faults. The major benefit was that it gave Rome a number of military commanders to operate under and this encouraged warfare and the gaining of glory, which were central tenets of the Roman aristocratic ethos. This allowed Rome to field a number of different armies at once. For a time (444–367 BC) the system of having two consuls a year was alternated with a special office known as the military tribunate with consular power, of which there could be as many as six a year. Thus one year might have two consuls, whilst the next could have six consular tribunes, dependant upon Rome's military needs. The major fault of this system was that having multiple commanders sometimes resulted in disagreement and division and the change of commanders every year led to a lack of consistency (though as time wore on commanders were allowed to remain in the field until the campaign had been concluded).

One key point needs to be made about the nature of the Roman army throughout the majority of this period, namely that it was a citizen militia, raised from the Roman citizens of Italy and their Italian allies. Each army was raised on a needs-only basis, campaigned for a season (spring and summer) and were demobilised for the autumn. As Rome's military commitments increased then so did the length of service, but the legionaries were still dismissed when the campaign was over. In other words, Rome had no standing army or professional body of soldiers, but given Rome's near-constant warfare throughout its early existence, this did lead to the creation of an aggressive and experienced citizen body of men.

The Foundations of Rome's Greatness

In the fourth century BC, two major aspects of the Roman system changed, one internal and one external. As with all city-states in the ancient world, there were internal political divisions over access to power. Although the citizenry could vote for proposed laws in the various assemblies[8], this process was controlled by the elite group of the aristocratic families known as the patricians, whose claim to power was based on ancestral descent from the original founding families from the time of the kings. Since the patrician families seized control of the Roman state in c.508 BC, they had been under pressure from those citizens who had been excluded from political power. These men formed a group known as the plebeians, though eventually this term came to be used for everyone who wasn't a patrician. The year 367 BC saw this struggle between the two groups (known as the 'struggle of the orders') achieve a breakthrough, with plebeians being admitted to the consulship, which became the sole chief political and military magistracy, with the consular tribunate being abolished. Thus the Roman command structure of two consuls became permanent and Rome had a far greater pool of talent from which to draw the best generals.

In 338 BC, Rome achieved such an unassailable dominance amongst the Latin city-states of central Italy that she was able to abolish the Latin League (the confederacy of Latin city-states of which Rome was the head), and replace it with a system of alliances that tied each of the city-states directly to Rome herself. It was this decision more than any other that laid the foundation for Rome's subsequent military success. The basis of each of these alliances between Rome and the other cities was that they would supply Rome with soldiers when called upon to fight for her. This essentially gave Rome an unlimited supply of military manpower and far more soldiers than a small city-state could supply from within her own citizenry. Rome's population in this period was upward of 250,000 citizens, of whom only a percentage would be of the right age and sex for military service. The additional allied manpower meant that Rome could regularly field armies of 40,000 plus and in emergences upward of 90,000 men.[9]

This new military manpower translated itself into a series of wars of conquest within Italy, most notably between the 330s and 290s BC when Rome fought a series of three wars against the other major Italian power, the Samnites. These ended in Roman victory and Samnite subjugation, followed by alliance to Rome. Thus, by the 290s BC Rome controlled the central Italian states. The next obvious targets for their attentions were the Greek city-states of southern Italy.

Given the massive disparity in military strength between Rome and these states, the Greek cities could not have hoped to stop Roman aggression. However, these city-states had long adopted a policy of seeking help from mainland Greece. During this period, Greece had seen the dream of a united 'world' civilisation under Alexander the Great end with his death in 323 BC. This was followed by the bloody break-up of his empire as his generals fought a protracted series of wars that saw the vast territories of the ancient world carved up between three major superpowers, along with a number of lesser powers.

One of these lesser kingdoms was that of Epirus (modern Albania) which was ruled by a young adventurous monarch, King Pyrrhus. It was to him that the Greek city-states of southern Italy turned when they needed assistance in fighting off Rome, and it was Pyrrhus who was the first enemy from the more advanced states of the eastern Mediterranean that the Romans faced. In many ways this first contact between the two civilisations set the tone for the future conflicts between them.

First Contact – The Pyrrhic Wars (280–275 BC)

The conflict between the Roman Republic and Pyrrhus was the first major interaction between the Greek civilisations of the east and the Roman one of the west, and its conclusion saw the Greek awareness of Rome reach a new height. It was also this invasion from the east that helped to set the tone for the next two hundred years of Roman foreign policy.[10]

The various Greek city-states of southern Italy were a loose collection of independent states which ranged from minor settlements to great cities. Of these, perhaps the most powerful was the city of Tarentum, which was the centre of the Italian woollen and ceramic trade and possessed a large army (for a city-state) of 15,000, along with a strong navy. Throughout the period of Roman expansion, Tarentum had enjoyed cordial relations with Rome, but in the 330s BC began a policy of inviting Greek kings over from the mainland to fight on behalf of the loose confederation of southern Italian Greek city-states. In 334 BC, King Alexander of Epirus, a brother in law of Alexander the Great himself, arrived in Italy in a campaign to protect these cities from the raids of their neighbouring Italian states. In this period, these enemies did not include Rome and the two parties concluded a non-aggression pact, which included a Roman naval exclusion from the Gulf of Otranto.

King Alexander's campaign, though initially successful, ended with his betrayal and death. He was followed in 303 BC by Cleonymus of Sparta and in 298 by Agathocles of Syracuse. Thus Tarentum had long established a pattern of inviting mainland Greek assistance whenever their borders were threatened, and Italy proved to be an exotic diversion for many a Greek king who was tiring of the wars and politics of the mainland.

The recent wars against the Samnites had brought Rome to the borders of the Greek cities and in 282 BC the Romans intervened in southern Italy to assist the Greek city of Thurii from raiders. This assistance took the form of a small land force and a small naval detachment that entered the Gulf of Otranto. It is doubtful that the Romans even remembered their earlier pact with Alexander of Epirus on this point, but the Tarentines interpreted it, quite understandably, as a blatant act of Roman aggression and retaliated swiftly, attacking and driving off both the land and naval force.

At the time the Romans had several other campaigns in other parts of Italy and merely responded by sending an embassy to Tarentum to seek reparation. This was soundly rebuffed and Tarentum once again turned to their usual policy and sought military assistance from the mainland. Once again they turned to the kingdom of Epirus and its current king, Pyrrhus. At this time Pyrrhus had the reputation of being one of the great generals of his day, who had been engaged in the wars that still raged in the Greek world following the death of Alexander.[11]

Weary of the fighting in Greece he eagerly sought a fresh challenge and arrived with 25,000 battle-hardened Greek veterans.

Thus the Romans found themselves at war with a general from the Greek world for the first time. This conflict was to be an instructive one all round. In 280 BC the Romans and the Greeks met in battle at Heraclea, where a force of 20,000 Romans was soundly defeated by Pyrrhus. Although the Roman legionaries held their own against Pyrrhus' pikemen, the Roman cavalry proved to be no match for his elephants. This victory saw the other Greek cities of southern Italy join his cause, along with the Lucanians and the Samnites.

The resultant push into central Italy, however, soon revealed the strength of the Roman alliance system, as Rome's older Latin allies remained loyal and soon provided Rome with fresh armies, forcing Pyrrhus to retreat back into southern Italy. These were the keys lessons that Hannibal learnt later in the century, but ones that he could not overcome. In 279 BC the Romans were sufficiently strong to give battle once again, this time at Asculum. Both sides numbered 40,000–50,000 and again Pyrrhus emerged victorious, though with heavy casualties.

Pyrrhus then attempted to negotiate with the Roman Senate to secure the freedom and security of the Greek city-states of south Italy, but his overtures were vehemently rejected. Instead Rome reached a new agreement with the North African power of Carthage, which was steadily advancing her empire through Sicily. In response, Pyrrhus moved his campaigning to Sicily to fight the Carthaginians in 278 BC. His absence saw the Roman armies advance into southern Italy and defeat many of his allies, forcing him to return to mainland Italy in 276 BC. Upon his return he again gave battle at Maleventum, but was defeated by two consular armies. This proved to be the end of the war for Pyrrhus as he returned to Epirus and left a garrison at Tarentum. By 272 BC he had tired of his Italian excursion and recalled the garrison leaving the city to the Romans. By the end of that year the Romans had overrun Tarentum and re-conquered the Samnites to become masters of the Italian peninsula.

This war was an important milestone for the Romans in particular, and the Mediterranean world at large, for a number of reasons. Rome had defeated a Greek incursion by one of the best commanders of the day and subjugated the Greek city-states of southern Italy. In doing so Rome had gained the attention of the other Mediterranean powers. The treaty with Carthage in 278 BC was followed by the establishment of diplomatic relations with the kingdom of Egypt in 273 BC, one of the 'big three' of the Mediterranean superpowers (the other two being Macedon and the Seleucid empire).

In addition, the Romans had adapted to Greek battle tactics, having met elephants in battle for the first time, and had eventually gained a victory over Pyrrhus. It was Pyrrhus himself who noted that the superiority of the Romans was not necessarily their ability to win victories, but their amazing ability to recover from losses in terms of manpower. In the ancient world, few states could recover from losing an army of 20,000 men in less than a generation. The Romans, thanks to their unique system of alliances (which placed an obligation on their allies to provide Rome with troops), could recover from these losses and actually outmatch their enemies. As Pyrrhus discovered after his first two battles, although he had emerged victorious and had inflicted more casualties upon the Romans, he could not sustain his own losses, as he could not replace his men as quickly as the Romans could. This led to his famous statement that he is alleged to have made, which provided the modern world with the concept of a Pyrrhic victory: 'If we are victorious in one more battle with the Romans, we shall be utterly ruined'.[12]

The Quiet Wars (275–200 BC)

First & Second Illyrian Wars (229–228, 219 BC)
First Macedonian War (216–205 BC)

Although you might have expected this initial conflict between Rome and the eastern powers to have been followed by a greater Roman involvement in the Greek world, this did not take place until later in the third century BC and then only on a limited scale. The key reasons for this were the two monumental wars Rome fought with Carthage: the Punic Wars (264–241 & 218–201 BC), fought for control of Sicily, Spain and ultimately the whole of the western Mediterranean. Although these wars lie outside of the scope of this work, they contained within them increasing interaction between the affairs of Rome and those of the Greek world, which can best be labelled as representing a 'quiet war'.

The aftermath of the First Punic War between Rome and Carthage had seen Rome gain control of the islands of Sardinia and Corsica, which were reorganised into Rome's first overseas provinces, as well as a dominant role in Sicily. This, and the previous dismantling of the Tarentine fleet, led Rome to consider her territorial waters for the first time, a task made all the easier by the construction of a permanent Roman fleet (another legacy of the First Punic War). With her western and southern coastal waters secure, Rome's attention turned to the Adriatic, where the cities and towns of the Illyrian coast (modern Croatia) had united under one ruler, Queen Teuta, and had taken up piracy as a major occupation.

Rome's initial response was to send an embassy (in 230 BC) to demand a halt to the piracy. When one of the envoys was murdered, however, Rome responded by sending both consuls to the Adriatic with a well-equipped army and a fleet.

The Illyrian pirates were soon swept aside and Rome established a protectorate over the towns of the Illyrian coast. This protectorate was not direct rule, nor was a formal treaty of alliance established, but for the first time towns on the Greek side of the Adriatic came under the influence of the Roman Republic. As part of a diplomatic offensive, the Romans sent embassies to the cities of Athens and Corinth and the Achaean and Aetolian federations (the two main alliances of mainland Greek city-states) to assure them of Rome's good intentions. Aside from formal courtesies, Rome was admitted into the Isthmian Games, a formal recognition of Rome's entry into the 'civilised' Greek world.

In 219 BC this protectorate over the Illyrian towns was challenged by an adventurer named Demetrius of Pharos, who had been an ally of Rome in the First Illyrian War. The resulting war was little more than a policing action, but it had one important consequence, as the soon-defeated Demetrius fled to Philip V of Macedon, the nearest of the big three superpowers.

On coming to the throne of Macedon in 221 BC, Philip V inherited a strong position. Macedon not only comprised the actual territory of the Kingdom of Macedon itself (see map 1), but operated a protectorate over mainland Greece as head of the Hellenic Confederacy, a position backed by the largest army in the Greek mainland. With Greece under his control and deadlock in the political and military situation in Asia Minor and the Aegean, Philip could afford to turn his attention to the emerging power of Rome. In 218 BC, not only did Demetrius of Pharos flee to his court and attract his ear, but Rome began the Second Punic War with Carthage, a war noted for the invasion of Italy in 218 by the famous Carthaginian general Hannibal. By 216 BC Hannibal had inflicted four defeats on Rome, including the devastating ambush at Lake Trasimene and the catastrophic defeat at Cannae, where the Romans lost upward of 50,000 men.[13]

Seeing Rome's plight, Philip took a decision that would ultimately turn out to have a disastrous effect on the Greek world and Macedon in particular, namely to set himself against Rome. Initially he started out on a small scale, with a plan to restore Demetrius to his Illyrian base and thus acquire a naval presence in the Adriatic for Macedon. When the Romans learned of this plan, however, they sent a fleet into the Adriatic (despite the situation in Italy) and forced Philip to abandon the scheme.

His next plan took on a greater boldness when he conducted an alliance between Macedon and Hannibal. Hannibal must have hoped that this would open up a second front against Rome and provide him with much-needed reinforcements. Philip's motives are less clear; certainly he wanted the expulsion of the Romans from Illyria (to be replaced by Macedonian influence no doubt), but whether he wanted to expand Macedonian influence over the Greek cities of southern Italy is not clear.

Philip's intervention sparked off what is now known as the First Macedonian War between Rome and Philip V, which was little more than a phoney war in military terms, but would have long-lasting political implications. The Romans were too occupied with fighting the Carthaginians to give the matter their full attention and, aside from deploying a force in Illyria, relied upon acting through other agents. They embarked upon a series of alliances with states that were enemies of Macedon, including the Aetolian League in Greece and the kingdom of Pergamum in Asia Minor, which led to fighting in Greece between Philip and the Aetolians. By 206 BC the Aetolians had come to terms with Philip and Rome also concluded a formal treaty with him in 205 BC, by which time the Carthaginians were on the back-foot and this so-called war was a distraction. Under the treaty Philip did acquire an outlet on the Adriatic coast, but at the cost of enduring Roman enmity and disunity amongst the mainland Greeks. For the Romans, although they had neither lost nor acquired territory (they still had their protectorate over Illyria), they had defended their presence in mainland Greece and had been drawn into the world of Hellenistic power politics, finding allies in both Greece and Asia Minor.

This short period of phoney war had seen little in the way of serious military action, but it had drawn Rome from the periphery of the Hellenistic world into a war with one of the big three and into military and political alliances with other Hellenistic states. This First Macedonian War may have been a non-event which ended in a stalemate, but Rome had been completely victorious in the western Mediterranean, with Carthage reduced to a minor city-state. This left Rome unchallenged in the west and with a new enemy in the east. Thus the foundation had been laid for the overthrow of the Hellenistic status quo and the establishment of a new world order.

The Liberation of Greece (200–188 BC)

Second Macedonian War (200–196 BC)
Spartan War (195–194 BC)
First Seleucid War (192–188 BC)

For the Romans the Second Punic War had been a life or death struggle, with Hannibal roaming Italy for sixteen years, inflicting heavy defeats upon them. This was accompanied by the ever-present threat of an attack on the city of Rome itself (which was a potent image in the Roman psyche, after a Gallic invasion had attacked and sacked Rome in 390 BC[14]). Yet despite these constant years of struggle, instead of enjoying their victory, the Romans embarked upon a further decade of warfare.

It is this decade that is perhaps the most momentous in Roman imperial history as it saw the Romans defeat two of the 'big three' Hellenistic super-powers, Macedon and the Seleucid empire (the two biggest at the time, in military terms). In just over a decade, the Romans went from being on the periphery of the Hellenistic world to being its most dominant power.

The cause of this rapid rise to dominance had its origins in Greece and the actions of Philip V of Macedon. With a stalemate against Rome in the First Macedonian War and his ally Hannibal defeated, Philip turned his attentions back to the Aegean. He formed an alliance with the Seleucid king, Antiochus III (the Great), for a joint attack on the empire of the third leading Hellenistic power, Egypt. Such an alliance alarmed the states who were opposed to Macedonian dominance, namely the Aetolian League of Greek city-states as well as Pergamum and the island state of Rhodes. The Aetolian League made the first move by sending an embassy to Rome in 202 BC to ask for assistance. Naturally enough, the Senate refused the request as they were still embroiled in a war against Carthage and were in the process of invading North Africa.

The following year Rhodes and Pergamum sent a joint embassy to Rome with the same request. In a surprising and momentous decision, the Senate agreed to their request to intervene militarily against Philip V. Why did they agree to this request when they had refused the one a year earlier? There are a number of possible reasons. Certainly this delegation, comprising perhaps the two strongest 'middle order' states of the Hellenistic world, carried more weight and offered the prospect of stronger allies than the weak Aetolian League. Furthermore, the war against Carthage had been successfully brought to a conclusion with Scipio Africanus' victory over Hannibal at the Battle of Zama. Rome now possessed more battle-hardened legionaries than at any time previously. Therefore, as well as having the opportunity, they now had the resources to fight a fresh war. An alliance between Philip and Antiochus, both considered to be the greatest military rulers of their day, presented a formidable opposition that could one day be turned against Rome, at least in the minds of the Senate.[15]

It is this last point that is perhaps the most important one, as the decision to go to war against Philip had no obvious physical cause; Philip was campaigning in the Aegean and was not threatening Roman territory or even their Illyrian protectorate and it was likely that he would be engaged there for a number of years to come. Yet to the Senate this seemed the perfect time, for three key reasons. Firstly, there was the euphoria of victory caused by the military triumph over Carthage, Rome's most dangerous enemy for the last sixty-plus years. This victory would have produced a sense of arrogance and invincibility in the minds of the Roman leaders. Secondly, the Roman state had been at war for eighteen years and now had a whole state geared for warfare, along with a huge number of seasoned troops and a new wave of victorious generals (with Scipio Africanus being the most famous). If they demobilised now then they might never assemble such military might again, especially if you consider the lack of a standing Roman army. Associated with this is the paradoxical sense of insecurity that the war had produced. Hannibal's invasion, shocking victories and sixteen-year rampage through Italy had deeply affected the Roman psyche, and on many occasions the spectre of a 'new Hannibal' was a powerful political image.

Many have argued that the Romans developed a concept of 'defensive imperialism', whereby a powerful state develops a policy of pre-emptive strikes against potential foes that they believe will one day, inevitably, attack them on their home soil.[16] This policy is usually prompted by a political or military shock. In Rome's case this shock was the Hannibalic invasion and the disastrous Battle of Cannae. Whilst there is little practical case for Philip representing an immediate threat to Rome, wars are generally started in politicians' minds first, and the Roman senators were no different to the politicians of today.

Added to this dangerous mix of arrogance and paranoia, backed up by a large military system, was a conscious desire to extend Roman pre-eminence from the western Mediterranean to the Greek mainland itself. This is not the same as a thirst for empire, as the Romans in this era had little desire for physical empire and the practicalities of imperial governance. The Romans had a clear concept of *auctoritas*, which best translates from the Latin as prestige. Individual Romans sought it through military and political careers and the Senate sought it for the state by defeating the other leading powers of the Mediterranean and establishing her influence over lesser states. The chance of extending Rome's benevolent (in her view) protection over the mainland Greek city-states, rather than just the Illyrian towns, could have been just too strong a temptation to resist. This would have been aided by the sense of cultural inferiority that the Roman elite felt towards the Greek mainland, though whether this was based on the Greece of the past, or the one that faced them, is hard to determine.

Thus the Senate voted for war with Philip, but then faced an immediate and unusual challenge to their decision. Under the Republic's unwritten constitution based on a tradition of 'custom and practice', matters of foreign policy were for the consuls and the Senate to decide, with the people seen as nothing more than a rubber stamp for their decisions. However, when the consul Sulpicius, who had been voted command of the war with Macedon by the Senate, put this decision before the assemblies for ratification (as was necessary under the Roman system), the people, weary after eighteen years of warfare and its consequences, and fearful of its continuation, voted decisively against the war. This rejection was an unusual occurrence and shows the depth of war-weariness that the people of Rome must have felt. Not to be deterred though, the consul Sulpicius went again to the people and put the question once more. This time, the people relented and reluctantly agreed to the war.

The Second Macedonian War saw Roman legions operating on the Greek mainland and the Roman fleet operating in the Aegean, for the first time. The rest of the Hellenistic states expected a long drawn-out affair, on a par with Rome's Punic Wars (twenty-three and eighteen years respectively). At first this war seemed to bear out their thoughts as the years 199–197 BC saw indecisive campaigning throughout the Macedonian region. Philip, lacking the resources for a protracted war, determined to bring the Romans, led by the consul Titus Quinctius Flamininus, to battle. The Battle of Cynoscephalae in 197 BC was the first battle between the Macedonians (the leading Greek army since the 350s BC) and the Romans (the new upstart power in the Mediterranean). After a long drawn out day of fighting the manoeuvrability of the Roman legionary, as opposed to the pikemen of the Macedonian phalanx, proved to be the decisive factor and saw the Macedonians defeated in a land battle for the first time in centuries. Macedon lay humiliated and Greece lay open to Rome.

What happened next summed up Rome's whole imperial attitude and surprised many of the Greeks. Arriving at the Isthmian Games of 196 BC, Flamininus proclaimed that, thanks to Rome, Greece had been liberated and that this freedom would be guaranteed in the future by Rome.[17] Macedonian garrisons were evacuated and their control over the Greek mainland was ended. Further military action ensued when the tyrant of Sparta, Nabis, attempted to use this situation to expand Spartan power. Sparta in these years was little more than a minor city-state and their swift defeat seemed to sum up the changing of the old order, with both Macedon and Sparta being humbled by Roman armies. By the end of this war, Flamininus remained true to his word: Rome took no territory and by 194 BC had evacuated her armies from mainland Greece.[18]

This evacuation illustrates an important point about Roman attitudes in this era. Roman policy can best be summed up by a desire for hegemony, rather than empire; that is to say the desire for pre-eminence amongst the states of the Hellenistic world (to be first amongst equals) rather than the annexation of territory, which the Romans would have considered to be both time consuming and cumbersome. Roman overseas territory at this stage was restricted to the islands of Sicily, Sardinia and Corsica, with the only substantial mainland territory being the south and east of Spain, which they took over from the Carthaginians and continued to hold merely to deny them a powerbase.

Rome's wish for a free Greek mainland was almost immediately put to the test, as the fall of Macedon presented a major opportunity to the other key figure of the Hellenistic world at that time. Antiochus III ruled the Seleucid empire which stretched from the Mediterranean to the Caspian Sea (see map 1). Not only was he considered the pre-eminent general of his age and the Seleucid empire the obvious remaining rival to Rome's new position in Greece, but in 195 BC Hannibal, Rome's implacable Carthaginian enemy, had fled from his home city to the court of Antiochus. To say that this move alarmed Rome would have been an understatement.

Rome's initial response was a cautious one. Asia Minor and the Middle East were far outside of Rome's experience and sphere of knowledge, and so diplomatic talks were entered into to sort out the issues between Rome and Antiochus. Talks between the two parties started at Rome and continued at Ephesus, but soon stalled. At this time in the Greek mainland, the Aetolian League, who had been Rome's ally against Macedon but considered that they had been poorly rewarded for their services, invited Antiochus to free Greece from Roman domination (as they saw it). Unable to resist the challenge, Antiochus accepted the offer and in 192 BC invaded the Greek mainland. Faced with a clear challenge of this sort and with the spectre of Hannibal once again threatening them, Rome quickly declared war. Thus, within the same decade as the Romans had fought Macedon, they found themselves at war with the Seleucid empire.

The First Seleucid War had two clear phases. The initial phase saw Roman armies, led by Marcus Acilius Glabrio defeat the Seleucid forces in Greece. This was accomplished at the Battle of Thermopylae, scene of the heroic Spartan last stand in the Persian Wars in 480 BC. Once again the defenders (Antiochus) attempted to hold the pass from the Roman forces and once again the invaders choose to go round the back of the pass and surround the defenders. Defeat at Thermopylae cost Antiochus his army and forced him to retreat back across the Aegean to Asia Minor. This left the Aetolian League alone to face Rome's wrath for their act of treachery. Attempts to negotiate were met with demands for an unconditional surrender. By 189 BC the Aetolians finally came to terms with Rome, with the league being reduced to impotence and being restricted solely to the Aetolian region and bound by treaty to Rome, thus ending their existence as an independent force. This incident perhaps shows how quickly the Roman dream of an independent Greece, living under the benevolent protection of Rome, had turned sour and foundered upon the deeply-engrained disunity and power struggles amongst the Greek cities.

With Greece safely back under Rome's wing, the issue of Antiochus came to the fore. Any invasion of Asia Minor required control of the seas and the fleet of Antiochus was faced by the combined fleets of Rome, Pergamum and Rhodes. The naval war raged over the years 191 and 190 BC and saw a Roman victory at Cape Corycus, the destruction of a Rhodian fleet at Samos and finally a decisive Roman/Pergamene victory at Myonnesus in 190 BC, which was the last decisive naval battle fought by Rome for over a century.

Having secured control of the Aegean, a Roman army led by the consul of 190 BC, Lucius Cornelius Scipio (brother of Scipio Africanus), crossed into Asia Minor, an act that would have been inconceivable to a Roman commander just ten years earlier. Despite the Roman force only being 30,000 strong, Antiochus attempted to negotiate, but Lucius deliberately set unacceptable terms. With no other option available, Antiochus gave battle in 190 BC at Magnesia.

Ranged against the Roman force was an army of roughly 72,000 men, backed up by elephants and heavy cavalry. However, the battle saw the Roman legionaries defeat the Greek phalanx once again. Antiochus' cavalry was routed by the Pergamene allied cavalry and his elephants were stampeded by Roman javelins (the Romans having learnt the tactic from fighting Pyrrhus and the Carthaginians). The result was the destruction of the Seleucid army and total defeat for Antiochus. The resulting peace settlement (the Treaty of Apamea, 188 BC) dismembered the powerbase of Antiochus, with a massive war indemnity, the loss of his fleet (bar ten ships), all of his elephants and the evacuation of all territories he held west of the Taurus Mountains. These lands were divided between Rome's two principle allies in the region: Pergamum and Rhodes. Antiochus was not allowed to attack any state on the European mainland or in the Aegean and any future alliances he made had to be approved by Rome. In short the Romans went far further than they had against Macedon and emasculated the Seleucid empire, setting it on a downward spiral that would eventually lead to its collapse and, inadvertently, to the rise of the Parthian empire (see next chapter).

Within just a decade the Romans had decisively defeated the strongest two of the three major powers in the ancient world and established themselves as the Mediterranean's leading power. Although they took no territory; the entire Greek mainland came under Roman influence and the Romans were now the guardians or 'policemen' of the Hellenistic world.

We have to ask ourselves how an outside power like Rome came to such prominence in such a short time. These wars came on the back of Hannibal's invasion of Italy and the near defeat of Rome in the Second Punic War. By 200 BC the Roman state had been at war for a generation, with a battle-hardened army and generation of able commanders, backed up by a near-endless supply of manpower and a uniquely flexible system of multiple commands, which allowed them to operate in a number of campaigns at once. Behind all this lay the Roman aristocracy and their twin motivations: the fear of 'another Hannibal' and the lust for military success (which would in turn lead to economic and political power). For Rome as a whole, there was the need to ensure that the security of Italy did not start at her own shores. Potential enemies were to be neutralised early, and the lands surrounding Italy were to be under her 'benevolent' protection. They had little desire for empire, merely seeking acknowledged dominance, and if that brought riches and power then so much the better.

After defeating Antiochus, Roman troops once again returned home and were demobilised. Yet this Roman world view had a number of flaws. Macedon was humiliated but not broken; the Seleucid empire had been emasculated without thought given as to what would happen if it collapsed; and the mainland Greeks had already shown their unwillingness to live at peace in a Roman-enforced freedom. Dealing with the consequences of this period would keep Rome occupied for the next century, in a process that would inexorably lead them to the plains of Carrhae in the summer of 53 BC.

From Liberation to Conquest (188 –96 BC)

Third Macedonian War (172–167 BC)
Fourth Macedonian War (149–146 BC)
Achaean War (146 BC)

The years that followed Rome's stunning successes provide an abject lesson in the dangers of a state attempting to police the world in the name of internal security and bringing 'liberation' to other peoples. Within fifty years of Flamininus' declaration of 'freedom for the Greeks', Greece and Macedon had been annexed to form the core states of the Roman Republic's eastern empire. This transition set the Roman state on a policy of conquest that changed the shape of the ancient world forever.

The immediate period following these wars saw the Romans using their newly-established influence to act as intermediary in the various conflicts that sprung up between the various states of the Hellenistic World, but through the use of diplomacy rather than warfare. A war between Pergamum and one of their neighbours, Bithynia, was settled with the assistance of Flamininus, who had been sent as a senatorial emissary. Perhaps the most famous of all of the senatorial emissaries was Gaius Popillius Laenas, who was sent as an intermediary when war broke out between Egypt and Antiochus IV of Seleucia, in 168 BC. Arriving in Egypt to find Antiochus besieging the Egyptian city of Alexandria, he ordered Antiochus to stand down and evacuate his army from Egypt, though he (Laenas) was only there with a small retinue of men. To make the point he drew a circle around the king in the dirt with his stick and ordered him to make his decision before he stepped out of the ring. Thus the might of Rome and its role as arbiter of Mediterranean affairs was made clear.

However, this policy of non-military intervention came to an end when Perseus came to the throne of Macedon in 179 BC. Perseus' accession followed the death of his father, Philip V, and the earlier execution of his more popular younger brother. Whilst maintaining the treaty relationship with Rome, he embarked upon a policy of rebuilding Macedon's pre-eminence amongst the mainland Greek states through alliances, backed up by an increase in Macedon's military capabilities. Again the Roman Senate sent emissaries to look into Perseus' activities, but by 172 BC, once more encouraged by Pergamum, the

Senate saw that the best policy was another pre-emptive war with Macedon, to ensure it remained in an inferior position.

Perseus called for the Greek city-states to assist him, but only received help from Epirus and one Illyrian chieftain. The rest of Greece had learnt from the example Rome had made of the Aetolian League. Nevertheless, Macedon still fielded an army of 40,000 men. The war started off well for Perseus, who defeated an advance force of the Roman army in Thessaly in 171 BC and another in Illyria the following year. He was aided by the Romans fielding a series of consuls with little military experience or drive. In 168 BC this all changed with the arrival of Lucius Aemilius Paulus, a veteran campaigner. He led his army into Macedon and forced a set piece battle at Pydna. Once again the manoeuvrability of the Roman legions proved to be superior to that of the Macedonian phalanx and the Macedonian army was comprehensively beaten. Perseus fled and the Macedonian cities surrendered.

The end of the war saw a number of disturbing new Roman traits, starting with the settlement of Macedon. Determined to end the threat of Macedon once and forever, the monarchy was abolished, the king interned, and all royal officials were deported. Having had its governing class removed, Macedon itself was split up into four independent regions, and each was given a republican government based on the Roman model. This exporting of a political system was repeated in the Illyrian kingdom that had allied itself to Macedon. This marked a change in the Roman attitude, with them no longer willing to let defeated enemies be, and began a process of changing the nature of the existing governments of long-established states. The kingdom of Macedon, with its long and illustrious history (home of Alexander the Great), was ended by Roman decree.

This new system was accompanied by a brutal crackdown on those perceived as being anti-Roman. Epirus, which had allied with Perseus and had been the home of Pyrrhus, was invaded and treated to a brutal repression, with upwards of 150,000 people seized and sold off into slavery. Rome's allies fared little better. Mainland Greece saw a purge of anyone suspected of harbouring anti-Roman sentiments. One thousand men were handed over as hostages to Rome by their allies in the Achaean League, including the future 'Roman' historian, Polybius. Rhodes, which had made an ill-judged attempt at mediation between Rome and Perseus, saw a motion being presented in the Senate for a declaration of war on them, as punishment for their perceived arrogance. In the end the Senate settled for stripping Rhodes of the territories that they had been given after the defeat of Antiochus III, an act which ultimately impoverished Rhodes and destroyed her status as a power in the Mediterranean. The king of Pergamum himself came under suspicion of collusion with Perseus, which is surprising, given his role in encouraging the war. For the next thirty years Pergamum was treated with suspicion by Rome.

The years that followed this crackdown were accompanied by an increasing Roman tendency to meddle in the internal running of the leading states of the Hellenistic world. Upon the death of Antiochus IV of Seleucia, the Senate sent a three-man commission into the empire to administer it until his son reached the age of majority. These commissioners took it upon themselves to enforce the treaty of 188 BC and finish the destruction of both the Seleucid fleet and their force of elephants, which sparked off a riot during which the chief commissioner, Gnaeus Octavius, was murdered. Things went from bad to worse when a rival claimant to the throne, Demetrius, 'escaped' from Roman custody, usurped the throne and was promptly recognised by Rome. A decade later, having angered Rome, he too was usurped by another pretender, who had also been encouraged and then recognised by Rome. This in turn sparked off a catastrophic civil war which saw the kingdom of Judea gain its independence, and the Parthians overrun Mesopotamia; both of which developments came back to haunt the Romans in the next century.

Egypt too suffered from internal chaos which was exploited by Rome. A civil war had broken out between rival claimants to the throne: Ptolemy VI and Ptolemy VII. Rome ruled in favour of Ptolemy VI after he visited Rome personally, again showing Rome's unquestioned status. A renewed conflict in the 140s BC led to the Roman general Scipio Aemilianus being sent to investigate. Thus the middle of the second century BC saw Rome dismantle the kingdom of Macedon, interfere and ferment civil war within the Seleucid empire, and determine who could rule Egypt. Allies and enemies were treated with the same disdain, yet Rome still showed little appetite for direct rule.

This situation changed in the 140s BC when Rome not only destroyed the city of Carthage (in what is referred to as the Third Punic War, but which was in fact nothing more than a three year siege of the city), but also went once more to war with Macedon, for the fourth and final time. The new constitutional settlement Rome had burdened Macedon with soon proved to be weak and incapable of maintaining order within the territories. A pretender to the Macedonian throne arose, who claimed to be a son of Perseus. He soon overthrew the weak Macedonian republics and once more united the kingdom, overrunning neighbouring Thessaly in the process and defeating a small Roman force which had been sent to deal with him. Therefore, in 148 BC, the Senate declared a Fourth Macedonian War, invaded Macedonia in force and easily removed the pretender. Once again the Romans found themselves in charge of Macedonia and were faced with a dilemma. Binding the Macedonian king by treaty had failed, deposing the monarchy and instituting an experiment in republican government had failed, so what alternatives were left?

In truth, in the eyes of the Senate and the Roman aristocracy, there was only one alternative, and so they took a momentous, and what they saw as inevitable, decision. The only method of securing Macedon and ensuring no further unwanted wars was outright annexation. Thus Rome gained her first imperial province in the east. To secure the province, Rome also annexed the neighbouring regions of Thessaly and Epirus, which could do nothing against the might of Rome. Almost as an aside, Epirus, the homeland of Rome's first eastern enemy, Pyrrhus, fell without a fight. After fifty years of resisting the notion of territorial empire, Rome had finally broken the last barrier. Once the floodgates were open they could not be closed. Not only was North Africa annexed, upon the destruction of the city of Carthage in 146 BC, but soon the rest of mainland Greece fell to Rome as well.

In 146 the tyrant of Corinth, Critolaus, alarmed by the Roman annexations in northern Greece, led the Achaean League (which for over fifty years had been a staunch ally of Rome) into overrunning central Greece. Such an overt challenge to the authority of Rome led to the Achaean War. With legions already in Macedonia, the conflict proved to be a short one and the invading Achaean forces were easily defeated. The Romans, led by Lucius Mummius, then invaded the Peloponnese and, after brushing aside the remaining Achaean forces, destroyed the city of Corinth, razing it to the ground and selling the survivors into slavery in one of the greatest acts of savagery the Greek world had ever seen. The Achaean League was dissolved and Greece was placed under the jurisdiction of the governor of Macedon, effectively annexing it. At a stroke the mainland Greek civilisations lost their independence, which they were not to regain until AD 1832.

In the decade that followed, this trend continued, as Illyria and Dalmatia were annexed to the province of Macedon in 129 BC. In 133 BC this process widened when the kingdom of Pergamum, which occupied the whole Asia Minor coastline, was gifted to Rome by the will of its last king Attalus III and by 129 BC became the Roman province of Asia. Thus, Rome had become the unquestioned master of the Mediterranean and the Hellenistic period was fast becoming the Roman period. Macedon, Athens, Sparta and Pergamum had all fallen under Roman rule. The remaining states of the east would have had a good idea what their future held; it was a case of 'when', rather than 'if'.

So, we can see that the period from the 160s to the 140s BC saw a hardening of the Roman world view, with liberation replaced by annexation and respect replaced by destruction. In many ways it represents a maturing of the Roman view of the Hellenistic world, with naivety turning sour and being replaced by cynicism. The sudden rise to power of the Republic and its shock overthrowing of the old order could never be reconciled with a policy of homeland security through intervention. The system of interplay between the states of the Hellenistic world, with the big three of Macedon, Egypt and the Seleucid empire and the lesser states of Rhodes, Pergamum, Achaea and Aetolia, was replaced with Rome as the dominant state and unquestioned arbiter of ancient world events.

This policy was bound to create resentment and opposition. When Rome's enlightened interventions became corrupted by the arrogance that accompanied their dominance, the path to annexation and empire was set. Interventions became more frequent, with a total of four wars with Macedon and three with Carthage. In Roman eyes, defeated enemies kept coming back and former allies kept turning on them (at least in the Senate's mind). When the policy of withdrawal failed, Rome turned to changing the local political systems and when that failed all that was left was either perpetual intervention and the accompanying feeling of perpetual insecurity, or annexation and direct rule, which provided Rome with the sense of security that she appears to have craved. Given the Roman mindset, the course they took seems inevitable, with the benefit of hindsight.

Despite the absence of outright warfare in the decades that followed these annexations, Rome still managed to acquire two new embryonic territories in the east. By 102 BC the eastern Mediterranean was suffering from a serious piracy problem, which indirectly was Rome's own fault. With the humbling of both the Seleucid empire and Rhodes, the two major fleets that patrolled the area, and which had kept piracy in check, had been removed, allowing the pirate fleets to flourish. The devastation which they inflicted on the trade of the remaining independent states of Asia Minor and the Middle East led to a number of Rome's allies demanding that Rome take action. Therefore, in 102 BC, with a diminution of Rome's other military commitments, particularly in North Africa, the Senate authorised a campaign against the pirates operating in the eastern Mediterranean. These operations were led by Marcus Antonius (grandfather of the more famous Mark Antony) and resulted in the annexation of the coastline of Asia Minor, which was then turned into the embryonic province of Cilicia (what is now southern Turkey). Nevertheless, the campaign achieved little more than a temporary reduction in the piracy in the region and the issue still remained. Secondly, in 96 BC the Egyptian king bequeathed the African coastal territory of Cyrene (modern Libya), west of Egypt, to Rome. Aside from formally acknowledging possession and arranging revenue collection, the Senate left the province to govern itself for the next thirty years.

Although the period of 129–96 BC saw Rome gain two further stretches of the Mediterranean coastline, Rome's focus was not on affairs of the east. This is understandable given the situation amongst the old powers of the Hellenistic world and the problems within Rome itself. In the east, with Macedon, Greece and Pergamum having been annexed, and with Egypt and the Seleucid kingdom having collapsed into civil wars, Rome's strategic position looked secure. Furthermore Rome had problems nearer to home, both militarily and politically.

A war broke out in North Africa between Rome and her former ally, Numidia[19] and two barbarian tribes (the Cimbrii and Teutones) invaded Italy.[20] Domestically, populist politicians were stirring up Rome's poor, resulting in political murders and open insurrection in the streets.[21]

It was during this period however, that Rome undertook a major reform of her military system. Faced with reversals in both Spain and North Africa, the populist figure Gaius Marius was elected consul and undertook a revision of the Roman military and its recruitment base. Rome's citizen army was replaced by a professional body of career soldiers, who no longer had to be demobilised to harvest the Italian farmlands. Further reforms of equipment, formations and tactics laid the foundations for the classical form of the Roman army, with legionary standards and unified equipment.[22]

Although Rome's neglect of her eastern policy is understandable, a number of threats arose in the east which were to have major consequences for Rome in the first century BC. As detailed above, one of these was a growing problem of piracy, a major issue given that Rome's food and trade were based on shipping. The other threats came from the collapse of the Seleucid empire, which resulted in the rise of new powerful states, the dangers of which the Romans were slow to see. In short, Rome seemed content with replacing the old order of Hellenistic states, but slow to realise that others would benefit from this collapse. Into this vacuum in the east came the Parthians (as will be detailed in the next chapter), the Armenians, and the rise of Mithridates VI of Pontus.

The Rise of the New Powers (96–63 BC)

First, Second and Third Mithridatic Wars (88–85, 83–82, 74–63 BC).
Armenian War (69–66 BC)

Pontus occupied the coastline and the interior of Asia Minor (see map 1) and was one of a handful of states to emerge from the fragmentation of the Seleucid empire in Asia Minor, the others being Pergamum, Bithynia and Cappadocia. The history of Pontus prior to the accession of Mithridates VI in 120 BC is difficult to chart, given the lack of surviving evidence, but the rise of the dynasty is generally dated to the period of 302–294 BC. Throughout the second century BC Pontus, along with the other kingdoms of Asia Minor, benefited from the diminution of the Seleucid empire at the hands of Rome. However, they always remained in the shadow of Pergamum, which was, by far and away, the leading power in the region. Pergamum's natural extinction and bequest to Rome removed yet another major barrier to the remaining kingdoms. In history, timing is crucial, and into this vacuum in Asia Minor entered the young King

Mithridates VI. Every inch the Hellenistic monarch, he was young, charismatic and an astute politician and general.[23]

Relations between Rome and Pontus had undergone a strain in the 120s BC. When organising Pergamum into the Roman province of Asia, the Roman commissioners were only interested in the western fertile plains, not the mountainous territories of the east, which would have been burdensome to rule. Therefore, Rome divided these lands up and granted them to the kingdoms of Pontus and Cappadocia, allies of Rome, with Pontus gaining the territory of Phrygia. However, this grant fell foul of Roman domestic politics and was soon revoked. The death of Mithridates V in 120 BC gave the Senate the excuse they were looking for to deny Pontus the promised territory.

Mithridates VI nevertheless ignored this slight and concentrated upon an expansion of Pontus through expeditions in the Black Sea region, bringing the Crimean region and the Black Sea trade routes under his control, which massively increased his powerbase. In 104 BC he made the first of his bold moves, taking advantage of Rome's inattention with regard to the area. Allied to his neighbour, Nicomedes of Bithynia, he annexed the kingdom of Cappadocia, vastly increasing his territory and his potential threat to Rome. At first Rome did nothing, though the populist general Gaius Marius (see above) did attempt to provoke a war with Mithridates in both 103 BC (by having Mithridates' envoys to Rome abused) and 98 BC (during a private meeting between the two). Marius was at political odds with the Senate in this period, so these attempts came to nothing.

In 96 BC, however, Mithridates fell out with his ally Nicomedes and the latter appealed to Rome. With its internal and external problems temporarily put to one side, Rome suddenly appeared to take notice of this new danger and sent Lucius Cornelius Sulla (who later became dictator of Rome in the 80s BC) to restore Cappadocia to independence. Realising his inferior military position vis-à-vis Rome, Mithridates acquiesced in this and the whole process was concluded without conflict. Mithridates soon made up for this setback through an alliance with the kingdom of Armenia, forged by marrying his daughter off to its king. It was during this period that Sulla met an ambassador from the Parthian empire, the other rising power of the region, for the first time (see chapter two).

This game of cat and mouse with Rome continued in the years 91–90 BC when, with Rome embroiled in a civil war with her Italian allies, Mithridates once again annexed the kingdom of Cappadocia along with Bithynia also. Despite the war at home, the Senate recognised the threat, especially to its vital province of Asia which was a vast source of wealth to Rome, especially vital at a time when its control over Italy was tenuous. They sent Marcus Aquilius to restore these kingdoms, commanding the Roman forces in Asia. At first Mithridates again pulled out of these territories, but Aquilius went too far and encouraged Bithynia to retaliate against Pontus with Roman backing, contemplating an attack on Pontus itself. Mithridates realised the inevitable and judged that it was now or never, especially given the situation in Italy and how few Roman forces were in Asia at the time. In 88 BC he launched a full scale onslaught, invading and conquering not only Bithynia, but also the Roman province of Asia. His army was larger and more experienced than the meagre Roman forces in the province and virtually all the native cities came over to his side on the back of a desire to end Roman taxation. This conquest was crowned by the massacre of all the Roman and Italian residents in Asia, happily enacted by the native populations, resulting in a total death toll of 80,000 or more.

This invasion and massacre sparked off the First Mithridatic War, which was by far the greatest challenge to Rome's dominance in the east in a hundred years and which led to a further twenty-five years of warfare between Mithridates and Rome, making him Rome's most durable opponent.

By 88 BC the civil war between Rome and her Italian allies was drawing to a conclusion, with Rome emerging as the victors. Three leading generals emerged from this conflict, each eager to take up the challenge of fighting Mithridates. Under normal circumstances, Mithridates' timing of his invasion would been judged to be too late, as Rome was emerging victorious from a war, with a large number of soldiers mobilised and being commanded by experienced and talented generals. Luck was on his side, however, as the three commanders, Gaius Marius, Lucius Cornelius Sulla (both of whom were known to him) and Gnaeus Pompeius Strabo, vied for this lucrative command (which was widely judged to be the greatest opportunity for a generation).

This contest appeared to have been settled when Sulla was elected consul and assigned the command by the Senate. Marius, near the end of his career and mindful of his earlier attempts to command a Mithridatic War, refused to accept this decision and had the the command awarded to him by vote of the assembly of the people (which, strictly speaking, was where the constitutional power lay). Sulla refused to be humiliated in this manner and actually led his own army in an attack on Rome itself, seizing power. Thus in Mithridates' view, the only Roman response to his invasion of Asia was the opening of another round of civil wars and total paralysis.

Again he used Rome's weaknesses to good effect and invaded the Greek mainland, which by then was dangerously undermanned. Not only did he have military superiority, but he again portrayed himself as a liberator from Roman misrule and championed the cause of Greek 'liberty'. We should not under-appreciate the irony of this, as a century earlier Rome had invaded from the west, espousing the same cause of Greek liberation; now the reverse had happened. The most notable success of this policy was the defection of Athens, where a pro-Mithridatic populist overthrew the ruling elite, which provided Mithridates with the Piraeus as a naval base from which to operate. Despite (or perhaps because of) sixty years of Roman rule, central and southern Greece quickly fell to Mithridates, setting Roman imperial policy back a century. Macedonia was next to fall, again with too few Roman troops for its defence. The beginning of 87 BC saw a new power rise in the eastern Mediterranean with Mithridates holding Greece, Asia Minor and the Black Sea. After one hundred years of warfare, the Romans were faced with what they had always feared: an enemy on its eastern shore.

By 87 BC, however, Sulla had finally restored some stability to Rome and embarked upon his delayed counter-invasion of Greece. Once there he immediately embarked upon a destructive siege of Athens. In the meantime, Mithridates' main force was in the process of completing the conquest of Thrace and Macedon, whilst a smaller force led by the Pontic general Archelaus engaged Sulla. By 86 BC, Sulla had retaken Athens after a protracted and brutal siege, and both armies advanced toward each other, meeting at Chaeroneia. In a long drawn-out battle, Sulla again showed the greater manoeuvrability of the Roman legions over Hellenistic forces (despite their use of scythe chariots), and defeated the Mithridatic and Athenian forces. Mithridates was forced to retreat back into Asia, followed slowly by Sulla, who retook Macedon en route.

However, matters took a turn for the worse for Sulla when a counter-coup in Rome took place in 87 BC and the pro-Sullan government was replaced by a hostile one. Sulla was declared an enemy of Rome, thus equal to Mithridates, and a second army was dispatched under Lucius Valerius Flaccus to deal with both Mithridates and Sulla, invading Asia directly in 85 BC. But, whilst in Bithynia, Flaccus was murdered by his deputy Gaius Flavius Fimbria, who then invaded the province of Asia and defeated Mithridates' forces at Rhyndacus. Sandwiched between the two Roman armies (of Sulla to the west and Fimbria to the east), the situation looked grim for Mithridates until the Roman disunity came to his rescue. Fimbria caught up with Mithridates at the city of Pergamum and would have captured him, but for the refusal of a Roman naval force under Sulla's lieutenant, Lucullus, to co-operate, which allowed him to escape.

Utilising this disunity, Mithridates conducted peace negotiations directly with Sulla (himself still a declared enemy of Rome). With neither side in a strong position, Mithridates managed to negotiate an extraordinary treaty with Sulla (the Treaty of Dardanus) in which he agreed to evacuate the conquered provinces of Greece and Asia, dismantle his Aegean fleet and pay a war indemnity. In return he was recognised as king of Pontus and an ally of Rome. Considering that he had invaded and conquered Rome's eastern empire (accompanied by massive bloodshed) and was facing two separate Roman armies, it was a diplomatic coup. Furthermore, the second Roman army would be dealt with by Sulla, which it promptly was when he persuaded Fimbria's army to mutiny and murder their commander. Sulla then departed to invade Italy in a renewal of Rome's First Civil War.

Thus ended the momentous events of the First Mithridatic War. A postscript to this conflict came in 83 BC when Sulla's governor in Asia, Lucius Licinius Murena, invaded Cappadocia and Bithynia (which were still under Mithridates' control) in an unauthorised incursion. This Second Mithridatic War soon ended when Mithridates defeated Murena in 82 BC and appealed to Sulla. Having just seized control of Rome for a second time, Sulla was in a weak position and wisely ended the matter there. Thus the second war was a minor affair.

If we look back at the first war, we can see that it saw a complete reversal of Rome's gains of the last century and turned the process detailed above on its head. It was not merely the case of a talented Hellenistic monarch exploiting Roman divisions. The interesting factor is the ease with which Asia and the Greek mainland defected to Mithridates. Both areas had been allied to Rome since the start of the second century and had been Roman territory for over fifty years. Yet the harshness of Roman rule and the resentment of being part of the Roman empire all seemed to have shown how superficial Rome's control of the east was. Both as a result of the fighting and its treachery during the war, mainland Greece suffered heavily.

It was obvious that the status quo between Mithridates and Rome would not last, especially given the retirement and death of Sulla (in 79 and 78 BC respectively) and the rise of a new generation of Roman generals eager for glory. However, in the short term, Roman policy in the east had a more pressing problem.

Once again the issue of the eastern pirate fleets came to the fore. Having recovered after the campaigns of 102–101 BC, the pirate fleets of the east flourished amid the chaos of the 80s BC. Again they caused major disruption to Rome's food supply and even subjected Italy itself to slaving raids, with a young Julius Caesar being their most notable captive. In 78 BC, the Senate commissioned Publius Servilius to tackle the problem. He campaigned until 74 BC but, apart from expanding the coastal province of Cilicia, he achieved little success. In 74 BC, another Marcus Antonius (son of the commander in 102–101, and father of the famous Mark Antony) took charge, possessing a far greater remit. The problem was so serious that he was given extraordinary powers throughout the whole Mediterranean. Despite success in the western Mediterranean he was defeated by a pirate fleet off Crete and died soon afterwards. As part of his campaign the area of Cyrene, technically Roman since 96 BC, was formally organised into a province.

By 69 BC, pirate fleets had sacked Delos and were starving Rome by attacking Rome's grain supplies from Egypt and the Black Sea. The Senate's response was a limited one, undertaking the conquest of Crete in 68–67 BC. The assembly of the people however, took decisive action and appointed Gnaeus Pompeius Magnus (Pompey the Great as he is more commonly known) to an extraordinary command of the Mediterranean, with total control of its resources (military and civilian). Using these massive resources (upward of 270 ships and 100,000 men) he swept the Mediterranean of all pirate fleets in a methodical process: defeating them at sea and then driving them inland into the hands of his infantry. Within three months the problem that had plagued the Mediterranean for a century had been cured.

Whilst this had been going on, tensions between Rome and Mithridates had been inevitably rising. In 76 BC, he agreed an informal alliance with the Roman general Sertorius, who was in control of Spain and fighting the pro–Sullan Roman government. He even had two Roman nobles, who were opposed to the pro–Sullan regime, with him in Pontus, training his forces.[24] In 74 BC, matters came to a head when the puppet king of Bithynia died without an heir and bequeathed his kingdom to Rome, which Rome promptly accepted. Faced with Roman control of the Bosporus, the entrance to the Black Sea, Mithridates returned to his original plan and once again invaded Roman Asia, thus starting the Third Mithridatic War.

Once again he acted faster than the Romans and had overrun Bithynia before they had a chance to react. By an ironic twist, the Roman governor of Asia and Cilicia was Lucius Licinius Lucullus, the man who had let Mithridates escape in 85 BC. Again utilising a two–pronged attack, Mithridates invaded Asia by land whilst sending a fleet into the Aegean to stir up the Greek states. The war in Asia soon ground down to a series of sieges and by 73 BC Mithridates had been pushed back to Pontus, which Lucullus then invaded. In 72 BC, Lucullus cornered Mithridates at Cabira and destroyed his army. This defeat was made worse by the defection to the Roman side of his son, Machares, who had been running Mithridates' Black Sea territories, thus denying him a vital powerbase. The years 71 BC and 70 BC saw Lucullus' forces slowly conquer the fortified towns of Pontus. With no other option, Mithridates sought sanctuary with his son–in–law, Tigranes, the king of Armenia.

Armenia represented a fresh challenge and one which highlighted the problems Rome faced with the consequences of its own earlier policies. Reducing the power of the Seleucid empire had led not only to the rise of Mithridates, but also the rise of Tigranes, who had annexed Cappadocia, Syria and non–Roman Cilicia, as well as part of Mesopotamia, which had been part of the Parthian empire (see map 2). When faced with Lucullus' demand to hand over Mithridates, Tigranes refused. In 69 BC, Lucullus crossed the Euphrates, another first for a Roman general, and invaded Armenia. However, this whole campaign was undertaken without senatorial consent and with a limited force of only 16,000 troops.

Without the forces or the backing for a concerted campaign, Lucullus brought Tigranes to battle at Tigranocerta and, despite having being greatly out-numbered, defeated his army (again utilising the greater flexibility of his troops' movement). This forced Tigranes into retreat and by 68 BC Lucullus was deep in Armenia pursuing the two kings when disaster struck. This took the form of a mutiny by his legions, who felt they were too far from Roman territory. Forced into a retreat, this ended Lucullus' pursuit of Mithridates and allowed him to return to Pontus and start a guerrilla war against Rome. This culminated in a further victory against one of Lucullus' lieutenants at Zela, in 67 BC. Given this loss and the preceding mutiny, the evasion of Mithridates and the illegal nature of his invasion of Armenia, Lucullus position was by now in danger. By 66 BC the situation presented Pompey with all the opportunities he needed, especially given his wintering in Cilicia after the successful end to the pirate campaign. Once again he made use of the assembly of the people and was awarded the coveted Mithridatic command.

The fortunes of Rome and Parthia again intersected when Tigranes was drawn into a war against Parthia, thus leaving Mithridates on his own to face a fresh Roman army of 50,000 men under Pompey. Mithridates found himself trapped and gave battle at Nicopolis, where his army was once again destroyed. Again, Mithridates gave the Romans the slip and managed to get to his Crimean kingdom, which he had managed to regain from his son. Still unwilling to give up the fight, he once again raised a fresh army and rumours soon spread that he was planning an invasion of Italy from the Balkans.[25] However, this outlandish plan was cut short by a rebellion which ended with another of his sons (Pharnaces) staging a coup and imprisoning Mithridates, who, faced with being handed over to the Romans, took his own life.

This ended the period of the Mithridatic Wars, which saw the opening of a new phase of Rome's relations with the east. Having defeated, annexed or humbled the established Hellenistic powers, Rome's attention wandered, distracted by domestic issues and other threats. This allowed the rise of new powers who had also taken advantage of Rome's humbling of the old order. The rise of Mithridates effectively mirrored the rise of Rome, a century earlier, from the rapid territorial expansion, to the invasion of Greece espousing the cause of liberation. The key difference being that he did not have the resources to compete with Rome. The Mithridatic Wars shook the Roman Empire in the east to its core, but Rome's recovery not only alerted Rome to the new dangers arising in the east, but acted as the spur to take Roman armies further than ever before. Even Mithridates' death was not enough to satisfy Pompey.

The Roman Settlement of the East (66–62 BC)

With Mithridates out of the way, the immediate threat to Rome had passed, but it was obvious to all at Rome that their previous settlement of the east was in serious need of re-assessment. Pompey, quite naturally, considered himself to be the man who could bring this security to Rome. Like Lucullus, the campaigns he undertook had not been authorised by the Senate, but, unlike Lucullus, he had a massive army and had the backing of the popular assembly of Rome and was therefore not overly concerned about what the Senate thought.

The emerging new powers of the east, Armenia and Parthia, who had just finished warring against each other, both conducted treaties of alliance with Rome (in the person of Pompey). During 66–65 BC, he undertook sporadic campaigns against the Albanian and Iberian peoples of the Caucasus region (modern Georgia) and made an abortive attempt to reach the Caspian Sea.

In 64 BC his attention turned towards the remnants of the Seleucid empire, which had been reduced to the province of Syria and was still undergoing internal strife. In addition, the kingdom of Judea was also undergoing a civil war in which he intervened. As a consequence, in 63 BC Roman forces captured Jerusalem after a three month siege. As a result of his several interventions, he created the new Roman province of Syria, which included the remnants of the Seleucid empire, whose existence was now terminated, and a chunk of Judean territory. The kingdom of Pontus was split into two, with the western half being annexed to the new Roman province of Bithynia. The eastern half was given to the new kingdom of Galatia, whose allegiance was to Rome. Pompey also extended the province of Cilicia to include the whole of the Mediterranean coast-line to join up with Syria (this process will be examined in greater detail in chapter four).

Thus, Pompey created a series of Roman provinces that guarded the Mediterranean coastline, protected by a series of client kingdoms in Asia Minor and Judea, supported by alliances with Armenia and Parthia (see map 3). This new eastern settlement protected Rome's interests in the Mediterranean and extended Roman influence further to the east than it had ever been before. It ensured that the Mediterranean would be centred on the Roman culture. The only significant free Mediterranean state of any note was Egypt, which was still crippled by internal strife and whose freedom from Rome remained tenuous. Only one power remained in the east whom Rome had not humbled into sub-mission; the Parthian Empire, whose rise in the east had mirrored Rome's in the west.

Summary

In the period from 200 to 63 BC the Roman Republic had overrun virtually the whole of the Mediterranean, overturning the Hellenistic world order and establishing Rome as the dominant power in the western world. For millennia, scholars have been examining the reasons for Rome's sudden rise to superpower status, and we do not have the space to re-open the debates properly here. What we have seen is that the Republic possessed both unique military institutions underpinned by a social and political order formed around an oligarchic aristocratic elite.

In terms of the military institutions, we can see that the system of alliances in Italy supplied the Roman armies with a near-endless supply of manpower, enabling Rome to deal with defeats which would have crippled any other ancient state. As early as the 270s BC, the Greek general Pyrrhus had identified this as being the crucial factor for Rome's military success. The organisation and structure of the legions and the legionaries themselves proved to be superior to their Greek counterparts. These two factors gave Rome military superiority in battle and an ability to recover from defeats if they encountered a general of superior ability, namely Pyrrhus or Hannibal.

On the social and political side, the consulships and the patrician-plebeian aristocracy gave Rome a pool of talented generals from which to draw. Underpinning this were the desires of the Roman aristocracy for military glory and economic benefit, all of which translated itself into political power within Rome. The Republic created the perfect circumstances for expansive warfare, with a competing aristocratic elite and a social order based on a mixture of personal and family success and the glory of the *res publica*. It was only when this balance between personal success and the good of the state was altered that the cracks started showing within the Republican system. What this analysis has only briefly touched on are Rome's internal problems, which led to the unique situation of an ever-expanding empire at the same time as increasing internal breakdown. As demonstrated during Rome's First Civil War, whilst this could hamper Rome in the short term, such as during Mithridates' invasion of Greece, ultimately the generals who had caused so much of this internal chaos could neutralise its effects on the empire, for now at least.

If we must touch on the debate between modern theories of 'defensive imperialism' and social and economic motivations, then we can see that it is neither one thing nor the other, but a mix of both. The Hannibalic invasion and near Roman destruction during the Second Punic War did clearly scar the Roman collective psyche for generations. To a great degree it was the underlying cause for the drive to military involvement in the east. However, as in all cases, the process soon took on a life of its own and became self-perpetuating. The question of when does one intervention to preserve your security become your primary foreign policy goal is one that all states have to face. In Rome's case, this policy of intervention, or 'defensive imperialism' if you will, struck a chord and interacted with the whole fabric of the Roman social order, which transformed occasional intervention into full-blown imperialism. The military, political, and economic benefits of overseas war were so attractive that it became a way of life. For centuries the Roman elites had waged war on their immediate neighbours. In the second and first centuries BC they found that they could continue this ancient practice, but on a far grander scale than their ancestors could ever have imagined. In the end, a legitimate desire for security became an imperialism that transformed the Mediterranean world, but ultimately consumed the Republic itself.

Chapter 2

Menace from the East:
The Rise of Parthia

Whilst the histories of this period tend to concentrate on the rise of Rome in the west, we must not forget that at the same time a new empire arose in the east, one that mirrored Rome's relentless push across the Hellenistic world. Unlike Rome, the Parthians represented a more traditional Hellenistic state, being a feudal empire united by force and ruled over by a dynasty (the Arsacids) that was considered alien to the majority of the peoples they ruled over. Yet the Parthians also represented a new force in history, a warrior race of horsemen from the steppes of central Asia who overran the traditional established kingdoms of the east. The Parthians ruled over an empire that, at its peak, stretched from the borders of India and China in the east to the Euphrates in the west and occasionally beyond.[26] Yet, despite the fact that for nearly four hundred years they were one of the two major superpowers of the ancient world, the Parthian civilisation has long been shrouded in obscurity. Even their very name, 'Parthian', is a western derivation.[27]

There are three major reasons for this. Firstly the Parthian empire was a hegemonic one, rather than a unified civilisation in its own right. The Parthian peoples were small in number and lacking in a distinctive culture, in comparison to the other peoples of the Middle East whom they ruled. Secondly, when the Parthian Empire collapsed in the 220s AD, they were replaced by a new dynasty, the Sassanids, who attempted to erase all traces of the Parthians, who they considered to be a non-native race. The third reason is one of chance, as a number of Parthian histories were written by the ancient Greek and Roman authors (a process given life by their victory at Carrhae), but none of them have survived into the modern world (see appendix three).

Therefore, we face a shortage of native documents and narrative histories, from either the east or the west. What we have left are scraps of information in the remaining western sources, archaeological information and numismatics (again see appendix three), though on occasions these can be contradictory, especially in terms of the origins of the Arsacid dynasty. Until they invaded and annexed Mesopotamia in the 140s BC the Parthians had largely escaped the

32

notice of the more advanced civilisations of the east, but from this point onwards, events involving the Parthians became part of the established historical record. The events of the previous century of the Arsacid dynasty of Parthia were also written about from this point onwards, though the chronology of these events is far less certain.

Parthia prior to the foundation of the Arsacid Dynasty

Whilst we have little detail for events in the region of Parthia prior to the 240s BC, we can recreate the broad picture. The region of Parthia lay to the east of the Caspian Sea, crossing what are now the countries of Iran and Turkmenistan. The region was on the edge of the central Asian steppes and was populated by a number of semi-nomadic Scythian tribes. References to the inhabitants of the region can first be found in the historical record when that area was conquered by Cyrus the Great, founder of the First Persian Empire (c.550–330 BC). The exact details of the conquest of this area are not clear, but for the first time the inhabitants of the region came into contact with the wider ancient world and found themselves on the edge of the first great empire of ancient history (stretching from the Indus to Greece). Apparently this new status did not agree with the inhabitants and as early as the 520s BC we find that the region of *Parthawa* was engaged in a revolt, which was subsequently crushed with a heavy loss of life.[28] From this point onwards it appears that the Parthians remained loyal subjects of the Persian Empire, being combined with the other races of the region into a *satrapy* (or province). Persian rule would not have been overly harsh for the Parthians, consisting of little more than a Persian *satrap* (governor) to admin-ister the area on behalf of the Persian king, though it may have forced them to settle down more as a people, given the Persian demands for tribute and men. Certainly it appears that along with the other races that formed the Persian empire, the Parthians supplied troops to their Persian overlords for the various Persian military expeditions, including the Persian invasion of Greece under Xerxes (480–479 BC).[29]

Other than these occasional glimpses in the sources and the archaeological remains, we have little trace of the Parthian region in these centuries. They remained a semi-barbarous tribal people on the fringes of a great empire, whose exact nature is impossible to determine. All this was to change with the arrival of the Macedonian king, Alexander the Great, who invaded the Persian empire in 334 BC. Once again we can find traces of Parthian troops fighting in the Persian army at the Battle of Gaugamela 331 BC.[30] With the defeat and sub-sequent death of the Persian 'Great King', Darius III, in 330 BC, the Persian empire collapsed and in its place stood the empire of Alexander the Great. Once again Parthia became a vassal state on the northern edges of another great empire, this time a Macedonian one.

With Alexander's premature death in 323 BC his dreams of a united ancient world empire died too and his territories were divided up between his various generals. These then entered into a generation of bloody dynastic wars which saw the emergence of a new order in the ancient world: the Hellenistic age. As these wars were well documented by the ancient sources, we find a number of traces of the Parthians in the following years. Upon the death of Alexander, his regent Perdiccas placed the satrapy of Parthia under the control of a man named as Phratapherenes.[31] In 321 BC, when another of Alexander's generals was in the ascendant, this time Antipater, Parthia found itself ruled by a Philip.[32]

By 317 BC the wars had reached Parthia itself. The satrap of Media, a man named Pithon, invaded Parthia and killed its satrap, Philotas (when he had replaced Philip is unknown). Pithon then placed his brother, Eudamus, as ruler of the province, but the other local rulers formed an alliance, invaded Parthia and drove both men from the region.[33] Thus Parthia, along with most of the region, found itself a pawn in a much larger game. What effect these invasions and changes of ruler had on the inhabitants of the region we cannot tell. Certainly it appears that Parthia was a useful region for the contestants to possess and later, at the Battle of Paratacene in 317 BC, we find Parthian troops in the army of Antigonus. Diodorus' account states that

'On one wing he stationed the mounted archers and lancers from Media and Parthia, a thousand in number, men well trained in the execution of the wheeling movement'.[34]

This is our first recorded glimpse of the Parthian military, and shows us the reputation that the Parthian cavalry had, even in this early period.

When the initial round of wars ended and the situation had stabilised (after the Battle of Ipsus in 301 BC), the Parthians again found themselves with a new overlord, as part of the newly formed Seleucid empire. This new entity was a loose federation of the races spread across the Middle East, from the Indus to the Aegean, which had been annexed by the Macedonian general, Seleucus. However, there were key differences between the empire of Alexander the Great and that of his successor. Firstly, Seleucus had neither the charisma nor the vision of Alexander, who had wanted to unite both the Greek and native peoples into one new civilisation. This new empire was to be ruled by the Greeks for the Greeks and this translated itself into distant rule from the region of Syria, Greek satraps, and a policy centred on the Mediterranean, rather than the east. Thus the Parthians found themselves at a neglected corner of a foreign empire.

Throughout this period, the tribes living in the region of Parthia occupied a space on the very periphery of the ancient world. They were fierce nomadic horsemen but apparently without any form of central government of their own. Although there are initial similarities between the position of Rome and Parthia (both civilisations being on the periphery of the civilised Graeco-Persian world), they represented two diametrically-opposed civilisations. Furthermore, whilst Rome always looked to the Graeco-Persian cultures, the region of Parthia lay at the juncture of a number of civilisations: the Indian states, the Chinese civilisation and the wild nomadic steppes of Central Asia. All of these would have a role in the shaping of this future world power.

The Foundation of the Arsacid Dynasty in Parthia

We must now consider the events that led up to Parthian independence and the establishment of the Arsacid Dynasty in Parthia, which is one of the most confusing episodes in Parthian history. The struggle centres around two different, but interrelating, processes: the decline of the central Seleucid power and the growth of the regions; and tribal migrations. At the centre of all these events is the semi-mythical figure of Arsaces, the first Parthian king. Although a number of histories were written about this process, none survive intact. We have three surviving ancient accounts of how Parthia achieved independence under Arsaces: a mention by the Roman writer Strabo in his work on world geography; an epitome (précis) of the history of Pompeius Trogus by a later compiler named Justin; and a fragment of a Parthian history by the Romano-Greek writer, Arrian (as reported by three later Byzantine writers, all in different forms).[35] By quoting all of these, we will soon realise the problems that we face in unravelling this process.[36]

In Strabo's *Geography*, written in the late first century BC or early first century AD, these three passages are relevant:

> But when revolutions were attempted by the countries outside the Taurus, because of the fact that the kings of Syria and Media, who were in possession also of these countries, were busily engaged with others, those who had been entrusted with their government first caused the revolt of Bactria and of all the country near it, I mean Euthydemus and his followers;[37] and then Arsaces, a Scythian, with some of the Däae (I mean the Apranians, as they were called, nomads who lived along the Ochus), invaded Parthia and conquered it. Now at the outset Arsaces was weak, being continually at war with those who had been deprived by him of their territory, both he himself and his successors, but later

they grew so strong, always taking the neighbouring territory, through successes in warfare, that finally they established themselves as lords of the whole country inside the Euphrates.[38]

At any rate, some say that Arsaces derives his origin from the Scythians, whereas others say that he was a Bactrian and that when in flight from the enlarged power of Diodotus [the rebel governor of Bactria] and his followers he caused Parthia to revolt. But since I have said much about the Parthian origins in the sixth book of my Historical Sketches and in the second book of my history of events after Polybius [both works now lost], I shall omit discussion of that subject here, lest I may be seen to be repeating what I have already said, though I shall mention this alone, that the Council of the Parthians, according to Poseidonius, consists of two groups, one that of kinsmen [of the king] and the other of wise men and Magi, from both of which groups the kings are appointed.[39]

In Justin's *Epitome of the Philippic History of Pompeius Trogus*, dating to the third century AD, these four passages are most helpful:

The Parthians, in whose hands the empire of the east now is, having divided the world, as it were, with the Romans, were originally exiles from Scythia. This is apparent from their very name; for in the Scythian language exiles are called Parthi.[40]

Subsequently, when the Macedonians were divided into parties by civil discord, the Parthians, with the other people of Upper Asia, followed Eumenes, and, when he was defeated, went over to Antigonus. After his death they were under the rule of Seleucus Nicator, and then under Antiochus and his successors, from whose great-grandson Seleucus they first revolted, in the First Punic War, when Lucius Manlius Vulso and Marcus Attilius Regulus were consuls [250 BC[41]]. For their revolt, the dispute between the two brothers, Seleucus and Antiochus, procured them impunity; for while they sought to wrest the throne from one another, they neglected to pursue the revolters.[42]

At the same period, also, Theodotus, governor of the thousand cities of Bactria, revolted, and assumed the title of king; and all the other people of the east, influenced by his example, fell away from the Macedonians. One Arsaces, a man of uncertain origin, but of undisputed bravery, happened to arise at this time; and he, who was accustomed to live by plunder and depredations, hearing a report that Seleucus was overcome by the Gauls in Asia, and being consequently freed from dread of that prince, invaded Parthia with a band of marauders, overthrew

Andragoras his lieutenant, and, after putting him to death, took upon himself the government of the country. Not long after, too, he made himself master of Hyrcania, and thus, invested with authority over two nations, raised a large army, through fear of Seleucus and Theodotus, king of the Bactrians. But being soon relieved of his fears by the death of Theodotus, he made peace and an alliance with his son, who was also named Theodotus; and not long after, engaging with king Seleucus, who came to take vengeance on the revolters, he obtained a victory; and the Parthians observe the day on which it was gained with great solemnity, as the date of the commencement of their liberty.[43]

Thus Arsaces, having at once acquired and established a kingdom, and having become no less memorable among the Parthians than Cyrus among the Persians, Alexander among the Macedonians, or Romulus among the Romans, died at a mature old age; and the Parthians paid this honour to his memory, that they called all their kings thenceforward by the name of Arsaces[44]

The following three extracts preserve parts of Arrian's *Parthica*, written in the second century AD. The earliest of these is Zosimus' *History* from the fourth or fifth century AD.

For after the death of Alexander the son of Philip, and of his successors in the empire of the Macedonians, at the period when those provinces were under the authority of Antiochus, Arsaces a Parthian, being exasperated at an injury done to his brother Tiridates, made war upon the satrap of Antiochus, and caused the Parthians to drive away the Macedonians, and form a government of their own.[45]

The next, Synkellos' *Chronology* dates to the eighth century AD.

During the reign of this Antiochos, the Persians [Parthians], who were tributaries to them from the time of Alexander the founder, revolted from Macedonian and Antiochid rule. The reason was as follows:

A certain Arsaces and Tiridates, brothers tracing their lineage from Artaxerxes king of the Persians [465–424 BC], were satraps of the Bactrians at the time of Agathocles, the Macedonian satrap of Parthia. According to Arrian, this Agathocles fell in love with Tiridates, one of the brothers, and was eagerly laying a snare for the young man. But failing utterly, was killed by him and his brother Arsaces. Arsaces then became king of the Persians [Parthians], after whom the kings of the Persians [Parthians] were known as Arsacidae. He reigned for two years and was killed by his brother Tiridates, who succeeded him, to rule for thirty seven years.[46]

The final version is in the *Bibliotheca* of Photius, writing as late as the ninth century:

> In the *Parthica* he [Arrian] gives an account of the wars between Parthia and Rome during the reign of Trajan. He considers the Parthians to have been a Scythian race, which had long been under the yoke of Macedonia, the Persians having been subdued at the same time, and revolted for the following reason.

> 'Arsaces and Tiridates were two brothers, descendants of Arsaces, the son of Phriapetes. These two brothers, with five accomplices, slew Pherecles, who had been appointed satrap of Parthia by Antiochus Theos (the Seleucid monarch), to avenge an insult offered to one of them; they drove out the Macedonians, set up a government of their own, and became so powerful that they were a match for the Romans in war, and sometimes even were victorious over them'.[47]

Furthermore, we have four later Graeco-Roman sources which comment on the Parthian origins. The first, Quintus Curtius Rufus, from the first century AD, backs the barbarian invasion version of events:

> the entire column was brought up by the Parthyaei, a race living in the areas which are today populated by Parthians who emigrated from Scythia.[48]

But the other three, from the second and third centuries AD, back the native revolt theory. We have Appian's account from the second century AD:

> He [Ptolemy] invaded Syria and advanced as far as Babylon. The Parthians now began their revolt, taking advantage of the confusion in the house of the Seleucidae.[49]

Dio Cassius' *History of Rome* written in the third century AD:

> when the successors of Alexander had quarrelled with one another, cutting off separate portions (of his empire) for themselves and setting up individual monarchies, the Parthians then first attained prominence

under a certain Arsaces, from whom the succeeding rulers received their title Arsacidae.[50]

And finally, Herodian's *History of Rome*, also from the third century AD:

> When these governors quarrelled and the power of the Macedonians was weakened by continual wars, they say that Arsaces the Parthian was the first to persuade the barbarians in those regions to revolt from the Macedonians. Invested with the crown by the willing Parthians and the neighbouring barbarians, Arsaces ruled as king.[51]

Thus we can now see the problem with which we are faced. There are two clear strands of thought, which sometimes overlap. One is that Arsaces was the leader of a tribe of Scythian barbarians which invaded and overran the region of Parthia, and the other is that there was a native revolt led by Arsaces who freed Parthia from Seleucid influence. Thus we have full-blown invasion and tribal migration (though Justin downgrades this to a small band of marauders) versus a native revolt led from within. Of the latter, the sources quoted above cannot make their minds up whether Arsaces was Parthian or Bactrian.

In connection with this problem, we have a number of further pieces of information. Firstly, we know that the Parthians had a dating system based on the accession of Arsaces to the throne and that it equates to the year 248/247 BC.[52] Secondly, we know that the neighbouring Seleucid province of Bactria revolted under its governor (as mentioned above, either a Diodotus or a Theodotus) and achieved full independence as the kingdom of Bactria. Added to this is the general collapse of the Seleucid empire in the 240s/230s period. The Third Syrian War (c. 246–241 BC), between the Seleucids and the Egyptians, saw heavy Seleucid losses and a collapse of Seleucid authority. This was followed by a fraternal civil war (c. 240–236 BC) which saw the Seleucid empire decline even further. Thus the decade from 246 to 236 BC was the perfect time for either a revolt or an invasion, with the Seleucids in no position to offer any resistance in the region.

A number of scholars have attempted to construct a narrative that ties all the elements together and attempts to make sense of them.[53] With due respect to them, the existing evidence makes that impossible to do without making great leaps of logic that are not supported by the remaining evidence. Lerner, however, does make one important point, namely that the dating of the founding of the Arsacid era (c. 248/247 BC) does not have to correspond to Arsaces' conquest of Parthia (which would place it before Seleucid power started to decline, directly contradicting both Strabo and Justin).[54] The date could relate to when Arsaces was crowned king (or ruler) of his tribe (either the Aprani or the Däae). We know that the Seleucids had been having problems with the Scythian tribes of the Caspian region, as it is recorded that the Seleucid general, Demodamus, was sent to the region c. 280 BC to suppress them.[55]

With this date issue opened up, we can now look at the two main elements that form the foundation tale, namely that Arsaces was both Scythian and was connected with Bactria. The first thing to note is that none of the sources speak of a full-scale barbarian migration to the area. Strabo states that Arsaces invaded with 'some' or 'certain' (τινάς) of the Däae, rather than many, and Justin tells us that he had a band of marauders. Thus we can conclude that this was not a full-blown barbarian migration, but was merely that Arsaces invaded Parthia, killed the governor, declared himself king and then led Parthia to independence. What are we to make of his Bactrian connection then? Attempts have already been made to connect the two elements of him being Scythian in origin and the Bactrian connection, by stating that his band/tribe attacked Bactria first and then were repulsed, but again there is nothing to back this up in the sources.[56] Given that we know that the governor of Bactria revolted, we can ask ourselves whether during this revolt he used Scythian tribesmen as mercenaries, and if he did so then might they be Arsaces and his warband? At the conclusion of the campaign to free Bactria from Seleucid rule, we can then suggest that Diodotus (the former governor of Bactria, now king) fell out with his mercenaries, as invariably happened, and they then invaded the neighbouring Seleucid province of Parthia and took over.

In this way we can construct a more logical sequence of events, which does not require a tight chronology. In 248/247 BC a man named Arsaces became the warchief of his band/tribe of Scythian barbarians, who occupied the lands bordering the Seleucid empire in the region of the Caspian Sea (in what is now modern Turkmenistan). During the period c. 246–236 BC, three major events occurred in the region which transformed Arsaces from tribal chief to king of an independent country. Firstly, Seleucid authority in the east crumbled due to a series of wars and setbacks in the west, allowing the governor of Bactria to declare independence. Secondly, this governor used Arsaces and his warband in his war of independence, but the two parties fell out at some point. Thirdly, Arsaces and his warband, which included his brother Tiridates, then invaded Parthia, killed the Seleucid governor and established themselves as the new ruling elite of the semi-nomadic province. Once they had established control, Arsaces then made himself king and declared Parthia to be independent. We even have a fragment of an ancient source that tells us where this event actually happened: 'the City of Asaac in which Arsaces was first proclaimed king; and an everlasting flame is guarded there'.[57]

Thus we have a chain of events that includes both traditions of Arsaces being Scythian, yet coming from Bactria. This only leaves us the Arrian-inspired events that include the Parthian governor and a homosexual angle. It is again possible that when Arsaces was driven out of Bactria he did not necessarily launch an immediate attack on Parthia, but could have offered his warband's services to the Parthian governor, against Diodotus of Bactria, with whom he had fallen out. It is then entirely possible that Arsaces promptly fell out with the Parthian governor (perhaps over his brother) and, rather than flee another province and finding Parthia far weaker than Bactria, slew the governor. He then established himself and his men as the new rulers of the Seleucid province of Parthia and declared independence, with himself as king. Thus we have a sequence of events that includes the main themes of each of the surviving sources without stretching the evidence too far or getting tied up with an exact time-frame. We can see that the foundation of the Arsacid dynasty in Parthia came about as a result of the temporary collapse of Seleucid rule in the east, which led to the revolt of Bactria and the Arsacid takeover in Parthia.

Therefore, the former Seleucid province of Parthia gained a new ruling elite; a Scythian warband, which seems to have been quickly accepted by the semi-nomadic peoples of the province, especially given a long rule of foreign (Persian and then Greek) governors. The fragments of Arrian all seem to contain traces of the Arsacids claiming descent from the first Persian rulers (the Achaemenids), which was probably done to help justify their rule.[58] It appears that the first capital of an independent kingdom of Parthia was the city of Nisa, which lies just east of the present city of Ashgabat (the capital of modern Turkmenistan), though the Parthian capital moved west as their empire grew.[59]

With this new ruling elite in place, the province was transformed into a state in its own right, but one that was still little more than an independent semi-nomadic region, which at the time appeared to possess few factors that would lead to the foundation of a new world power. If anything, it was neighbouring Bactria, with its numerous cities and control of the eastern trade routes, that looked more likely to become the dominant power in the region. Although Arsaces appeared to have established Arsacid rule firmly within Parthia, he still faced two massive external threats. Not only did he have a dominant Bactria on his eastern flank, but he had the Seleucid empire to his west, which, when it recovered from its internal difficulties, would be eager to regain its lost territories.

The Struggle for Independence (c. 240s–176 BC)

Before we examine the drawn out Parthian struggle to remain independent, we must first deal with the problem concerning the length of Arsaces' reign. Here we have two totally contradictory sources. The first is Synkellos:

He reigned for two years and was killed by his brother Tiridates, who succeeded him, to rule for thirty-seven years.[60]

and the second is Justin:

Thus Arsaces, having at once acquired and established a kingdom, and having become no less memorable among the Parthians than Cyrus among the Persians, Alexander among the Macedonians, or Romulus among the Romans, died at a mature old age[61]

We have two differing traditions at play here. One has Arsaces ruling for a long reign, being succeeded by his son, who in turn is replaced by a grandson of Tiridates, named as Priapatius (who ruled as Arsaces III). The second tradition has Arsaces being murdered by his own brother (the very one that he had saved from the clutches of the Parthian governor) within just two years, who then goes onto rule for a long reign until he is succeeded by his grandson Priapatius. So which are we to believe?

It is suspicious that none of the earlier sources mention this fate of Arsaces, and that it mirrors the origins of Rome (with Romulus killing his brother Remus). Furthermore as one modern author puts it

the importance of Arsaces I is far greater in the later imagination of the Arsacid Empire . . . Why would the Parthians recall a leader who had held power for not two or three years, and never in fact ruled in Parthia proper at all, on every coin they ever issued, and in the name of every king they ever had[62]

Therefore, the most obvious way to proceed is by accepting that Arsaces did indeed rule for a long period, down to c. 211 BC in fact, and was the man who did so much to free Parthia from Seleucid domination and build it up into a strong regional power. Having dealt with this issue, we can now turn our attention to the rest of Arsaces' reign. It appears that both he and his men did not dwell upon their new status long, as we are told that the Parthians (as we can now call them) soon invaded the neighbouring Seleucid province of Hyrcania and annexed it, thus increasing the size of Parthian territory and Arsaces' power-base.[63] By c. 236 BC, the Seleucid king, Seleucus II, had settled his empire sufficiently to allow himself to mount a campaign to recapture the provinces of Hyrcania, Parthia and Bactria. Once again the details of the period are sketchy, but it appears that he targeted Parthia first and allied with Diodotus of Bactria in an anti-Parthian pact. This was followed by a full-scale invasion of Parthia and the total defeat of Arsaces, who was forced to flee the country altogether and find shelter with the nomadic tribes of the Caspian steppes.[64] At this point it appeared as though the Parthian rebellion had been crushed and Parthia would be once again relegated to a footnote of history.

Instead, Arsaces managed to engineer a remarkable turnaround. Fortunately for him, it appears that Diodotus of Bactria soon died, leaving his throne to his son. Diodotus II soon realised the danger from a resurgent Seleucid empire; it was clear that once Parthia had fallen Bactria would be next. It appears that he therefore reversed the policy of his father and allied with Arsaces, preferring an independent Parthia as a buffer state between Bactria and the Seleucids. With Diodotus' backing, Arsaces managed to raise a fresh army and challenge Seleucus once more. Justin presents us with the following:

> within a short time, Arsaces joined battle with king Seleucus who had come to punish those who had seceded and he [Arsaces] remained the victor. Ever since, the Parthians celebrate this day with solemnity which they have fixed as the beginning of their freedom.[65]

Arsaces' defeat of the army of Seleucus finally established Parthian independence. It appears that this victory was made the more complete by the capture of Seleucus himself, who remained a Parthian hostage for some time.[66] He was eventually released, but the terms must have been the recognition of Parthian independence.[67] With independence secured, Arsaces then established the foundations for a strong Parthia:

> while Arsaces, having put the Parthian kingdom in order, assembled an army, laid the foundations of a fortress, strengthened cities, and founded on Mt. Apaortenon the city of Dara, the location of which is such that there is no other city of a more fortified character and more fascinating.[68]

During this period, Parthia was at peace with Bactria and had a de facto peace with the Seleucid empire.[69] However, in 223 BC the Seleucids gained a new and powerful king in the person of Antiochus III, also known as the Great, who did much to restore the Seleucid empire to its former glory. The death of Arsaces (c. 211/ 210 BC) and the accession of his son, Arsaces II,[70] along with the breakdown of Parthian-Bactrian relations, presented Antiochus with a golden opportunity to recover the eastern provinces.[71]

In 209 BC, Antiochus invaded Parthia with a huge army, quoted in one ancient source as being 120,000 strong, though we must question such an extravagant figure.[72] The new Parthian king, Arsaces II, retreated ahead of the Seleucid forces, destroying the infrastructure as he went. Nevertheless, his forces were defeated at Mount Labus and he could not stop Antiochus invading Hyrcania, where the new Parthian capital of Hecatompylus lay.[73] The details of the rest of the campaign have been lost, but the war ended with Parthia's defeat and a peace treaty which established a compromise situation. The Arsacid dynasty were recognised as rulers of Parthia, but Parthia itself was reduced to being a federal dominion of the Seleucid empire, without being a formal province. Whilst we have no exact details of the nature of this status, it is clear that Parthia was reduced to being a federated ally of the Seleucid empire.[74] Thus the many gains of Arsaces I had been overturned and, although the Arsacids remained in control of Parthia, the country had lost both its independence and its fledgling empire.

We know nothing else of the reign of Arsaces II and it is probable that he kept a deliberately low profile following his defeat. We know that he was succeeded on the throne by Priapatius, who designated himself as Arsaces III. This was the first time this appellation had been taken by a member of the family whose real name was not Arsaces. According to Justin this took place c.191 BC, but it has recently been argued that Priapatius seized the throne from Arsaces II and established the rule of the junior branch of the Arsacid family, which descended from Arsaces' brother Tiridates.[75]

Though the coup remains speculation it does appear that from this point onward, although they all claimed descent from Arsaces, all subsequent Parthian kings were descended from Tiridates, which may explain the growth of the variant tradition that Arsaces I died quite soon after leading the Parthians to independence and that Parthian power was laid by Tiridates instead.

This defeat and diminution of status was a major setback in the history of Parthia and we know nothing of the internal events that took place for the rest of Priapatius' reign. The rise of Parthia to superpower status might have ended there if it were not for the help they received from an unusual and unknowing source. As we have seen, with the east secure, Antiochus III turned his attention to the west and mainland Greece, then under Roman protection. A disastrous war with the Romans resulted in the destruction of Seleucid power in the west and shook his whole empire. This defeat appears to have had no immediate effect on Parthia. In c.176 BC Priapatius was succeeded by his son, Phraates (who ruled as Arsaces IV), and it is only from this date that we see the Parthian fightback.

It is difficult to gauge the status of Parthia during the years c. 208–176 BC, given the lack of surviving source material. We can certainly assume that following their defeat and Priapatius' accession to the throne (whether by coup or not) the Parthians kept a deliberately low profile in fear of angering Antiochus III. We do not know for certain that the Seleucids left a garrison in Parthia, but given the trouble that they had caused the empire, we can assume that it was the case. We can also assume that Antiochus' war and defeat against the Romans would have seen that garrison removed and thus allowed the Parthians to rebuild their own forces and re-establish her independence from Seleucid interference. Following the peace terms imposed on them by Rome, the Seleucids were unlikely to be able to stage a campaign on the scale of Antiochus' invasion of 209 BC, virtually guaranteeing Parthia's independence from them.

Thus the actions of Rome on one side of the ancient world saw important repercussions on the other, revealing the delicate balance of the ancient world order. Once again we can see that Rome's interference with the established Hellenistic order was allowing new states to emerge that would ultimately threaten Roman security, a result of Rome's haphazard policy with regard to the east.

The Rise of a New Power (176–138 BC)

With Rome's humbling of the Seleucid empire, the way was open for Parthian expansion to the west. It is the next two monarchs, Phraates I (c.176–171 B.C) and Mithradates I (c.171–138 B.C), that led the Parthians on the road to imperial status. Although he only reigned for five years, Phraates disregarded over thirty years of Parthian stagnation and launched aggressive wars against his immediate neighbours, both to the west and south, subduing the tribes that lived there. Upon his death, this expansionism was taken up by his younger brother, Mithradates I (no relation to the monarchs of Pontus). At the same time as Mithradates' accession, the king of Bactria was overthrown by a usurper, plunging Bactria into chaos. Mithradates took this opportunity to invade Bactria (Parthia's closest rival in the region) and annexed the bordering territories of Tapuria and Traxiana, though we are unsure of the exact date of this campaign (most likely during the early 160s BC).

A potential threat to Parthia from the new Seleucid king, Antiochus IV, was averted in 163 BC, when he was murdered whilst campaigning in the east of the empire. With Bactria cut down to size and the death of the Seleucid king, Mithradates again showed his strategic abilities by launching an invasion of the Seleucid-controlled region of Media (a major regional power in its own right) in the 150s BC (though again this is hard to date exactly). After a long and protracted war, whose exact details are lost to us, by 148 BC Media had been conquered. Rather than ruling it directly, Mithradates appointed a governor to rule the province in his name, thus creating the first proper imperial province of the Parthian empire. This was not the only way in which the Parthian empire was taking shape, as this conquest had brought Parthian territory to the river Tigris itself, beyond which lay Mesopotamia, the cradle of all great eastern empires, containing the great cities of Babylon and Seleucia.

Building upon his already-great success, Mithradates determined to continue and launched his most ambitious campaign yet. In 141 BC he invaded Mesopotamia, thus reversing two hundred years of conquest from the west. Defeating a general of the Seleucid king, Demetrius II, Mithradates accepted the surrender of the strategic cities of Seleucia and Babylon and had himself re-crowned as 'King of Kings' in Seleucia.[76] However, Mithradates had to break off the campaign to return to Parthia proper; for what reason we do not know, though border raids by barbarians are suspected. Nevertheless, the Parthian army had developed in such a way that he was able to leave a force to complete the conquest of Mesopotamia, under an unknown general, whilst he himself campaigned on Parthia's eastern borders, perhaps to repel raiders from China.

In his absence, the Seleucid king attempted to re-capture Mesopotamia but was defeated in battle by Mithradates' general (in 139 BC). The king himself was captured and transported back to Parthia, where he lived as an honoured captive and was even married off to one of Mithradates' daughters. Mithradates returned to the west in person and added the minor kingdom of the Elymaeans to the Parthian empire, as well as the old Persian capital city of Susa. In addition to this territory, the Parthians took a considerable amount of loot with them back to Parthia, taken from the Greek cities and temples of the region.

Having achieved these great conquests, in the winter of 138/137 BC Mithradates died peacefully, being justifiably labelled as the true founder of the Parthian empire. On his accession, Parthia was a small regional power just recovering from forty years of Seleucid domination. On his death, thirty-three years later, the Parthian empire was the unquestioned dominant power in the region. Bactria had been humbled, Media and Mesopotamia had been conquered and the Seleucid empire driven back west of the Euphrates. The reigning Seleucid king had been made a captive and a subservient son-in-law. For the first time in two hundred years, the great cities of Susa, Babylon and the whole Mesopotamian region were free from Greek rule. In historical terms the tide had turned and the Greek advance eastwards had now turned into a retreat back towards the Mediterranean.

During these years, the Parthian army had developed into a devastating fighting machine, defeating armies from both the east and the west. Although its exact nature is unknown, we can surmise that it was in this period that the Parthians perfected their legendary cataphract cavalrymen to complement their mounted archers. Certainly by 138 BC, just as Rome was the dominant power in the Mediterranean, Parthia was dominant power in the east, and designated heirs to the first great Persian Empire. An attack on the remnants of the Seleucid empire and a push for the Mediterranean seemed inevitable, especially given the presence of a captive Seleucid monarch who could act as a puppet ruler.

Unlike the rise of the Roman empire in the west, however, the Parthian empire had one crucial difference; as with all eastern empires, they were reliant upon the brilliance of the individual monarch. Arsaces had established a strong independent Parthia, but his successors had overseen its decline. Mithradates had overseen Parthia's rise to being the region's superpower, but could his successors hold onto it?

The only possible way out of this dilemma was to create a command structure that would allow competent generals to develop and as the Parthians' Mesopotamian campaign had shown, there were certainly encouraging signs in this direction; the crucial victory over the Seleucid forces had been won by one of Mithradates' generals (whose identity is lost to us). Furthermore, the Babylonian chronicles record that the Parthian king appointed five generals to command the Parthian forces in the region. From their names, Antiochus, Nikanor, Hyspaosines, Philinos[77] and Enius[78], it appears that generals of Greek or local origin were employed there rather than using Parthian generals.

This policy had both benefits and drawbacks. The benefit being that they had local knowledge and could rule the area in Parthia's name without looking like foreign oppressors. Furthermore, they would not be a threat to the Parthian throne, as a powerful Parthian general would be. The drawback was that their loyalty could be in question, as happened when the general Antiochus betrayed the Parthians to a local regional power, Elam.[79] However, we know little of the Parthian military command structure or how much the king relied upon non-Arsacid generals overall.

By contrast, the Romans in this period did not suffer from this weakness. The nature of the republican system and the ruling oligarchy provided Rome with a multitude of able commanders (along with the inevitable poorer ones). This is one of the key factors that allowed for the seeming relentless progress of the conquests of the Republic. When the Romans eventually abandoned their republic in favour of an empire then they too succumbed to this 'dilemma of command'.

Collapse and Recovery (138–88 BC)

In the case of Parthia, Mithradates' son, Phraates II, came to the throne in 138 BC, but the decade of the 130s saw little in the way of preparations for a campaign against the remnants of the Seleucid empire. It appears that the whole Seleucid issue had been allowed to deteriorate. Despite his luxurious treatment, the captured Seleucid king, Demetrius, attempted to escape captivity and reach his homeland on two separate occasions, both of which ended in his capture and subsequent pardon. Furthermore, the situation in the Seleucid empire itself had stabilised. Defeat and the loss of Mesopotamia and the king had led to a usurper,

Tryphon, seizing the throne, which sparked off yet another Seleucid civil war. Yet the Parthians failed to capitalise on this opportunity, perhaps waiting for the situation to deteriorate even further. Instead, however, a 'legitimate' Seleucid claimant seized the throne and unified the empire under his leadership. This was Antiochus VII, who was perhaps the last great leader the Seleucids produced. With the throne secure, he immediately turned his attention to recovering Mesopotamia, if not the rest of the eastern lands.

This failure to capitalise on Mithradates' conquests could be used as evidence for the weaknesses of the Parthian (and Seleucid) systems, namely their reliance on kings with dynamism. In their defence, it was possible that the Parthians were distracted by the migratory activities of the tribes on their Chinese border, who we know to have been active in this period. In any case, the Parthians certainly neglected events in the west and paid the price for it. In 130 BC, Antiochus VII invaded Mesopotamia with an army of over 80,000 men (the largest for a generation).[80] Again we possess little exact detail for the subsequent war, but what is clear is that it was a disaster for the Parthians, who were defeated in three separate battles. We only know the location of one of them, on the River Lycus, where the Parthian general Indates was defeated.[81]

These defeats were followed by the revolt of the city of Seleucia and the murder of its Parthian governor, Enius, with the city of Susa soon following.[82] Clearly this showed the tenuous nature of the Parthian conquest of what had been Greek territory for two hundred years (again another factor to bear in mind for the later Roman campaign).

By the end of the year, Parthia had not only lost Mesopotamia, but also the military reputation that Mithradates had taken three decades to establish. As a consequence, Antiochus advanced into Parthian-held Media, gaining allies from all the tributary races and cities that had previously sworn allegiance to the Parthians. In a move that showed that he was clearly not in the same mould as his father, Phraates attempted to negotiate, although it is possible that he was buying time. Antiochus' terms were the destruction of the Parthian empire through the return of all of its conquered territories, outside of Parthia proper, to the Seleucid Empire.

Finding the terms totally unacceptable and being unable to defeat Antiochus in open battle, Phraates resorted to underhand tactics. Firstly, he released Demetrius and sent him back to Syria, something that would undermine Antiochus VII; secondly, he set about undermining Antiochus' military position in Media. Antiochus had ended the campaign of 130 BC by wintering in Media rather than withdrawing back to Mesopotamia. Thus the burden of feeding and housing such a large army fell on the native populations of the region, who naturally resented this treatment at the hands of the Greeks. This resentment was fanned by Parthian agents into full scale revolt.

In the spring of 129 BC in a superb piece of planning, the cities of Media rose up and attacked the scattered, resting army of Antiochus, just as Phraates took to the field himself and advanced into Media. Despite being advised to retreat, Antiochus offered battle, which, given the disorganised nature of his army, was only ever going to have one outcome. The Seleucid army was destroyed, along with Antiochus and his dreams of the restoration of the Seleucid empire. Phraates had succeeded through a use of cunning and brute force, where brute force alone had failed. Phraates advanced into Mesopotamia, which was easily re-conquered. Having turned defeat into victory, Phraates prepared for an invasion of Syria, now controlled by Demetrius once more. Victory would have put the Parthians on the Mediterranean coast of the Middle East, some sixty years before the Romans annexed it. Unfortunately for the Parthians however, imminent victory in the west was undermined by a new perilous threat from the east.

For a decade or more, the lands bordering Parthia's eastern border had seen the advance warnings of a full-scale barbarian migration, as periodically occurred all over the ancient world. This is perhaps what had caused Mithradates to return eastwards in the 130s BC and what had delayed Phraates in his campaign against the Seleucids. Pressures in the northern steppes had led to a fierce nomadic tribe known as the Saka moving into the region adjoining the Parthian border, from where they mounted raids across the border. Phraates had clearly tried to solve this problem earlier by a policy of co-option, as the sources indicate that a large number of Saka tribesmen had been hired to fight for Parthia in the war against Antiochus. However, they were still making their way westwards towards Media when Antiochus' army was destroyed. Unwilling to demobilise empty handed, they then turned on the Parthians and ravaged the territories of the empire, penetrating as far west as Mesopotamia.[83]

Phraates' policy of co-option had allowed a dangerous barbarian enemy into the heart of the empire. It was a lesson that he was slow to learn. In the short term, the Parthians' problem with the Saka became considerably worse, when it turned out that the tribesmen who were now raiding their territory were merely the advance guard, with the whole tribe approaching Parthia's northeastern border. Between the Parthians and the Saka lay the kingdom of Bactria, which proved to be no match and was devastated.

Abandoning the invasion of Syria, Phraates made for the eastern border, but not before making an ill-advised and ultimately fatal error. Believing that he would need a large force to defeat the Saka, he conscripted a large number of the Greek soldiers from Antiochus VII's defeated army. He chose to ignore the fact that the Greek cities had recently revolted and that the Saka mercenaries were still ravaging his territory. With an army containing a large number of Greeks soldiers whom he had just defeated, Phraates returned to the east to engage the Saka in battle.

In 128 BC, in an unrecorded location on Parthia's eastern border, the Parthian army met the Saka barbarians in battle. During the battle the inevitable occurred when the Greek soldiers deserted the Parthians, allowing them to be routed and slaughtered. Phraates himself perished in the fighting, making him the first Parthian king to die in battle. Parthia now found herself fighting for her existence in the face of a barbarian onslaught and the situation soon got worse. The new king, Artabanus I (the uncle of Phraates) resorted to buying the Saka off, which appears to have worked in the short term. However, a second wave of migrating barbarians followed the Saka, named in the sources as the Tochari, and Artabanus met them in battle in the region of Bactria in 124 BC. He too was killed in battle (at the point of a poisoned arrow) and another Parthian army met defeat (the fifth in a decade).[84]

When Mithradates II succeeded to the throne in 124 BC, he faced an empire in crisis. Not only were the eastern borders, nearest to the Parthian homeland, being overrun by barbarians (who had killed the last two kings in battle), but the province of Mesopotamia was undergoing serious problems of its own. The governor installed by Phraates II in 129 BC, Himerus (or Euhemerus), had engaged in a policy of retaliation against the Greek inhabitants for their revolt the previous year, thus provoking them to the point of open insurrection once more.[85] Furthermore, a new kingdom had been created on the mouth of the Tigris (where it emptied into the Persian Gulf). During the several conquests of Mesopotamia in the preceding decade, the minor city of Antiochia had found itself ignored by both warring sides, due to its southern position. The Seleucid governor, Hyspaosines, seized the opportunity and declared independence, changing the city's name to Spasinou Charax (the city of Hyspaosines) and making it the capital city of the new kingdom of Characene. Taking advantage of the Parthian weakness, he then invaded Mesopotamia proper and by 127 BC had conquered both Babylon and Seleucia.[86]

Thus Mithradates II faced problems in both the east and the west of the Parthian empire. For the next thirty years he worked tirelessly as ruler of Parthia and re-established the empire as a major power. The exact details of his campaigning have been lost to us, but it appears that the barbarians in the east had eased up on their westward push, settling in the Afghan regions of Helmand-Quandahar and the Punjab in India. This allowed Mithradates to deal with the western problems first. In 122 BC he re-invaded Mesopotamia and attacked the kingdom of Characene. Within the year the Parthians had re-occupied both Babylon and Seleucia and had soundly defeated Characene, which now became a vassal state of the Parthian Empire.

With the west secured, Mithradates turned his attention back to the east. Again our sources provide us with little detail, but it is clear that he fought a number of campaigns against the barbarian tribes on, or within, the borders of the Parthian empire. We have no dates, but Chinese sources appear to indicate that the Parthians had secured the border city of Merv by 115 BC. Other sources state that he defeated the barbarians on a number of occasions and added a number of Bactrian cities to the his empire.[87]

It is clear that by c.100 BC the eastern border of the empire was secure enough to allow the trade routes with the Han empire of China to flourish (leading to the establishment of the great Silk Road). Chinese records show that the Han dynasty sent an embassy to the court of Mithradates sometime in the period 120–90 BC to formalise trade relations, showing both the stability and the powerful role of the Parthian empire (see appendix III). It is clear that Mithradates II had ended the barbarian threat which had threatened the very existence of the empire, for which he was given the title 'The Great'.

These threats dealt with, Mithradates began a fresh period of expansion in the west, attacking and defeating the newly emerging kingdom of Armenia. He did not occupy the territory, but he did take hostage the heir to the Armenian throne, Tigranes (who, as we have seen, later went to war with the Romans), to ensure future Armenian good behaviour. When the old king died in 94 BC, Tigranes was installed on the throne of Armenia with the aid of Parthian forces, in return for which the Parthians received seventy valleys worth of territory.[88]

Thus, by the late 90s Mithradates II had not only stabilised the Parthian Empire but had once again established it as the superpower of the region. His eastern borders were secure and had established firm relations with the Han empire of China. To the west, Mesopotamia was firmly under Parthian control and no further threats were posed by either Seleucids or Characenes, while Armenia was now a subservient ally. Parthian policy appeared to have changed from one of outright annexation to one of suzerainty over its neighbours.

The focus of Parthian rule had moved westwards with the seat of government moving from Parthia proper into Mesopotamia and a new winter capital city of Ctesiphon, on the Euphrates (the summer capital being Ectabana in Media). The reasons for this are unclear, but, as the Saka invasion had shown, the old Parthian capitals of Nisa and Hecatompylos were vulnerable to barbarian incursions from the northern and eastern steppes. The province of Mesopotamia was now firmly in Parthian hands and provided a western outlook to the empire, and the monarchy inherited a more Hellenistic nature. Having a capital city in Mesopotamia also provided a powerful political and cultural statement (in many ways mirroring Peter the Great's decision to move the Russian capital from Moscow to St Petersburg in the 1700s). In addition, with all the great eastern empires having centred their civilisations on that region, the Parthians could claim to be the natural heirs to the Persian empire, rather than the failing, and alien, Hellenistic states.

It was also in Mithradates' reign that the Parthians took their first step in relations with the wider western world, in the form of the first contact between Parthia and Rome. Whilst both empires would have been aware of the other, neither would have considered the other a serious threat prior to the 90s BC (though had Parthia invaded Syria then this would have undoubtedly changed). As we have seen, by the 90s BC Rome had realised that their neglect of the east had allowed new states to rise from the ashes of the Seleucid empire, in partic-ular Mithridates VI of Pontus. By 92 BC, Rome had become so alarmed by the rise of Mithridates VI that the Senate commissioned the governor of Cilicia, Lucius Cornelius Sulla, to intervene in the Asia Minor region and restore the independence of the kingdom of Cappadocia (which had been annexed by Mithridates VI). Whilst for Rome, the immediate threat was the kingdom of Pontus, they would have been well aware of the advance of the Parthian empire. Armenia had recently been defeated in battle and was now under Parthian influence. As detailed in chapter one, the Romans were never slow in spotting, or even inventing, new dangers to their much sought after security.

The details of how the Romans and Parthians arranged their first meeting are unknown, but what is known is that Sulla met with a Parthian ambassador, Orobazus, by the Euphrates. Whilst the details of the meeting are obscure, it does appear that there was a sharp cultural difference between the two sides (inevitable given one was an oligarchic republic and the other an oriental monarchy). It does not appear that either participant had the authorisation to conclude a treaty, so the meeting took the form of a mutual exchange of good-will. Orobazus appears to have been treated in high-handed fashion by Sulla, a fact which cost the former his life upon his return to the Parthian court.[89]

Whatever the result, it is highly doubtful that the Parthians and Romans agreed on a line of demarcation between the two empires, as this would have run against both sides' aims and interests in the region. In any event, soon after this meeting, Tigranes of Armenia, a client of Parthia, conducted an agreement with Mithridates VI of Pontus, placing the Parthians, if not on Pontus' side, then nearer them than the Romans. Events in 88–87 BC did little to calm Roman fears, as the Parthians expanded this policy of suzerainty over the remnants of the Seleucid empire, which was once again in the midst of another civil war. It appears that the Parthians intervened on the side of one contender, Philip, against the reigning king, Demetrius III. Demetrius was defeated and captured by Parthian forces and, like his namesake, was sent into comfortable exile in Parthia proper at the court of Mithridates II.[90] An intervention of this sort placed the Seleucid empire (what was left of it) firmly in the orbit of Parthia, whereas it had traditionally fallen to Rome to interfere in Seleucid affairs in this way. It had shown how far the balance had tipped between Seleucia and Parthia and how far Roman influence had waned in the region, especially given the invasion of the Roman empire by Mithridates VI in 88 BC and Rome's own subsequent descent into civil war.

Thus the reign of Mithradates II, shows us both the strengths and weaknesses of the Parthian empire. When controlled by a monarch of ability and determination, the Parthians proved to possess a formidable military machine, capable of defeating any of their neighbours. This military success was accompanied by a shrewd policy of economic and diplomatic links with the states on her borders. By the end of Mithradates' reign (87 BC), the Parthian empire was the unchallenged master of the Middle East, with a firm hold on Mesopotamia demonstrated by the establishment of a new capital on the Euphrates. The states not directly under her control, such as Armenia and the Seleucid empire had been humbled and brought under Parthian influence. In the east, her borders were secure and trade was flourishing with China, benefiting the Parthian economy immensely. The barbarians had been defeated and old rivals such as Bactria had fallen.

But was this due to the strength of the Parthian system or the brilliance of one man? The answer is of course an element of both, but Parthia's history had shown that in the hands of an able monarch they were capable of massive expansion, as with Arsaces I and Mithradates I. Yet both these periods had been followed by periods of massive decline, as less-talented monarchs proved unable to build upon these achievements. Was this again to prove the case in the aftermath of Mithradates II?

The Eclipse of Parthia (87–58 BC)

It is difficult to say who exactly was ruling the Parthian empire in this period, as for the years from 87–70 BC we appear to have three kings; Gotarzes I, Orodes I and Sinatruces I. All three appear to have overlapping reigns, including Gotarzes who first appears with the title 'King of Kings' circa 91 BC. Whilst there are no records of a civil war in these years, it is clear that the Arsacids in particular and their empire in general entered a period of confusion and uncertainty, which some scholars refer to as a Parthian 'Dark Age'. It is likely that Gotarzes and Orodes were in conflict with each other. By 76 BC, however, we hear of a Sinatruces being offered the throne, a man who was 80 years old at the time. It appears that he was the candidate raised to bring an end to the dissensions between the rivals and formed a new branch of the Arsacid line.

The effects of this internal strife were clear and twofold. Not only was the Parthian empire not able to capitalise on the seeming collapse of Rome's eastern empire (following the invasion of Mithridates VI of Pontus), but their own position as the dominant power in the Middle East was severely challenged. Seeing both Rome and Parthia collapsing into civil strife, Tigranes of Armenia threw off the role of vassal state and made a bid to turn Armenia into the regional power. On the death of Mithradates II, and feeling that all personal ties were now broken, Tigranes launched an invasion of both the Parthian and Seleucid empires. Northern Mesopotamia, untouched for forty years, fell to the Armenians, as did the whole of the remaining Seleucid empire (see map 2). He invaded Media and burned the Parthian imperial palace there to the ground.[91] The only check on the advance of the Armenian armies proved to be the arrival of the Roman armies in the region, in the 70s BC.

In 70 BC, the aged Sinatruces died and his son Phraates III came to the throne, ushering in a period of relative internal stability. The position he inherited, though far worse than the one left by Mithradates II, showed signs of improving, but only thanks to the actions of the Romans, as will be detailed later. Phraates' reign came to a sudden end in 58/57 BC when he was murdered in a palace coup organised by two of his sons, Mithradates III and Orodes II. Once again the Parthian monarchy collapsed into instability and on this occasion, with Rome free of civil war, it gave their enemies the opportunity they had been looking for.

Summary

We can see that there are parallels between the eastward expansion of the Roman Republic and the westward expansion of the Parthian Empire, though they took different forms. Ostensibly Parthian expansion was created by a desire for independence, borne out of the revolt of the 240s BC and it was clear from the start that for Parthia to survive the Seleucid empire needed to be overthrown. Likewise, no conscientious Seleucid king would accept the loss of their eastern territories, not to mention the creation of a dangerous rival. Up until the end of the reign of Mithradates II, the viability of the Parthian state was still at stake. Unlike Rome, however, many of the Parthian problems were of their own making. Periods of expansion, under Arsaces I, Mithradates I and Mithradates II were all followed by periods of contraction. This was contrasted with the Roman Republic which expanded and rested, but rarely contracted (the Pontic invasion of 88 BC being the notable exception).

Central to this whole process was the Parthian monarchy. A strong monarch could utilise Parthia's military and economic powerbase to dominate and ultimately conquer her neighbours in the east, which led to them becoming the superpower of the region. Yet a weak monarch, or a series of weak monarchs, could throw all this good work away, as happened in the 200s, the 120s and

70/60s BC. Nevertheless, despite the system's unpredictability, the Parthians ultimately always seemed to find a monarch who could undo a period of decline and take the empire to new heights.

Thus, in the 50s BC a clash appeared to be inevitable between two seemingly unstoppable juggernauts, one driving eastwards and the other westwards. Neither had shown any inclination to live with a rival of equal power. The very existence of a state with the power to rival their own was enough for the other to feel threatened.

The Roman oligarchy saw any other powerful state as a threat to their security and a potential invader of Italy, as the recent experiences with Mithridates VI had shown. However, a threat to them was also seen as a golden opportunity for glory and economic gain, as the clash between commanders for the opportunity to fight Mithridates VI had also shown. Thus the Romans operated from a mixture of paranoia and opportunity. To the Parthian kings and the aristocracy any rival power was considered a threat to their existence and a potential invader of the Parthian homeland, as their recent experiences with Armenia had shown. Thus, both states would have felt threatened by the presence of the other, a situation that could only have a single outcome: war.

Chapter 3

Marcus Crassus and the Lure of the East

With the background to the rise of the two great empires dealt with, we must now turn our attention to the man who led the Roman forces at the Battle of Carrhae and who will forever be associated with the battle. His name was Marcus Licinius Crassus and at the time he was one of Rome's two leading men (the other being Gnaeus Pompeius Magnus, more commonly referred to as Pompey the Great). Despite his contemporary status, history mostly remembers Crassus only in clichés; his supposed insatiable greed, his crucifixion of the defeated slaves of Spartacus, his sponsoring of Gaius Julius Caesar and his defeat and death at the hands of the Parthians (which is most commonly attributed to his supposed military inexperience and incompetence). If we are to examine the Parthian campaign and the Battle of Carrhae in detail, we will need to move away from these clichés and gain a clearer picture of the man who was the driving force behind the campaign.

In 55 BC Marcus Licinius Crassus was elected, along with his sometime ally, Pompey, to the consulship. This was the second time that the two men had been paired in this office (the first being in 70 BC) and both were elected unopposed, due to their use of bribery and intimidation to prevent anyone else from standing. Despite their dislike for each other and their long term rivalry, both men had a history of working together when it suited their needs and, when combined, their resources outstripped the rest of the Senate put together. Both men were incredibly wealthy and had scores of magistrates, senators and businessmen in their patronage. This was the third such time that these two men had worked together (the others being in 71–70 and 60–59 BC) and once again they had been brought together by the twin motivations of opportunity and mutual protection (as will be seen later).

Once in the consulship, both men ensured that they received extraordinary five year military commands, with Crassus being awarded Syria as his province. In addition to the extended term of command, he secured a number of additional legions to take with him, as well as the power to make war and peace as he saw fit (without reference to the Senate or people). There can have been little doubt in Rome, or amongst the peoples of the east, as to the intentions of such an extra-ordinary command. Parthia was in the grips of a fraternal civil war and Crassus' predecessor as governor of Syria (Aulus Gabinius) had already accepted an appeal for Roman help from one of the two royal brothers, Mithradates III. What Crassus' exact aims were in this war will be analysed later. Firstly however, we need to acquaint ourselves with what nature of man Rome had placed in charge of her first war with Parthia and the extension of the Roman imperium in the east. To do this we need to look beyond the traditional stereotypes to see this man who was one half of Rome's dominant political partnership.

Background and Early Life

Marcus Licinius Crassus was born into one of the two branches of the Licinius Crassus family (or *gens*), a leading plebeian senatorial family. He was the second or third son of Publius Licinius Crassus, who had been consul in 97 BC and censor in 89 BC. The Licinius Crassus family were descended from the wider Licinius family (which had been involved in Roman politics since the fifth century BC) and had formed their own distinctive branch, shown by the use of the additional name Crassus, in the third century BC. The family emerged and came to prominence during the Second Punic War, when mounting aristocratic casualties allowed for rapid political advancement. From that time onwards, the Licinii Crassi had been a solid aristocratic family, achieving consulships in each of the succeeding generations[92]. Two distinctive branches of the family had formed, with one branch receiving the additional name of *Dives* (rich). Ironically Marcus Licinius Crassus belonged to the other branch.

Thus, Marcus was born into a solidly senatorial family that belonged in the upper echelons of the aristocracy, but one that had done little to stand out from the rest of such families. To date they had avoided being closely connected to any of the major military or political events that had shaped the republic in the second century BC. As a second or third son (we are unsure which) Marcus could have looked forward to a good senatorial career, possibly even a consulship (though his elder brother would have taken preference). As it happened, events conspired to advance his career far beyond such uninspiring beginnings.

We have no exact date of birth for Marcus, though Plutarch states that he was sixty when he set out for the Parthian campaign, giving us a rough date of 115 or 114 BC. As we will see later, however, this information is open to question. Despite their senatorial status, his upbringing appears to have been a humble one (for an aristocrat). We have little detail about his early years, but one event that we do know of was the death of one of his brothers (who is unnamed in the sources, but not the eldest one). Marcus then married his brother's widow, Tetulla. This in itself was a common enough practice within the Roman aristocracy, especially when the family wanted to keep the bride's dowry, but does indicate one or two useful things. The bride's name indicates that she was not from the leading aristocracy, which perhaps suggests that the family had chosen a rich provincial bride, making them a typical example of an aristocratic, but relatively cash-strapped, family. It would also indicate that Marcus was the third son, with his two brothers being married, but not him. He remained married to Tertulla for the rest of his life, though, as is typical in our sources, we have no further detail about her. The union produced two sons, Marcus and Publius (the latter would be with his father at Carrhae), both born in the late 80s BC.[93]

In terms of upbringing, the sources talk of Crassus being well educated with a polite and courteous manner. He also appears to have been an excellent orator which led him to establishing a career as a lawyer of some note.[94] Given his age, it is likely that he served on his father's staff when his father was fighting in Spain as proconsul during 96–93 BC, which was usual for a young aristocrat and for which we have an oblique reference from Plutarch.[95] This would have been his first taste of warfare, in a particularly difficult campaign against the peoples of Spain (the Lusitanians in this instance) for which his father was awarded a triumph. When war broke out in 91 BC between Rome and her Italian allies (referred to today as the Social War[96]), Marcus' father served as a legate of Lucius Julius Caesar and again it is likely that Marcus was present as a junior officer, again establishing his early military credentials.

This period also produces the first evidence of a link between the Licinii Crassi and Julii families. After serving as a legate of Lucius Julius Caesar (great uncle to the more famous Gaius Julius Caesar), Marcus' father then held the censorship with him. This gives us a clear indication of the links between the two families, with Marcus later nurturing a young Gaius Julius Caesar. Thus far Marcus' career had followed the traditional path: military service in his teens and twenties in preparation for a political career in his thirties. However, this was not to be, as in 88 BC Rome's first civil war broke out.

Marcus Crassus and the First Civil War

In 88 BC, following a dispute over who would command the campaign against Mithridates VI of Pontus, the two consuls of Rome, Lucius Cornelius Sulla and Quintus Pompeius Rufus, marched their army on Rome. The action caught everyone unawares and the city fell with little resistance. The attack on Rome itself was relatively bloodless, with twelve of Sulla's enemies being outlawed, several of whom were killed. The vast majority of the Senate, including the Licinii Crassi (father and sons) were unaffected. However, when Sulla left Rome for the east to fight Mithridates, his enemies planned their return. In 87 BC the consul Lucius Cornelius Cinna copied Sulla's tactics and also marched his army on Rome, along with Sulla's leading opponent, Gaius Marius. This time the city was defended and put up a brave, but ultimately one-sided resistance, and when the city was stormed it was accompanied by a vast massacre. Aside from the general slaughter that accompanied the taking of an ancient city, Gaius Marius used this opportunity to rid himself of the many political enemies that he had made in his long career. Most of Rome's leading senators were butchered along with many of their families; on that list (for reasons we cannot determine) were Publius Licinius Crassus and his eldest son, Publius. At a stroke Marcus became the head of his branch of the family branch. Yet despite his father and eldest brother being murdered, he himself remained untouched and this must be analysed.

The standard reason given by scholars is that he was too young (only twenty-eight or nine) and was not politically active, and so had not yet amassed any enemies. Yet the same could be said of his elder brother and that did him little good. Furthermore, given the general slaughter and the fact that he would be honour-bound to seek revenge for the deaths, leaving Marcus alive makes little sense. Plutarch reports that Marcus avoided the immediate slaughter as he was too young and later fled to Spain, along with three friends and ten servants.[97] It is far more likely that as a politically inactive young man he would not have been involved in defending the city or attending the Senate and thus had more time to make his escape when the city fell. Perhaps his father had made provision for his youngest son to escape in the event that the city fell, thus ensuring the family's survival should the situation in Rome turn for the worse.

In any event, Marcus sought refuge from the slaughter by fleeing to Spain. Plutarch tells the story of how Marcus spent eight months hiding in a cave, aided by the generosity of a stranger.[98] Whilst not wanting to spoil the romance of such a tale, Plutarch does overlook two major factors. Firstly, Marcus apparently fled Rome with three friends and ten slaves (making it a very crowded cave); secondly, thanks to his father's efforts in Spain, the Crassi would have had a number of friends and supporters in the region, and possibly even own property out there. Thus Marcus fled Rome to a comfortable exile in Spain, probably on a family estate, surrounded by friends and allies, whilst he waited for the situation in Rome to calm down.

It is apparent that he spent the years 87–84 BC in Spain, during which time Rome was ruled by Lucius Cornelius Cinna. During this time Sulla was in the east fighting Mithridates, but a clash between him and Cinna seemed inevitable. In 84 BC, however, as Cinna was awaiting Sulla's invasion of Italy, he was murdered by mutinying troops. With Cinna gone, the faction that held Rome began to disintegrate and it was at this point that Marcus Crassus came off the fence and made a crucial decision. Despite having held no political office and having no official mandate, he raised an army of 2,500 men (an understrength legion). He achieved this by recruiting men from amongst his father's veterans, who had been settled in the area (which was possibly another reason why he fled there in the first place). How quickly he managed to raise a legion without any overt authority merely demonstrates how lawless the Roman Republic had become and how little central authority Rome itself exerted. Crassus then used this army to extort money from the neighbouring Spanish cities to pay for his campaign, one of which, Malaca, he was accused of sacking.[99] He was then able to collect enough ships to transfer his men from Spain to Roman North Africa, where one of Sulla's lieutenants, Quintus Caecilius Metellus Pius, was stationed.

In his early thirties, then, Crassus had proclaimed himself a general, raised an army and entered into the civil wars, which all demonstrate considerable leadership and ambition. Such actions also mirrored the early career of Pompey who had taken similar actions in Italy. Once in Africa, though, he soon fell out with Metellus, who was there with an official command and was a man of traditional values who would therefore have no time for an upstart commander. Unperturbed, Crassus decided to join Sulla directly and so took his fleet and army to Greece to meet up with him in person. When he arrived in Greece, Sulla did not concern himself with the legality of Crassus' command, but made him one of his trusted lieutenants, being grateful for the military support and the political message that it sent out, having the scion of a consular family joining his cause. When Sulla invaded Italy in 83 BC Crassus was at his side, unlike Pompey who had remained in Italy awaiting Sulla's arrival.

Once in Italy, Sulla entrusted Crassus with raising fresh forces from the Italian states, a task which he accomplished with considerable success. By 82 BC, he was operating alongside Metellus and Pompey, successfully campaigning in Northern Italy. Crassus again distinguished himself in battle, successfully besieging the city of Tuder and working in a joint operation with Pompey to defeat the general Carrinas. The outcome of the First Civil War was settled at the Battle of the Colline Gate, just outside of Rome itself, later that year.

It was here that Crassus had his first decisive military victory. Sulla commanded the centre of his army and placed Crassus in charge of the right wing. As the battle progressed, Sulla's central detachment of soldiers were overwhelmed and the centre of the line collapsed, which left him facing defeat. Crassus however had triumphed on the right wing and succeeded in routing the enemy forces, who then turned and fled back into the rest of their army, causing total mayhem in the enemy's ranks. This saved Sulla and allowed his army to regain their formation and rout the opposing forces, who were now in disarray. Thus, whilst Sulla is credited with winning the Battle of the Colline Gate and thus ending the war, it was Crassus who had made the telling contribution and brought about the victory.

It is clear that the First Civil War was a key period in Crassus' life. From being born as a lesser son to an undistinguished senatorial family, he became the head of the household and a key lieutenant of the ruler of Rome. Crassus' actions during the war showed that he had excellent leadership and martial skills, through raising his own army and equipping it, then raising a fleet and transporting his men by sea (first from Spain to Africa, and then from Africa to Greece). In battle he acquitted himself against the best Roman commanders of the time and made the decisive contribution in the engagement that won the war.

It was following Sulla's victory, however, that the less savoury aspects of Crassus' character emerged and he became embroiled in a scandal that forever tainted people's views of him. Upon his victory, Sulla's thoughts turned to the elimination of his surviving enemies and planned a purge, known as the proscriptions. This involved the production and publication of a list of his enemies. Anyone whose name appeared on the list could be killed on the spot, with the killer then receiving a reward. The dead man's property was then confiscated by the state and used to pay off the demobilised soldiers. The man that Sulla turned to in order to implement this bloody programme was Crassus. Despite fulfilling Sulla's orders and eliminating his enemies, and thus gaining a vast reserve of wealth for Sulla's demobilisation programme, Crassus himself emerged from the process with a vast personal fortune. Not only was he accused of profiteering by buying up the confiscated property on the cheap, but he was also suspected of adding to the list the names of men whose properties he had his eye on. Not only did this make Crassus a great deal of money, but it also earned him a reputation for greed and avarice which was to remain with him for the rest of his life and even beyond. In the short term his actions also led to an estrangement between him and Sulla.

Crassus' new fortune was based on a spread of different types of property, ranging from silver mines in Spain, to massive landed estates in the country and a considerable number of properties in Rome itself. The landed estates could be sold off or kept to produce a steady annual income as could the property in Rome. Furthermore, his portfolio of aristocratic properties in Rome presented him with an additional political opportunity. To replenish the numbers of the Senate (most of whom had been killed in the civil war, or the proscriptions that followed), Sulla had created over 450 new senators, many of whom were without a house in Rome itself. This allowed Crassus an excellent opportunity to sell these men some of his recently acquired properties at a knock down rate and thus earn their gratitude, which was an invaluable political commodity.

Despite the unsavoury reputation that this whole episode had given him, and his resulting estrangement from the inner circle of Sulla's supporters, Crassus himself was one of the new inductees into the Senate, as his birth and rank demanded. By the time that Sulla retired from power in 79 BC, Crassus was in his mid-thirties. Although the civil war had interrupted his normal progression on the political career structure (he had yet to hold a magistracy), and although he was technically just a junior senator, Crassus entered the post-Sullan period with an enviable military reputation, great personal wealth and a growing circle of patronage. On the downside, he had gained an unsavoury reputation for greed and a number of political enemies

Nevertheless, the war had shown Crassus' considerable military skills, both tactically and logistically. He had raised an army from scratch and transported it across a war-torn Mediterranean. He became one of the first defectors to Sulla's cause and was at his side on the invasion of Italy. He had established himself as a good field commander in the campaigns of 83/82 BC, despite his youth, and had played a crucial role in the victory at the Colline Gate, turning potential defeat into a war-clinching victory. He then amassed a considerable fortune and gained entry into the Senate, creating a formidable basis for a future political career.

Out of the Shadows: The Spartacus Slave Rebellion

During the period from the retirement of Sulla in 79 BC to the outbreak of the Spartacan Slave Revolt in 73 BC we know little of Crassus' activities. It is not to say that there was little of importance occurring, it is just that the surviving sources do not mention him in connection with them. Furthermore, the sources all focus on the rise of Pompey. In 78–77 BC, Rome was rocked by the attempted coup of the consul Lepidus, who marched an army on Rome but was stopped by two armies raised by the Senate, one of which was commanded by Pompey. The other major events of this period concerned the Senate's attempts to re-conquer Spain from a dissident Roman general by the name of Sertorius (who had fled Italy upon Sulla's invasion) and the third war against Mithridates VI of Pontus. After Lepidus' attempted coup, the main domestic agenda focussed on the over-turning of Sulla's reforms of the office of tribune.[100]

We have no detail of Crassus' role in any of these events, and it is here that we find him being overshadowed in our sources by the figure of Pompey. Crassus was the elder of the two by eight or nine years, but both men had had similar early careers, raising armies without authorisation and joining and fighting for Sulla in the civil wars.[101] In 78 BC Crassus was the rich senator, whilst Pompey was still a young man, too junior for political office. Yet whilst Crassus spent the 70s working within the system, Pompey chose to work outside of it. His favourite tactic was to threaten to use military force, or imply the threat, if he did not get what he wanted. It was in this manner that Pompey gained a command against Lepidus and was later sent off to Spain to help fight against Sertorius.

Both men had been given a taste of power during the Sullan period at a very young age. When the Senate attempted to restore the standard model of republican government, both men found themselves potentially deprived of this power and both decided to struggle to keep their previously high position. For Crassus, this could be done within the senatorial system, by using his wealth and guile to build up a political powerbase within Rome. Pompey however was still technically too young to hold anything other than junior positions, in either political or military life, and thus chose the maverick's route. Both men, however, shared the same problem; they were both considered to be young and dangerous upstarts by the ruling senatorial clique of Sullan supporters, men such as Lucullus, Metellus and the like, on account of their unorthodox methods during the Sullan period.

Although we have no direct account of Crassus' political activities in these years 79–74 BC, Plutarch does give us one anecdote that may shed some light on his position in these years. In the mid 70s one of the main agitators for the restoration of the powers of the office of tribune was Lucius Sicinius, who led political attacks on a number of leading senators. Plutarch records a story that Sicinius was asked why he did not attack Crassus, to which he replied that Crassus 'had hay on his horns'.[102] Romans used to put hay on the horns of bulls that were dangerous and gored people. We have no way of telling whether the quote is genuine, but it illustrates nicely that in this period Crassus operated in the shadows of Roman politics, steadily building power and influence. One area where we do have evidence for Crassus' activities lies in the legal field, as we know that he regularly engaged in defence work. This gave him the chance to exercise his powers of oratory and to gain a high profile. Furthermore, it allowed him to build up a network of patronage amongst the men whom he had (successfully) defended.

Crassus is not recorded as having held a political office until his praetorship of 73 BC. Under normal circumstances he would have held the tribunate in the 80s BC followed by the quaestorship (both of which were junior offices), but the war put paid to holding those. The next stage would have been the aedileship, at some point in his mid-thirties. We have no record of him holding this office, which may be an omission, but it could indicate that he did not need to hold such a junior position, given his strong powerbase already. It was only the praetorship and consulship that carried the power of *imperium* (the right to military command). Under Sulla's new constitution, no one could hold the office of praetor until they were 39 years old, which Crassus would be in 76 or 75 BC. We do not know why he waited until 73 to hold the office as there is no record of him having any difficulty in being elected (unsurprising given his wealth and influence), but perhaps it indicates that the date of birth we have given him (based on

Plutarch's statement), is wrong. Perhaps this indicates that he was indeed 39 years old in 74/73 BC which gives us a possible date of birth of 113 / 112 BC.

In any event, he passed his year as praetor in Rome quietly enough. Nevertheless, the year was notable for a slave revolt in Capua, not an uncommon occurrence in itself. However, on this occasion the revolt was started by a group of trainee gladiators led by a man known as Spartacus. At first it was assumed that they would either disperse (as revolting slaves usually did) or be swiftly dealt with by the local Capuan militia. The Capuan militia however were soon defeated, and this gave the slave force a supply of real weapons as well as acting as a clarion call to all other slaves in the area, many of whom flocked to join this new slave force. The sources also report that a number of freeborn Italian peasants joined the group, which illustrates how Italy must still have been recovering from the devastation of ten years of warfare during the previous decade.[103]

It was at this point that the Senate began to take notice and dispatched one of the praetors with a force of 3,000 men to end this rebellion. The sources are confused over his identity; he was either a Claudius Glaber or a Varinius Glaber.[104] Either way, he soon had the slaves trapped and surrounded on a hilltop, but was outmanoeuvred when they climbed down the blind side of the hill and launched a surprise attack on the Roman force, defeating them. Once again the slaves gained greater notoriety along with an enhanced arsenal of Roman weapons, both of which in turn led to more recruits joining them as they continued to ravage the countryside.

After the defeat of a praetorian army, the Senate determined to wipe out this rebellion, which threatened to upset the whole economic and social fabric of Italy. Another praetor was sent to deal with them, either a Publius Varinus or a Publius Valerius (again the sources are confused).[105] Spartacus' force engaged the praetor's army on several occasions and ultimately defeated him, killing or capturing his junior officers and forcing him to flee on foot (as the slaves had also captured his horse).

By the beginning of 72 BC the Senate was in a state of panic. Two praetors had been defeated and this slave band had now swelled into a large army capable of defeating major Roman forces. On a personal level, many of the Senators had properties that were being plundered and had slaves absconding. This revolt could not have come at a worse time for Rome. Italy was still recovering from the civil wars and Rome was fighting wars on two other fronts, against Sertorius in Spain and Mithridates VI in the east. Much of Rome's military manpower, and virtually all of her leading generals, were overseas.

Crassus' attitude during this year would be interesting to know. Two of his colleagues had been dispatched to deal with an apparently-minor problem, both had been defeated and now this problem was turning into a national emergency.

It is unlikely that during 73 BC Crassus would have wanted the task of fighting some runaway slaves, but by 72 BC the situation now presented a remarkable opportunity. At the end of their year in office, the praetors were expected to leave Italy to govern a province. Crassus however stayed in Rome. This has usually been ascribed to the fact that he already had military experience and wealth and therefore did not need, or want, to spend a year away from the centre of politics. There may have been a more powerful motivation for Crassus to stay in Rome, however. Not only were all the choice military commands already taken (in Spain and the east), but the situation in Italy was deteriorating rapidly and would make a wonderful command in its own right. This is more likely to have been the motive that led him to stay in Rome in 72 BC.

Unfortunately, the Senate turned to the consuls of the year, Gellius Publicola and Cornelius Lentulus, neither of whom had any significant military experience. Both were dispatched against Spartacus, with two legions each. At first it looked as though this plan would work as Publicola cornered a slave army led by Spartacus' deputy, Crixus, and annihilated it. Spartacus headed north for the Alps and freedom, with both consular armies trailing him. But then, instead of flight, he turned about and in separate battles defeated both consuls. He followed this by defeating the governor of Cisalpine Gaul (Northern Italy) at the Battle of Mutina, destroying an army of 10,000 men. It was at this point that he made a surprise return to central, and then southern, Italy. His motives for this were never known, but having destroyed three Roman armies in the space of a few months, perhaps he now thought of toppling the whole Roman system.

In Rome, the Senate and the people were in full-scale panic. Three armies had been destroyed and both consuls defeated (both of whom had escaped and slunk back to Rome in shame). Italy lay open to Spartacus and there was talk of the city itself being besieged. Publicola and Lentulus had proven themselves to be incapable of defeating Spartacus and established generals such as Lucullus, Metellus and Pompey were all fighting overseas. It was at this point that Crassus made his bid for glory. The exact sequence of events is obscure, but what is clear is that Crassus offered his services to the Senate to take command of the war against Spartacus and put his experience and wealth at their disposal.

It appears that Crassus timed this move to perfection. We have no record of dissenting voices and apparently both the defeated consuls approved, surrendered their military commands and remained in Rome, probably due to a deal having been worked out between themselves and Crassus.[106] Given his acknowledged military experience, both on the battlefield and at organisation, such a choice seemed ideal. For those who harboured doubts about his questionable ethics, the crisis was too grave for such concerns to matter. Thus, in his late thirties, Crassus was called upon to save the Roman state and given proconsular authority in Italy. We can see that if both the Senate and the assemblies conferred the command upon Crassus in such an emergency, then there can have been few people who doubted his military capabilities.

Not only had he been called on to save the state (which, if he was successful, would reap massive political rewards), but he had also trumped his rival Pompey. The war in Spain against Sertorius was drawing to a conclusion (following the latter's assassination) and Pompey's name was being mentioned in connection with a recall to fight Spartacus and save Rome himself. Crassus' move would, therefore, not only secure his own success but would deny Pompey the chance of the command and would allow him to match, or even surpass, Pompey's successes in Spain.

With the command secure, Crassus once again showed that he was a superb military organiser. In addition to the remnants of the two defeated consular armies, he raised six fresh legions, which he financed out of his own pocket. Furthermore, rather than recruit raw and inexperienced men, he recruited men from amongst the veterans of Sulla's armies from the civil war, many of whom had been settled in Italy. This immediately gave him an army of 40,000–45,000 seasoned soldiers with which to face Spartacus. We are told that he also took with him a number of ambitious young senators on his general staff, thus again not wasting an opportunity for political patronage.[107]

His initial strategy was to secure the area around central Italy and force Spartacus into battle. This plan appeared to be working, when one of his subordinates, Mummius, rashly attacked Spartacus's army in a bid to gain glory for himself. He met with the same fate that all previous Roman commanders had and was defeated. It appears that the men he had under his command were from the two defeated consular armies and during the battle had turned and fled. It was at this point that Crassus showed his ruthless side once again. In order to restore discipline in the army, he resurrected the ancient Roman punishment of decimation, where one man in ten of the retreating soldiers was chosen at random and brutally clubbed to death by their fellow soldiers.

With this act fresh in his men's minds, Crassus attacked Spartacus and defeated him in battle for the first time. Spartacus however, managed to retreat to the south and attempted to leave Italy, either for Sicily, or further afield. Having been betrayed by the Cilician pirates, who had promised to transport his army but then double-crossed him when they had been paid, he found himself trapped in the toe of Italy. Dividing his army into two, Spartacus broke out of the south and made inland, with Crassus in close pursuit. Crassus soon caught up with the lesser of the slave armies, led by Castus and Cannicus, trapped them between the two wings of his own army and slaughtered them. As part of the spoils of victory, Crassus recovered five legionary eagles and twenty-six lesser standards, along with a number of magisterial badges of office, all of which had been taken from defeated Roman armies.

Prior to the battle Crassus had split off a part of his own force in order to shadow Spartacus' army, led by his officers, Tremellius Scrofa and Quinctius. Once again Spartacus showed that he was still a match for ordinary Roman commanders and defeated this force. Crassus however had marched on immediately after his own victory and caught up with Spartacus' army before it could retreat. Spartacus gave battle but proved to be no match for Crassus, who annihilated the slave army. Spartacus himself died in battle with his body never being recovered (despite the more famous ending of the film version). As a deterrent to future slave revolts and to show Rome that the danger had passed, Crassus then ordered the now infamous crucifixion of 6,000 of the captured slave army, with their live bodies lining the road from Capua (the origin of the revolt) to the gates of Rome.

Crassus' achievements in this war cannot be overestimated. As Appian states: 'Crassus accomplished this in a space of six months and because of it immediately acquired a reputation to match that of Pompeius'.[108] He had comprehensively defeated an enemy who, at his peak, had looked capable of attacking Rome itself and was a threat to the Republic's very existence. As a private citizen, he had come to Rome's aid, when Rome's chosen consuls had failed. He raised and paid for a massive veteran army himself and ended the menace of the slave army. In the eyes of the Senate and the people of Rome, he had saved the state from destruction, as he would no doubt remind them any chance he got. In military terms, this was his crowning achievement. Once again he had shown that he possessed considerable ability in raising and equipping armies for the field and that he was a superb battlefield general. His tactical abilities cannot only be seen in comparison to those generals who were defeated before he took command, but also by the two defeats that his officers suffered when they attempted to fight Spartacus on their own. Crassus ended the campaign having three clear victories to his name, two over Spartacus and one over the lesser slave army of Castus and Cannicus.

However, just when it looked like he was on course to reap the benefits of his victories, his old rival and constant shadow, Pompey, once again appeared on the scene. Pompey had been returning from Spain and was making his way back through Italy with his army, obviously hoping to take part in the action against Spartacus. As he came through Northern Italy he ran into a group of slaves fleeing from the defeat, which he easily dispatched. He then sent a message to the Senate stating that although Crassus had defeated the slaves, it was he who had ended the war; a typical piece of Pompeian one-upmanship. Though as Velleius reports, it was clear in Rome where the credit lay: 'The glory of having ended the war wholly belongs to Marcus Crassus'.[109]

Even so, for all concerned (the Senate, Pompey and Crassus) victory over Spartacus was quickly overshadowed by a new and potentially far worse situation. Pompey and Crassus were both approaching Rome with their armies.

Neither man got on with the other, both would expect to be rewarded for their victories and both would expect further political advancement. In 71 BC the situation in Italy was on a knife-edge. With the bloodshed of the civil wars fresh in everyone's minds, Sulla's two most unscrupulous generals, both at the head of loyal armies, were approaching Rome – and each other.

Away from the Abyss: the Rise of the Duumvirate (71–70 BC)

With the stage set for a tense encounter between the two rivals and the Senate and people holding their breath and fearing the worst, the two men did the last thing that anyone expected: they decided to join forces and seize the consulships for the next year (70 BC). We lack the detail of how this deal came about, who made the first move, or what terms they reached, but it was clear that both men had everything to gain from working together and everything to lose from allowing the Senate to set them against each other. This duumvirate (a body of two) presented a formidable unit and was easily more powerful than the Senate itself. Pompey had massive popularity amongst the common people, whilst Crassus had significant backing amongst the equestrian businessmen of Rome. Both had victorious armies and Crassus had his massive wealth and political patronage. The only opposition to this duumvirate came from the Senatorial aristocracy, who had influence but little real power in the face of such opposition.

For Crassus, a consulship was a just and legitimate goal. Under the Sullan constitution he was the correct age (over forty-two) and had had a three year gap between his praetorship and his running for the consulate. For Pompey, however, such a desire was blatantly illegal as he was only thirty-four years old and had never held a political office. So, for Crassus this was an interesting move. He would have almost certainly have gained the consulship for 70 BC without an alliance with Pompey, so we can legitimately ask what he got out of it, especially given that Pompey's illegal consulship would taint his own. Running on a joint ticket would assure that Crassus tapped into Pompey's popularity with the common people of Rome, but more importantly it would ensure that neither man would have a colleague who opposed his measures, especially if the Senate had got one of their number elected. We must assume that both men had proposals which they wanted to implement and thus worked out a programme of legislation beforehand, ensuring that both would get what they wanted.

In the build up to the elections, both men refused to disband their armies, with Pompey claiming that he was waiting for the rest of his returning Spanish armies in order to celebrate his triumph and Crassus claiming that he would disband only after Pompey had. It is likely that both men had agreed this ruse in advance and thus appeared to play each other off. Both men presented the Senate with

claims for triumphs for their military endeavours and a demand for the consulships of 70 BC. Given the overwhelming power of this joint ticket and the implied
threat in the refusal to disband their armies, the Senate gave way on both
proposals. Pompey received dispensation from the Sullan laws in order to be
eligible to stand as consul and both men were duly elected. We are unaware if
anyone else even ran in opposition to them, but such an act would have been
extremely foolhardy.

Thus, possessed of an extraordinary mandate, both men entered the consulships of 70 BC. In terms of the victory parades, Pompey celebrated a triumph for
his victories in Spain whilst Crassus received an ovation (a lesser triumph). This
has often been misinterpreted as a snub to Crassus by the Senate and Pompey,
showing his inferior status to latter. In actual fact, Crassus could not have claimed
a triumph due to the fact that he was not fighting a foreign enemy, but defeating
a rebellion. Nevertheless, Crassus ensured that he was not outshone by Pompey.
He received special dispensation to wear a laurel crown on his head during his
parade (only ever reserved for triumphs, making him the only man to have this
honour during an ovation). Furthermore, Crassus dipped into his own personal
fortune to outstrip Pompey, setting up 10,000 tables for the people to feast off
during his parade and then giving them each a free gift of three months supply
of corn (the staple food of the common people). By such largesse Crassus ensured
that he rivalled Pompey in popularity with the people. He went further when, as
an act (calculated, no doubt) of piety, he dedicated a tenth of his entire personal
fortune in honour of Hercules, when tradition only required that a victorious
general dedicated a tenth of his campaign spoils. Again we see Crassus using his
wealth to counter Pompey's popularity.

In political terms, the consulships of Crassus and Pompey are noted for two
key constitutional changes, both of which indicate the mindset of the men. Most
famously, they passed a law restoring the powers of the tribunate of the plebs (a
radical political office), whose powers of legislation were technically unlimited
and could be used to undermine the Senate's decisions (as it had been in the past).
Agitation for this restoration had been growing throughout the 70s, and it is clear
that Pompey had been claiming that, if he gained the consulship, he would restore
them. Though we can see that this measure was inspired by Pompey, the
tribunate's usefulness would not have been lost on Crassus, and both men made
use of tribunes in the later decades.

The second major constitutional change was the restoration of the office of
censor, which had lapsed under Sulla (if it had not been formally abolished). The
choice of the new censors was an interesting and potentially revealing one.
The consuls of 72 BC (Cornelius Lentulus and Gellius Publicola) were chosen.
Given that both men had suffered defeat at the hands of Spartacus, neither was
held in high esteem. As it was these two men whose command Crassus had taken

over in 72 BC, then we can perhaps see one of the main reasons that they stood aside so easily (other than not wanting to fight Spartacus again). It is likely that in return for their complicity in Crassus' command, they would be later honoured by him, in the form of being the first newly restored censors, a distinguished honour in the Republic.

Furthermore, given that the censors controlled the issuing of all building and other economic contracts, we can see why it would have appealed to Crassus. We have no details of any contracts awarded by the censors of this year, but it is a fair assumption that there were a number of them and that Crassus benefited, either directly or indirectly, by them. In addition, the censors enrolled the millions of Italians who had recently gained full Roman citizenship, thus allowing Pompey and Crassus the opportunity to take the credit and the support it brought. The censors also traditionally revised the list of Senators, and now sixty-four were expelled by them for moral or financial irregularities. Clearly these men would have been no friends of either Crassus or Pompey.

Thus this duumvirate consolidated their control over a number of aspects of the Roman Republic, revising the constitution, the citizen list and the Senate. It is clear from the sources that the two men quarrelled a lot, but aside from a natural rivalry, it is unclear how personal this really was.[110] During their consulship the sources report a story of the people becoming alarmed at a rift between these two, which led to a very public reconciliation between them.[111] Although there was a natural competition between them, you cannot help but wonder whether this was played upon by both men and how far this reconciliation was staged to some degree for political effect. Both men were consummate politicians after all.

With their consulships coming to an end, both men took the unusual step of refusing the customary governorship of a province the following year, and both retired back into normal political life. Certainly they had already achieved spectacular military success and at the time the only ongoing major military campaign was against Mithridates VI of Pontus in the Third Mithridatic War, which was already being commanded by Lucullus. Crassus returned back into the quiet and unseen political machinations that were his forte, whilst it appears that Pompey was biding his time and wished to remain in Rome, awaiting a further military command. Thus the duumvirate, which had been brought together by circumstance and opportunity, was retired and both men returned to their separate political lives.

Rome's Two Masters (69–62 BC)

Scholars, both ancient and especially modern, have always tried to define Crassus' actions throughout the decade of the 60s BC in terms of reacting to those of Pompey. In 67 BC Pompey used a tribune to gain an extraordinary military command for himself to dispose of all pirate activity in the Mediterranean. At the successful conclusion to this campaign, he used another tribune to assign him the command of the war against Mithridates VI. Crassus meanwhile spent the decade in Rome (at the heart of domestic events). It can be legitimately asked whether Crassus tried to stop Pompey from gaining his extraordinary commands or whether he wanted his rival out of the way. Thus again Crassus and Pompey reverted to their respective routes to power: Crassus through domestic politics and Pompey through military campaigns. In that respect, the 60s showed them both at the top of their respective fields.

From 69 to 66 BC we can again find little direct evidence of Crassus' activities. In general we can see that Crassus pursued two quiet and consistent policies in this period. Firstly he had his legal work as a defence advocate, at which he is portrayed as being quite accomplished. This is not a case of Crassus needing the money, but more a case of him building up a system of politicians who would owe him and whom he could call upon in the future to repay the favour. Secondly there was his sponsorship of young, rising noblemen. The two essentials that every aspiring young politician in Rome needed were money and contacts; Crassus had both in ample supply and was only too willing to lend his support to young aristocrats embarking on a political future. A number of these young men had started out serving under Crassus in the Spartacan campaign. This policy would again lead to a network of men in important positions upon whom he could call to repay a favour. The most famous of all of these protégés was a certain Gaius Julius Caesar, who fell under Crassus' wing in the mid-60s. Thus Crassus continued the expansion of his network of political influence.

In terms of more concrete actions, the revival of the censorship in 70 BC meant that the next censors would be elected for the period 65–64 BC (as it was held only once every five years). Unsurprisingly, Crassus stood for and was elected as censor, along with a Quintus Lutatius Catulus, a staunch senatorial man. We must assume that Crassus had his own appointment in mind when he had the office resurrected five years earlier. During his censorship Crassus proposed two major policies. The first was the granting of citizenship to the area of northern Italy known as Transalpine Gaul. The second was that Rome should annex Egypt (which had been willed to Rome by Ptolemy X, an act which had never been taken up by Rome until this point). On both points, however, Crassus was opposed by his colleague Catulus. The relationship between the two men deteriorated to such a point that both resigned before their term of office had ended. Again the sources do not record the issuing of any building or other economic contracts, but it is entirely possible.

Crassus' Egyptian proposals are an interesting topic and one that bears further consideration. Certainly Crassus used a tribune to propose the Roman acceptance of King Ptolemy's will, showing that Crassus too could benefit from a restored tribunate.

It has been suggested that Crassus was actually proposing a commission to determine who the rightful heir to the Egyptian throne was, an issue that had been continually in dispute for the whole of the first century BC. As was later shown (in the 50s) when another such dispute was settled by Rome, whoever was responsible for the winning claimant being put on the throne could hope to profit from it handsomely. It is more than likely that Crassus had himself in mind to command the expedition that went to Egypt. This would have been especially attractive to him given Pompey's campaigning in the east and would have allowed Crassus to keep pace with his rival nicely. In any event, the plans were opposed not only by Catulus, but by the renowned orator Cicero and many in the Senate[112].

Crassus next became embroiled in the series of events known as the Catilinarian Conspiracies, in 66 and 63 BC. In both cases the events were centred on Lucius Sergius Catiline and his attempts to gain the consulship. In 66 BC he attempted to stand for the Consulship of 65 BC, but was barred by the Senate as he had a pending corruption charge to face. Sources report that he then attempted a coup, which came to nothing.[113]

Suetonius reports that the real instigator of the coup was Crassus, who would have been made dictator, with Caesar as his deputy.[114] Apparently, this view was supported by Cicero's secret memoir, which was only published after his death and used by many later sources, though it does not survive today.[115] It must be pointed out, however, that there is no real evidence that there ever was a plot in 66 BC, let alone that Crassus was behind it.

This is typical of the speculation and myth that flourished around Crassus and his political manoeuvrings, most of which were never recorded. It is also typical of the need for scholars, both ancient and modern, to have Crassus as the force behind every major event of the decade, all forming part of some grand scheme to stop Pompey. The truth is likely to be far more mundane. Crassus was by far and away the leading man in Rome (given Pompey's absence) and operated a network of political patronage for his own ends, rather than some grand anti-Pompeian strategy.

Catiline again stood for the consulship of 63 BC where one of his opponents was the orator Cicero. Cicero came from a non-Roman background, as his family were Italians by ancestry and this put him at a distinct disadvantage to Catiline, who came from old Roman stock. Cicero countered this by spreading rumours about Catiline and the non-plot of 66 BC. Enough mud stuck to ensure that Catiline was defeated and Cicero elected. This time it appears that Catiline did plan on seizing power in a coup as he could not get himself elected. The coup consisted of Catiline raising an army in Italy, supported by a conspiracy in Rome to murder the consuls. However the conspiracy was soon revealed and the men involved arrested and executed by the Senate. With the conspiracy in ruins, Catiline's small force (about 3,000 strong), eventually gave battle at Pistoria (62 BC) and was comprehensively defeated, with Catiline dying in battle.

Crassus' role was undetermined at the time and has remained so ever since. Certainly he did have links to Catiline, as it appears that he was one of the young men whose political careers Crassus had been underwriting. This did not make him the mastermind of the plot, especially one as incompetent as this one. In the senatorial debate over the fate of the conspirators, Crassus was actually implicated directly by a witness, but this was dismissed by a large number of senators, most of whom were probably in debt (financial or political) to Crassus. If he was involved, then it is likely that he soon realised that Catiline was not competent enough to carry out a coup and manoeuvred Cicero and the Senate into dealing with him.

This last point showed the astuteness of Crassus' political senses. Catiline, for all his faults, was popular with the people due to a number of promises he had made them and whoever disposed of his allies would be extremely unpopular with them. When the day came for the vote on in the Senate on the conspirator's sentence, Crassus absented himself and thus avoided any complicity with the quasi-judicial death sentence passed. At the time Cicero took great delight in claiming responsibility for the demise of Catiline's allies, which was later to cost him dear, when in 58 BC he was tried and exiled for his role in their execution.

Crassus simply returned to his standard policies of political networking and soon secured Caesar's election to the praetorship for 62 BC, along with a governorship of one of the Spanish provinces, where, as we have already seen, Crassus had great influence. Furthermore, he secured Caesar's election to the post of Rome's chief priest (the *pontifex maximus*) through considerable bribery. This paid off in 61/60 BC when Crassus was elected to the College of Pontiffs (an horrific priestly college in Rome).

The Return of the Duumvirate (62–59 BC)

By late 63 BC, all thoughts in Rome turned to Pompey's triumphant return from his eastern campaigns. The sources record that Pompey sent a legate (Quintus Caecilius Metellus Nepos) to Rome for various meetings with the Senate, to agree the details. It is more than likely that Pompey used him to act as an emissary to Crassus in some early discussions over his return, though what was discussed was never recorded. Certainly Pompey would have wanted to gauge his possible reception amongst the Senators, after being away for over five years and given the way he usurped the eastern command. Therefore, some line of communication between Rome's most powerful general and Rome's most powerful domestic politician would have been essential. All too often the assumption is that these two men were permanently hostile towards each other, but we must never forget that, although they were rivals, they had a record of working together when the need arose. Pompey was guaranteed a hostile reception in the Senate and would need allies in order to get land for his soldiers' demobilisation and his settlement of the east ratified.

One of the key pieces of information here, and one that is little noted by most commentators, is that early in 62 BC Crassus left Rome (an unusual act in itself) and is reported as reappearing in Asia Minor.[116] We are not informed of the purpose of his visit, but given the proximity between himself and Pompey, the most logical assumption is that the two men met, away from Rome, in order to work out a deal that would enable Pompey's return. Again we do not know what was discussed, but it is possible that the duumvirate was resurrected in some form. Certainly Crassus retuned to Rome and Pompey arrived back soon after and confidently dismissed his armies upon landing.

If there was any kind of agreement between the two men in the years 61 and 60 BC then it appears that it was not working very well. Pompey easily ensured that he had one of his lieutenants elected as a consul in both years (Marcus Pupius Piso in 61 and Lucius Afranius in 60 BC). However, he soon found that the Senate and the opposing consul managed to frustrate his plans and block his lieutenants. On certain occasions, the sources report that Crassus himself opposed Pompey in the Senate over the ratification of his eastern settlement.[117]

By 60 BC, however, both Crassus and Pompey threw their weight behind another candidate for the consulship of 59 BC. This time they chose Gaius Julius Caesar, who had already been working with Crassus and had now returned to Rome seeking a consulship and nursing a grudge against the Senate for trying to block his standing for election. With the backing of Crassus and Pompey, Caesar was duly elected consul, but again the Senate ensured that one of their own number (M. Calpurnius Bibulus) was elected as the other consul, which looked as though it would lead to another year of frustration.

Several factors ensured that this would not be the case. We cannot be sure how much support Crassus was actually giving Pompey in the years 61–60 BC and it was most likely that he was playing both sides to ensure that Pompey's aims would be frustrated. By 59 BC, however, two things had changed. The first factor was that on this occasion the duumvirs had chosen an ambitious and accomplished politician to be consul for the upcoming year, in the form of Gaius Julius Caesar. The second factor was that Crassus found that he now needed measures of his own passed into law. Crassus had always prided himself as being the chief political patron of the equestrian businessmen in Rome and a particularly powerful cartel had overbid for the contract to collect the Roman taxes in Asia but now wanted it renegotiated. They naturally turned to Crassus, who in turn needed the Senate to overturn the contract. It was only now that he threw his full weight behind Caesar.

The dynamics between the three men proved to be interesting. Crassus had been Caesar's old political patron, but Caesar astutely arranged a marriage alliance with Pompey whereby Pompey married Caesar's daughter (despite the two men being roughly the same age). Once this marriage alliance had been conducted, the rest of the Roman political elite began to take notice and worried that a new and dangerous alliance had been formed. The Roman writer Varro wrote a political treatise called *Tricaranus* ('three-headed monster').[118]

This term has led to a number of scholars to misrepresent the balance of power between the three men. Caesar may have been consul, but he was entirely dependant on the backing of Crassus and Pompey, who were Rome's two most powerful men. Rather than a triumvirate, in reality it was a duumvirate once again. Given the rise to prominence that Caesar achieved later in his life, ancient and modern historians have a tendency to make Caesar's role in this period far greater than it actually was.

As it happens, Caesar succeeded where his predecessors failed. Through the use of violence and intimidation, his colleague (Bibulus) was virtually reduced to house arrest, leaving Caesar to pass the measures that his two paymasters desired. Crassus got his clients' tax contract renegotiated, as well as the great honour of being designated as the first man to speak in senatorial debates. Pompey got land for his men and the ratification of his eastern settlement. As a bonus, and showing his own political acumen, Caesar ensured that his own future was taken care of and secured the governorships of both the provinces of Gaul for a five year period, thus setting out on a path that would lead him to his future success.

From Duumvirate to Triumvirate (58–55 BC)

With Crassus and Pompey having achieved what they wanted, the arrangement between the two men came to an end. When Caesar left to take up his governorship of Gaul for five years and then become embroiled in a lengthy campaign of conquest, Rome was faced with the rare and dangerous situation of having both Crassus and Pompey in Rome at the same time, for a lengthy period. Thus it may not have been much of a surprise that Rome, in the years 58–56 BC, descended into a period of turmoil and violence, with armed political gangs controlling the streets of Rome. The chief instigator of this violence was the populist politician Publius Clodius. Clodius used the tribunate, supported by his armed street gangs, to launch attacks on a number of senior targets. High on his list were Cicero, Caesar and Pompey. Cicero was exiled by the people for his role in the execution of Catiline's allies in 63 BC. Caesar's actions in passing the legislation as consul in 59 BC were questioned as unconstitutional, as was his five year command in Gaul. Pompey was harassed in the street by Clodius' gangs and placed under virtual siege. To pay for his populist programmes, Clodius had the assemblies pass a bill annexing the island of Cyprus to Roman rule. At the time, Cyprus was ruled by Egypt, but had technically been bequested to Rome earlier in the century by Ptolemy X. Naturally there was little the Egyptians could do about this annexation.

The only notable figure who seemed to sail through this period unscathed was Crassus. Unsurprisingly we can find close ties between Crassus and Clodius going back into the 60s. In 61 BC Crassus defended Clodius from a sacrilege charge and ensured his acquittal thanks to outrageous (even for those times) amounts of bribery. Now, this is not to say that Crassus was behind every one of Clodius' actions (Clodius did not have the temperament to take orders in such a manner), but it does appear that Crassus was backing his actions. Again this would keep his political enemies on the backfoot and allow him to go about his political business unimpeded. Such a view was indeed expressed by Cicero himself in several of his letters. In August 59 BC he wrote: 'I think that Pompey, under pressure from Crassus, may waver'.[119] And in a letter to a friend on 5 October 58 BC: 'but I am still afraid of Crassus'.[120] In a letter to his brother Quintus, in February 56 BC, he elaborated:

> Pompey replied warmly, making oblique reference to Crassus and assaying plainly that he intended to take better care of his life than [Scipio] Africanus had done, whom Gaius Carbo murdered [in 129 BC .... Pompey has information, and talks about it to me, that a plot against his life is in progress, that Crassus is backing Gaius Cato and supplying Clodius with funds.[121]

Again we can see Crassus as the arch manipulator and a man at the centre of the murky world of Roman politics. But by 57 BC Clodius was on the backfoot, with Pompey creating his own armed street gangs under the leadership of Titus Annius Milo and paving the way for Cicero to be recalled from exile. The biggest foreign policy issue at this time was Egypt. In the 60s Crassus had led the attempts to annex Egypt, which had come to nothing. However, in 58 BC a popular revolt had led to the Egyptian king Ptolemy XII being ousted. He promptly fled to Rome and, thanks to significant bribes or the promise thereof, ensured that the Senate confirmed him as the rightful king. The only undecided issue was who should lead the expedition to restore him. The sources tell us that naturally both Crassus and Pompey wanted it for themselves, whereas the Senate was keen to ensure that neither man had access to even more wealth and patronage. The result was deadlock. Ptolemy left Rome disappointed and retired to a villa in Asia.

Indeed, deadlock best describes the situation of Roman politics in this period. Crassus and Pompey were both in competition with each other and with the Senate, and the streets of Rome had been turned into a battlefield between the supporters of Clodius and Milo, fighting a proxy war that neither of their sponsors could afford to lose. Elsewhere, two significant developments occurred that would have a profound effect on the future of Rome and its empire. In Gaul, Caesar was proving to be an inspired military commander and had annexed large amounts of territory, taking Roman rule to the Rhine and the Channel. In the east, the Pompeian-backed governor of Syria, Aulus Gabinius, had accepted an invitation by one of two brothers locked in a civil war over the Parthian throne and was preparing an invasion of Parthia, of which more later.

Therefore, both Pompey and Crassus were beginning to look increasingly irrelevant, being locked into domestic disputes in Rome, whilst the key events were taking place elsewhere. Both men had built careers on a mixture of political acumen and military success and yet the military glory was now being enjoyed by others. Caesar in particular was proving increasingly successful at using Crassus' and Pompey's techniques for his own ends. The people at Rome, faced with political turmoil and battles on the streets, now had a new hero in Caesar, who was engaged in a war of conquest against Rome's traditional barbarian enemy, the Gauls. Caesar also benefited from his absence from direct involvement in the chaos at Rome and from the glowing reports from Gaul describing his victorious campaigns, which he sent back to Rome to be read to the people.

Nevertheless, Caesar was facing an increasing problem of his own. Despite the positive reports which he sent back to Rome, the conquest of Gaul was proving to be an arduous affair, with rebellions breaking out as soon as he subdued an area and an increasing array of tribes opposing him. Added to this was the approaching termination date of his five year command in Gaul. The campaign would not be finished by the expiry date of his command (54 BC) and it was highly likely that the Senate would not only block any extension to his command, but would appoint another man to finish the campaign off and thus steal his glory. If this wasn't bad enough there was talk in the Senate of having him prosecuted for his actions as consul in 59 BC (in steamrolling through the laws he passed for Crassus and Pompey). To say that he was in a quandary would be putting it mildly. It was clear that he needed help and thus the idea was born to resurrect the old combination of Crassus and Pompey once more, though this time on a more even footing, as a triumvirate, rather than a duumvirate.

However, this was easier said than done given the political manoeuvrings between the two men and the running battles between their clients. Both men had ties to Caesar, Crassus as his old patron and Pompey as his son-in-law, but neither would be expected to do him any favours for free. Furthermore, given his military success and subsequent rise in popularity, not to mention control of a large army north of Italy, both men had a lot to gain by seeing a rival force eliminated. In 56 BC, however, at two crucial meetings, this situation changed, and it was a change with far-reaching consequences for the future of the Roman Republic.

Whilst most historians focus on the meeting between the three men at Luca, in April 56 BC, the sources record that there was an earlier meeting between Caesar and Crassus in Ravenna.[122] We do not know what was discussed at this meeting, but it was likely that Caesar was sounding Crassus out about the renewal of an alliance between the two men. The outcome however was clear: a second meeting was needed between all three men to forge an alliance. This gave Crassus a clear advantage over Pompey, as this first meeting had given him time to work out the terms that he wanted to demand in making this arrangement, which would most likely have been the Egyptian command. Events soon proved that Crassus was using this opportunity to think on a far larger scale.

In April 56 BC, at the town of Luca in Northern Italy (which was the southern most point of Caesar's province), the three men held a meeting that was to change the direction of the Roman Republic. It was hardly a private affair as the sources report that over two hundred senators also attended, showing the influence of the three men.[123] Again we have no direct evidence for what was agreed at this meeting, but subsequent events give us a good idea. What Caesar wanted was clear enough: a significant extension to his command in Gaul, in order to give him enough time to finish his conquests. The key issues here were not just what price Crassus and Pompey would extract from Caesar, but firstly whether the two men would work together once more (this would be their third alliance) and what price they would extract from each other.

Once again it appears that the two men realised that they could accomplish more together than they could apart. They came to the conclusion that this time they would need to push through the measures they needed themselves, as they had done in 70 BC, rather than work through agents, as was done in 61–59 BC with mixed results. Thus both men determined that once again they would hold the consulship, though this was not actually accomplished until early in 55 BC, due to the opposition that the two men faced. Once again Crassus and Pompey, through a mixture of bribery, intimidation and downright open violence stood unopposed and were duly elected consuls.

This time around there appears to have been none of the dissension between the two men that marked their previous term in office together (both older and wiser perhaps). Their first major action was to secure Caesar a five year extension to his command in Gaul, and they then turned their attentions to securing their own futures, which they did with great success. They had a tribune pass a bill through the popular assemblies that effectively partitioned the Roman empire. As well as Caesar having a five year command in Gaul, Crassus and Pompey both received five year commands. Pompey received the two provinces of Spain and the right to rule them *in absentia*, whilst Crassus received the province of Syria, seven legions and the right to make war and peace as he saw fit (without having to refer his decisions back to the Senate or people for agreement).

Thus, for the first time in its history, the armies and imperial possessions of the Roman Republic were effectively partitioned between three men. Caesar had the armies of Gaul in the north, Pompey those of Spain in the west, and Crassus those of Syria in the east. Furthermore, it is clear that the triumvirs were also determining Rome's foreign policy, with Gabinius being recalled from Parthia and sent to restore Ptolemy XII to his throne in Egypt.

Of the three men, it can be seen that Crassus emerged as the clear winner out of this deal. Caesar got an extension to his command and Pompey got armies under his control in the west whilst staying in Rome, at the centre of events. In addition, it was his man who got the plum Egyptian command. However, these gains were all overshadowed by Crassus, who negotiated his usurpation of the command to intervene in the Parthian Civil War.

This represents a serious step up for Crassus. Up until 57 BC, he must have been thinking about the Egyptian command. However, when Gabinius, sponsored by Pompey, set about an intervention in Parthia, he saw his chance for an eastern command that would prove to be the culmination of his career (which in a sense it was, though not as he had envisaged it). Rather than another Egyptian intervention, he now commanded Rome's first war against the Parthians, and whilst Gabinius may have had a limited intervention in mind, the raising of seven legions showed that Crassus was thinking on a far grander scale. Furthermore, he had ensured that it was he, rather than Pompey, who secured this command and had thus stolen a march on his rival. He now had his chance to place him in the shade militarily, whilst Pompey stayed in Rome. In many ways this was a reversal of roles, as traditionally it had been Crassus who stayed at Rome immersed in the politics, whilst Pompey was campaigning in the east.

Summary

This analysis of Crassus' career reveals a completely different picture to the stereotype that is most commonly reported today. For thirty years he had been at the centre of the key events that shaped the Roman Republic in the first century BC, in both the political and the military sphere. He had entered the First Civil War on Sulla's side, raising an army on his own authority and proving crucial to Sulla's success in the key battle that ended the war. He had master-minded Sulla's bloody proscriptions, making himself one of Rome's richest men in the process. He had been responsible for defeating Spartacus and saving the Republic from the slave rebellion. He had jointly been responsible for over-turning the Sullan constitution and had dominated the subsequent fifteen years of Roman politics using his powers of political and financial patronage. He had held the consulship and censorship and, now in his late fifties, had secured a second consulship and the chance to lead Rome into its first war with Parthia, which if successful would push Roman control past Mesopotamia and earn him his place in history.

We can see, therefore, that Marcus Licinius Crassus was a talented politician and general, who at the time of his departure for the east was one of the two leading Romans of his day. History up to now has judged the man for the failure of this subsequent campaign and shrouded his achievements before it, hopefully now we can see otherwise. With the background to the First Romano–Parthian War complete we can now move on to the war itself.

The War

Chapter 4

An Unnecessary War?
The Origins of the First
Romano–Parthian War (96–55 BC)

Before we examine the details of the campaign, we need to take stock and look at the origins of the war and see how this affects the way we view the campaign that followed. This is a necessary step as most ancient and modern sources portray this war as being nothing more than unwarranted Roman aggression, fuelled by Crassus' greed, ambition or sense of military inferiority, all of which have been suggested at some time.[124] The contention here is that this war was not simply dreamed up by Crassus against a state which had done nothing to warrant it, but an inevitable clash between the two rising superpowers of the ancient world. Thus we need to draw together the strands that we covered earlier (in chapters one and two), remove them from a purely Roman or Parthian perspective and combine them to provide a more rounded view of the whole process.

As we have seen, by the second century BC the great powers that had emerged from the ashes of Alexander the Great's empire were in decline, with a new generation of states rising to prominence and challenging the established order. We must not make the mistake of looking at this process from a narrow European or Mediterranean perspective, as Rome was not the only rising new power. To view the ancient world in such a way limits our perspective and gives the rise of Rome a certain degree of inevitability. As well as Rome there was Pontus, Armenia and Parthia. The first century BC saw these new powers clash with each other in a round of wars that would determine which civilisation would emerge as leading power of the ancient world.

By the 50s BC there were only two candidates left in this field, Rome and Parthia. In a way it was fitting that it came down to these two powers, as they both represented opposing civilisations, both coming from the extremities of the so-called 'civilised' ancient world. If we analyse the events of the century preceding the outbreak of the First Romano-Parthian War, it can be seen that there are four distinct phases of contact between Rome and Parthia and that the war that broke out in the 50s BC was not due to the actions of any one man, but was the result of the wider forces of history.

Contact Avoided

It would be misleading to start the relationship between the two empires with the point that they first physically met. It is clear that for the first century of its existence the Parthian empire occupied only the fringes of the consciousness of the ancient world, a problem for the Seleucids and nothing more.[125] That all changed in 141 BC when Mithradates I invaded and annexed Mesopotamia and took the Seleucid king (Demetrius II) hostage. Such an action would have made the ancient world stand up and take notice of this new power from the east, and none more so than the Romans. The Romans had come to see the Seleucid empire as within their sphere of influence, often interfering in her domestic affairs, so the rise of a new power threatening Seleucia must have raised some concerns in Rome.

There is a terrible tendency for the ancient and modern scholars of Rome to ignore Parthia until the first century BC. Yet by 141 BC, Parthia stood poised to invade Syria itself and either annex it outright or, more probably, install a puppet ruler (Demetrius II) on the throne. Such an action would have been seen as direct interference in Roman affairs and would have seen a new empire appear on the shores of the Mediterranean, an event which would have surely demanded Roman intervention. Such a worry can only have been inflamed by the defeat and death of Antiochus VII in 129 BC when, once again, Parthia stood poised for an invasion of Syria. As it happened, the question of whether Rome would have intervened or not became an academic one, as Parthia suffered a barbarian invasion from the east which would occupy her for a generation. Rome, too, as described earlier, suffered from a lapse of concentration with regards to the Near East, occupied with bloody political infighting at Rome, as well as wars in Africa and Northern Italy. For the next thirty years both empires neglected affairs in the Near East and were far more occupied in other parts of their empires or with affairs at home.

The intriguing aspect of this period is just how close the two great empires came to clashing and just how far back the roots of the clash between the two can be traced. Parthia does not appear to impinge on the Roman consciousness until the first century BC. This is the image that the surviving ancient sources appear to depict, a view echoed by their modern counterparts. There is often the impression that Parthia had reached its natural boundary of the Euphrates and that Syria was always a part of the Roman sphere of influence. Yet we have seen that Parthia had designs on Syria far before the Romans ever considered annexing it to their growing territories. In 129 BC, when a Parthian invasion looked imminent, the Romans had only just gained a territorial foothold in Asia Minor, never mind the Middle East. As it happened, events conspired to keep both empires away from clashing over Syria until seventy year later.

The main beneficiaries from the inattention of the two empires were the states of Pontus and Armenia. But, by the 90s BC, both had come to the attention of the great powers, who, having recovered from the various difficulties each had faced, once again turned their attention to the region. Parthia struck first, invading and defeating the Armenians. Although Armenia remained nominally independent, the heir to the throne, Tigranes, was taken as a hostage and Armenia became a vassal of Parthia. Upon the death of the old king, Parthian forces installed Tigranes as king of Armenia and received a handsome parcel of land for the Parthian Empire, only referred to as the 'Seventy Valleys'.[126]

The relationship between Parthia and its vassal Armenia was a crucial one in this period as Tigranes allied himself, by marriage, to Mithridates VI of Pontus, which created a super-alliance of the two states that could dominate the Asia Minor region. Although the links are never clearly expressed in our surviving sources, lurking behind this alliance is Parthia, as the sponsor of Tigranes. The paucity of our sources will never allow us to unravel the tangled motivations here, but we can speculate about the role of Parthia in this alliance and what they were hoping for. Mithridates of Pontus was clearly pursuing an anti-Roman policy in the region and this alliance was bound to upset Rome. Perhaps Mithradates II of Parthia was playing a clever game by overseeing the creation of a regional alliance that would rival Rome and yet keep Parthian hands clean?

Whatever his intention, this Pontic-Armenian alliance did soon come to the attention of Rome. When Mithridates VI invaded and annexed Cappadocia, Rome's focus returned to the east once again and they resumed the role of arbiter of international relations in the region, determining that a powerful kingdom of Pontus was clearly a strategic threat to Roman interests. The Senate demanded that Cappadocia be granted independence once more. Mithridates agreed to this, but no sooner had the Cappadocians elected a new king then the other wing of the alliance, Tigranes of Armenia, struck. The Armenians invaded Cappadocia, overthrew the new king and installed a puppet king who was loyal to Mithridates of Pontus.

It was at this point that Rome decided that they had to act, or allow the establishment of the new regional power of Pontus-Armenia on their borders. They too would have been well aware of the renewed Parthian threat, possibly sponsoring this alliance and using it as cover. Lucius Cornelius Sulla, one of Rome's most promising generals was dispatched to free Cappadocia from outside rule and restore the overthrown king. Little detail remains of the campaign itself, but the Romans invaded Cappadocia and defeated a joint Cappadocian-Armenian army. The puppet king was removed and the old king restored. This marks the first occasion that Roman forces clashed with the Armenians. It is at this point that the first meeting between the representatives of Rome and Parthia took place and the background to this meeting should not be ignored, though it all too often is in the modern sources.

First Contact

In 92 BC the Roman pro-praetor, Lucius Cornelius Sulla, met with an emissary of the Parthian king, named Orobazus. Also present at the meeting was the newly-restored Cappadocian king. This historic meeting is little covered by our surviving sources, yet has proved fertile ground for modern misinterpretations.[127] It appears that the Parthians initiated the meeting, ostensibly to offer friendship between the two empires, though it will be recalled that neither representative had any authority to negotiate a treaty. A lack of sources will never permit us to ascertain the Parthian intentions here, but the timing is perhaps indicative. Parthia's vassal, Armenia, had just been defeated by the Romans and the meeting could have provided the chance for the Parthians to assess Rome's intentions towards Armenia. It is also possible that they intervened, as the power behind the Pontine-Armenian alliance, to diplomatically shore up a situation that had been lost militarily. Certainly Rome took no further action against either Pontus or Armenia.

We have no clear record of what was discussed at the meeting, though we do know that Sulla physically placed himself between the king of Cappadocia and the Parthian emissary. This was a move designed to show Rome's dominant position and a breach of protocol that amounted to a slap in the face to Parthia, which cost the Parthian emissary his life when the Parthian king found out about it. What is certain is that no treaty was agreed between the two powers, and certainly not one that bound the Parthians to keep to the east of the Euphrates. Not only is none recorded in the sources, but neither participant had the authority to conduct such an agreement. In any case, Mithradates II swiftly acted on his aggressive intentions towards Seleucid Syria.

It is unclear what message Mithradates II took from this meeting, with both sides offering friendship, yet warily eyeing each other up. Certainly the Pontic-Armenian alliance had been defeated in Cappadocia, but they were still a threat to Rome in Asia Minor. Not only was Rome entangled in this region, but in 91 BC a civil war broke out in Italy between Rome and her Italian allies. Uncoincidentally, it was in this period that Mithradates II moved on Seleucid Syria. In 88 BC, Parthian forces intervened in a civil war between the Seleucid king, Demetrius III, and his brother Philip, capturing the former and replacing him with the latter. The newly-crowned Philip II owed his throne to the Parthian king while his brother might be the perfect puppet if one were needed to be placed upon the Seleucid throne.

At this point it appeared that the Parthians were on the verge on overrunning the Middle East, with vassal kings on the thrones of Armenia and Seleucid Syria. This dominance was reinforced by the outbreak of the First Mithridatic War between Rome and Mithridates VI of Pontus, a nominal Parthian ally, but not one with a direct connection to Parthia. By the end of 88 BC, the Romans had lost Asia and Greece and had been pinned back to Italy, added to which was a further outbreak of civil war between Rome's leading generals, with the city of Rome itself being attacked. It appeared that victory lay within Parthia's grasp, which is usually the time that one is most vulnerable. And so it proved in this case, when the death of Mithradates II in 87 BC resulted in a complete collapse of Parthian power.

Thus the period of the 90s BC not only saw the first diplomatic contact between Rome and Parthia, but also saw a proxy war break out between the two, with Parthia backing the creation of a regional power block of Pontus and Armenia, which would keep the Romans occupied in Asia Minor, allowing Parthia the time and space to annex Syria. Once again however, the Roman and Parthian empires mirrored one another, when, within two years (88–87 BC), both collapsed into civil wars and both once again lost impetus in the region.

The disasters that befell Rome and Parthia proved to be a golden opportunity for Armenia. With Rome in the midst of a civil war, Parthia undergoing dynastic struggles (which may well have resulted in full scale civil war[128]) and Pontus recovering from the war with Rome (which ended with Mithridates' defeat in Greece), Armenia was the sole regional power able to take advantage of the situation. Tigranes invaded both the Seleucid and Parthian empires, annexing Syria and taking a large swathe of Mesopotamia and Media from Parthia (see map 2). It is ironic that the first regional power to annex Syria was neither the Romans nor the Parthians, but the Armenians.

Collapse and Recovery

During the decades of the 80s and 70s BC the regional superpower was Armenia, but the basis of this position was the weakness of both Rome and Parthia, and it was the alliance with Mithridates VI of Pontus that was ultimately to lead to their downfall. Such an explicit alliance with a determined enemy of Rome was one that Parthia had avoided in this period. Parthia had neither the ability to intervene in the Mithridatic Wars, due to her own internal troubles, nor, it would appear, the intention. Even if Mithradates II had still been alive it is unlikely that the Parthians would have intervened directly. It was more likely that they would have strengthened their dominant position in the region, whilst keeping Rome busy fighting their agents.

Nevertheless, just as Armenia's links to Pontus brought her to Rome's attention, Parthia's links to Armenia ultimately did the same. By 74 BC Rome had recovered from her civil wars sufficiently to engage with Mithridates VI of Pontus for the third and final time.[129] Despite again starting the war slowly, the Romans, under Lucius Licinius Lucullus, soon defeated Mithridates and drove him from Pontus, as related previously. Mithridates turned to his allies for help. Tigranes of Armenia, by now the dominant regional power, stuck by his alliance and offered him refuge, whilst the new Parthian king, Sinatruces, refused to get involved, which was a good move given Parthia's relative weakness in this period.[130]

Tigranes, however, had fatally miscalculated when he granted Mithridates sanctuary in Armenia, as the Romans were in no mood to compromise. Lucullus, operating well beyond his legal mandate, invaded Armenia in 69 BC and, in an act of desperation, both Mithridâtes and Tigranes appealed to the new Parthian king (Phraates III) for help against the Roman invaders. Tigranes even offered the restoration of the Parthian lands taken from them by Armenia as an inducement. Phraates was no fool however, and realised that Parthia was still in no shape to go to war with Rome and rightly gambled that he could regain those territories from a defeated Armenia. His assessment soon proved to be accurate as the Armenians were comprehensively defeated at the Battle of Tigranocerta, which perhaps created a false impression in the Roman minds about the fighting capacity of the armies of the region.

Following the battle, Lucullus turned his attention to the Parthians, sending them a clear warning not to get involved. According to the sources Phraates was negotiating with both sides, assuring them of his support for their cause, whilst determining to stay neutral[131]. Parthia was now negotiating with Rome from a position of weakness, a fact that both sides were aware of. Phraates' price for supporting Rome was the restoration of the provinces of Gordyene and Adiabene in Mesopotamia from the Armenians.

It was at this point that Romano–Parthian relations took a decisive turn for the worse. Lucullus, tiring of the drawn out negotiations, sensing the weak position of Parthia vis-à-vis Rome and having defeated two of the three regional powers (Pontus and Armenia), apparently determined to attack Parthia.[132] How seriously he intended this campaign to be prosecuted we will never know, as Lucullus suffered the twin blows of a mutiny of his troops and political manoeuvrings at Rome. Certainly it was a bold move, but Lucullus had too few men and had not yet finished off either Mithridates or Tigranes. Nevertheless it marked a clear change in the Roman line of thinking; a clash with Parthia now seemed inevitable.

As it happened, Lucullus' position had been fatally undermined and, with no clear end in sight to the wars with Mithridates or Tigranes, his command was usurped by Pompey, who got the popular assembly to grant him an extraordinary command in the east. One of his first actions when he reached the east was to reopen negotiations with the Parthians. The sources disagree over the terms of this first formal treaty between Rome and Parthia. Either it secured Parthian neutrality or the arrangement was that the Parthians invade Armenia and open up a second front.[133] Given the strength of Pompey's forces, and the improbability of Pompey wanting to rely on foreign help, coupled with his later reaction to Parthian forces actually attacking Armenia, it seems unlikely that Parthian aid was required, merely their guarantee of neutrality. In any event, in 66 BC the Roman and Parthian empires forged their first treaty of alliance.

Perhaps emboldened by this, Phraates decided to take the offensive, rather than sit back. He supported the son of Tigranes in a bid against his father and Parthian forces invaded Armenia. No sooner had he invaded Armenia than his caution got the better of him and he withdrew, leaving the younger Tigranes to be defeated by his father. It was an ill-judged and tentative intervention and one that only served to further sour his relationship with Rome.

By 65 BC, both Mithridates and Tigranes had been defeated, leaving Rome, and Pompey in particular, as the dominant force in the Middle East. Now Romano-Parthian relations took another sharp downward turn. Whilst Pompey was in the Caspian region, his *legate* (deputy) Aulus Gabinius undertook a raid deep into Armenian territory, crossing the Euphrates and reaching the Tigris. Alarmed by such a deep Roman incursion into former Parthian territory, Phraates invaded the former Parthian province of Gordyene and seized control of it. He then sent ambassadors to Pompey demanding a final resolution of the previous year's agreement, ensuring the return of the former Parthian territories from Armenia and the determination of the Euphrates as a line of demarcation between the two empires.[134] It is likely that this last demand was more to limit the sphere of Roman activity than bar the Parthians from their traditional goal of securing Syria.

Pompey's reply did nothing to assuage Parthian fears. He demanded the Parthian evacuation of the newly-seized province of Gordyene and on the matter of a line of demarcation, merely stated that 'whatever border he determined would be a just one'.[135] Upon encountering Parthian prevarication, Pompey ordered another of his legates, Lucius Afranius, to recover the province of Gordyene, by force if necessary. This was the first encounter between the forces of Rome and those of Parthia and appears to have ended with the Parthians withdrawing their forces rather than fight Rome.[136] Afranius then pursued the Parthian forces back into the Parthian Empire, across the River Tigris and then returned to the Roman sphere of control by way of Mesopotamia during the winter of 65 BC, actually passing through Carrhae in 64 BC and finishing up in Syria.[137]

This tour by Afranius' army was a clear sign of the impotence of the Parthians in the face of overwhelming Roman military superiority. If nothing else, it makes a mockery out of the claim that either Lucullus in 68 BC, or Pompey in 66 BC, had agreed to the Euphrates being the boundary between the two empires. There is no reason to believe that any Roman commander negotiated a clear border beyond which they could not pass. At the time Rome was militarily superior and Parthia visibly the weaker of the two and the whole concept would have gone against Roman notions of their imperial dignity.

By 64 BC, Pompey had still not decided to return the province of Gordyene to the Parthians. Phraates then engaged upon a dangerous gamble and once more invaded Armenia and waged war on Tigranes, who had been retained as king of Armenia by Pompey and who now was technically an ally of Rome. As the war dragged on into a stalemate, it is said that Pompey contemplated an invasion of Parthia.[138] Unlike Lucullus, he now had a legitimate cause for a war and had the mandate and the forces. In the end he pulled away from such a confrontation, for reasons that have never been made clear, and brought all sides to negotiation. The fate of the former Parthian territories, held by Armenia, was to be decided by a three-man Roman commission, who decided that Gordyene was to remain Armenian (a key province in terms of access to Parthia) whilst Adiabene was to be returned to the Parthians.

Thus the Parthians regained part of their Mesopotamian territories, but were denied Gordyene by order of Rome. We will never know why Pompey pulled back from the brink of war with Parthia, caused by his own needling of them over the province of Gordyene. Certainly he would have given little regard for whether his mandate covered it, which it technically did, nor would he have cared much for what the Senate thought, as he had the popular assemblies on his side. Ultimately it would appear that he did not want to prolong his stay in the east with a potentially long campaign and it was clear (or so the Romans thought) that the Parthians were weak and did not require a war to deal with them. What Pompey did do, however, was to change his mind over the fate of Seleucid Syria and annexed the kingdom as a province of Rome. This about-face was probably due to his desire to keep Parthia in check and deny them access to the Mediterranean. In many ways Phraates' desire for a Euphrates line of demarcation appears to have backfired on him, with the Romans annexing the territory west of the Euphrates.

Thus the period 74–64 BC saw a radical shift in the balance of power between Rome and Parthia. Up until this period, both Rome and Parthia had appeared to mirror each other in regards to the east. Both were successful when the other was, and then lost focus when the other did. In 87 BC Parthia appeared to have the upper hand, with client kings on the thrones of Armenia and Syria, and Rome having to fight off a Mithridatic invasion of Greece. The

80s BC saw both civilisations undergo massive internal strife and civil war, but, although the Roman civil war was far more devastating, they actually emerged from the period far stronger than Parthia. During Parthia's weakness, Armenia had taken advantage and established herself as the dominant regional power.

By 64 BC Parthia had been reduced to bargaining with Rome for the return of her former territories and had been militarily humiliated by both Armenia and Rome. Both Lucullus and Pompey had contemplated war with Parthia, whose grip on her western territories was weak. By the time Pompey returned to Rome, Armenia was now a client state of Rome (with the strategic province of Gordyene as a hold over Parthia), Syria had been annexed and had two legions permanently stationed there. Annexing Syria took Roman territory up to the Euphrates and gave the two empires a common border for the first time (if you include both empires' client kingdoms). This situation was the result of circumstance rather than treaty and it is highly unlikely that Rome had ever agreed not to cross the Euphrates. As Afranius' campaign in 65/64 BC had shown, the Romans now had experience of operating in Mesopotamia.

In Roman eyes, and probably in reality, Parthia under Phraates III was weak. Parthian forces had refused battle in 65 BC and had been chased deep into Parthian territory, with Rome operating throughout Mesopotamia with impunity. The scene was clearly set for a future confrontation. Yet before Crassus entered the stage as the commander of a Parthian War, another man nearly got there before him.

The Phoney War

The years 62–57 BC marked a lull in Roman interest in the east. This was to be expected, given the defeat of Rome's enemies and the lack of tangible threats in the region. Furthermore the focus of the Roman elite was on domestic politics, with the return of Pompey to Rome and the various activities relating to his return by his allies and enemies. In 58 BC, however, Aulus Gabinius, Pompey's former legate (and one of the two commanders who had crossed the Euphrates in 65 BC), gained the consulship (with Pompey's backing). His assigned province was originally Cilicia, but he managed to have it altered to that of Syria. The ostensible reason was to defend it against Arab raiders, who had always been a nuisance in that area. Nevertheless this did not warrant it being made a consular province, nor did it require a three year command and a substantial grant of legionaries and money (both unspecified by our surviving sources[139]). Clearly this indicated a substantial military campaign of some type and one backed by Pompey.

It is against this background that events in Parthia take a central role. In 58 or 57 BC (the sources are unclear on the specific year) the weak Parthian king, Phraates III, was murdered by his two sons (Mithradates and Orodes). Mithradates, being the elder, took the throne under the title of Mithradates III, but was then removed in a second coup by a group of nobles led by Surenas, who then installed Orodes as king. Mithradates was relegated to governor of Media, where he soon contacted the Romans to aid his restoration.[140] Thus a second Parthian civil war was sparked off. At some point in 57 or 56 BC Gabinius agreed to side with Mithradates. By 55 BC a Roman army led by Gabinius crossed the Euphrates with the intention of putting Mithradates back on the Parthian throne as a client of Rome.[141] Therefore the first war between Parthia and Rome looked set to begin, with Gabinius as the general in charge and the first Roman general to invade Parthia in an aggressive war.

Events in Rome intervened, however, when Pompey, Crassus and Caesar created their political alliance. As well as determining the consulships for 55 BC (for Pompey and Crassus) and another five year command for Caesar to complete the conquest of Gaul, the question of Parthia and Egypt came up, with the triumvirs apparently determining Roman foreign policy. It appears that during the conference at Luca, Pompey and Crassus agreed that the relatively easy job of invading Egypt and restoring Ptolemy XII to the throne of Egypt would be given to Gabinius, who already had an army in the east, whilst Crassus would undertake the proposed war with Parthia.[142] Thus Gabinius duly received a letter from his patron ordering him to turn back, withdraw from Parthia and invade Egypt instead, which he duly did. Entering Egypt in 55 BC, he restored Ptolemy XII to the throne, who then handsomely paid Gabinius and Pompey for their actions. Gabinius then turned to Judea and defeated an anti-Roman rebellion in the client kingdom there.

Summary

Through this brief analysis of Romano-Parthian relations, it can be seen that the war of 55 BC was not suddenly sprung on the Romans by a greedy and unscrupulous Crassus, as many sources would later claim. The war had probably been decided on in 58 BC by Pompey and Gabinius, the latter of whom had actually got as far as invading the Parthian empire before having to hand the command over to Crassus. Roman foreign policy in the east was now in the hands of the triumvirs and not the Senate. Pompey, and later the triumvirate as a whole, had come to the conclusion that the time was right to reduce Parthia to a client kingdom, as had been done with Armenia and Egypt. This decision was based on the experience of the previous decade, which had seen Parthia humiliated by

Rome, with Parthian territory being decided upon by Roman commissioners, and the Parthian army allowing themselves to be chased out of their former territories rather than fight the Romans. If that were not enough then Parthia had just seen two successful coups against the reigning king and Rome now had a pliant candidate to place on the throne. In every way Parthia now resembled the other weak states of the region, ripe to be converted into a Roman client. It is against this background that we must consider the First Romano-Parthian War, as it alters our whole perspective on the campaign.

Chapter 5

The Invasion of the East (55–53 BC)

We must now turn our attention to the war itself, and the events that led up to the Battle of Carrhae, which only occurred after over a year's worth of campaigning by the two sides. Again we must be aware that both sides were involved in this process and must not limit ourselves to merely analysing the Roman campaign and imagine that the Parthians sat there complacently waiting for Crassus' army to arrive. In point of fact, as we will see, the Parthians did just the opposite and forced the Romans to alter their plans; an alteration that was to have profound effects on the campaign that followed.

Initial Strategies: Rome

The surviving sources do not provide us with any detail on what Crassus hoped to achieve apart from Plutarch's grandiose statement that:

> he would not consider Syria nor even Parthia as the boundaries of his success, but thought to make the campaigns of Lucullus against Tigranes and those of Pompey against Mithridates seem mere child's play, and flew on the wings of his hopes as far as Bactria and India and the Outer Sea.[143]

Again our surviving sources paint us a picture of Crassus as a new Alexander, hoping to bring the whole of the east under Roman control, a fine ambition for a man of near sixty, seeking a legacy. Our sources also appear to be emphasising how out of his depth they considered him to be and how outlandish the whole campaign was. The one factor that they do not mention is the request from Mithradates III to the Romans (accepted by Gabinius, Crassus' predecessor as governor of Syria) to intervene in the Parthian civil war. Following Gabinius' withdrawal from Parthia, Mithradates remained with Gabinius during his subsequent invasion of Egypt. This is only recorded by the Romano-Jewish historian Josephus, who provides us with several key and unique aspects of this war. The role of Mithradates here is a highly interesting one and raises a number

94

of important questions.[144] Josephus goes on to tell us that in 55 BC, after accompanying Gabinius on his campaigns, Mithradates was sent away when the Romans were in Jerusalem (quelling another civil dispute). Mithradates subsequently turned up in Mesopotamia, whereupon he restarted the civil war and seized the cities of Babylonia and Seleucia, which he made his base of operations.

It is interesting that Mithradates went from being a refugee, living on Gabinius' hospitality, to a returning prince who set up his own kingdom in Mesopotamia, and all in advance of Crassus' arrival in Syria. It is tempting to speculate that Mithradates was sent back into Parthia to rekindle the civil war and thus destabilise the Parthian empire, and the Mesopotamian region in particular, prior to the arrival of Roman forces. Whilst the Romans did not provide him with any forces, it is more than possible that some of the spoils of Gabinius' Egyptian campaign accompanied him back to Parthia, to make his triumphant return from exile all the more palatable for the elites of the two great cities of Seleucia and Babylonia.

Thus Rome's initial strategy (or to be more exact, the triumvirs' original strategy) appears to have been to use Mithradates as a stalking horse, and inflame Parthia's civil war to their own ends. Not only did Crassus have an ally in southern Mesopotamia, controlling the major Greek city-states there, but the Parthian military would be split and not able to focus on any impending invasion, which by now was obviously coming.

It is curious that this does not appear to have been picked up in Rome. The surviving sources record hostility from the Senate and the people to this apparently uncalled-for war. Nevertheless, as described elsewhere (see appendix two) the sources are all hostile to the whole campaign based on its outcome. Many of the objections would have been to the triumvirate's highjacking of Roman foreign policy and the prospect of Crassus being in charge of a victorious campaign in the east furthering his and the triumvirate's power.

In spite of all this, a law passed by the tribune Gaius Trebonius granted Crassus the province of Syria for five years and seven legions with which to fight any campaign. Furthermore, he was given the power of declaring wars and creating treaties as he saw fit (thus undermining many of the ancient sources who object to there being no formal cause for a war between Rome and Parthia[145]). However, even the passing of this law did not receive unanimous consent. In particular, one of Trebonius' colleagues, Gaius Ateius Capito, attempted to block this law, but was overruled. He continued to campaign against Crassus and this command throughout the year, and in particular made a colourful contribution, as will be seen shortly.

With the domestic opposition sidelined, Crassus still faced one important obstacle: namely how to raise seven legions worth of men. It was one thing to be voted seven legions by law; it was another to raise the numbers of men willing to serve. Here Crassus had several problems. Not only had Caesar recruited a large army for his Gallic campaigns from the men of Italy, but Pompey was also recruiting for his Spanish provinces. Furthermore, Pompey could turn to his veterans from his eastern campaigns to bolster his new armies. Crassus had not fought a campaign since the defeat of Spartacus, some fifteen years earlier. Such a timespan would have prevented many of his former troops being capable of fighting a fresh campaign.

However the outlook was not all negative for Crassus, as his projected campaign was against a rich eastern power and held out the prospect of being a repeat of Pompey's highly successful eastern campaigns of the 60s BC, during which the soldiers reaped handsome rewards. Compared to fighting barbarians in Spain or Gaul, this campaign would have seemed the far more attractive one. We know that Crassus recruited men from Lucania, Apulia and amongst the Marsian regions of Italy.[146] The important point here is not the ethnicity of his troops, but their quality. It is likely that the vast majority of his legionaries were young and inexperienced, as opposed to the army he had faced Spartacus with. Such an inexperienced army would require training, not that there was much time to do so in Italy.

Despite all the sources stating that Crassus had difficulty recruiting, Plutarch makes an interesting observation that is not often remarked upon. In a section commenting on Crassus' dealings with an Arab chieftain, he states that a number of Crassus' men had served with Pompey in the 60s and had encountered this particular Arab chieftain before.[147] The key thing here is that Plutarch appears to tell us that Crassus had managed to recruit an unknown number of veterans from Pompey's campaign in the 60s. This would suggest that whilst the bulk of his seven legions were inexperienced men, Crassus' army did posses a core of experienced Roman soldiers, in the form of veterans from the eastern campaign of the previous decade. Not only would these men bring precious fighting experience, but they had been in the region before and would have knowledge of the local conditions. Even though these men were veterans of Pompey, the lure of another lucrative eastern campaign would have been a strong incentive to sign on once again and they may have done so in greater numbers than we previously believed.

We know that Crassus left Rome to meet up with his army in late 55 BC. We have a letter of Cicero from what now equates to 14 November 55 BC, which states that Crassus had left the city recently.[148] His term of office as consul was coming to an end and he was eager to reach his province before the campaigning of 54 BC could begin. This was quite the normal practice in Rome, especially given the distance he had to travel.

Crassus' departure from Rome is a story in itself. When the day came, Crassus made a public show of it, accompanied to the city gates by Pompey. We hear that

Caesar also sent a letter wishing him good fortune. As he approached the city gates, the tribune Gaius Ateius Capito once again attempted to scupper the whole proceedings by ordering his attendants to arrest Crassus. This failed when Capito's tribunician colleagues blocked him. Not to be thwarted quietly, Capito then went onto curse Crassus and his whole campaign. Plutarch provides us with the most dramatic description of this:

> but Ateius ran on ahead to the city gate, placed there a blazing brazier, and when Crassus came up, cast incense and libations upon it, and invoked curses which were dreadful and terrifying in themselves, and were reinforced by sundry strange and dreadful gods whom he summoned and called by name.
>
> The Romans say that these mysterious and ancient curses have such power that no-one involved in them ever escapes, and misfortune falls also upon the one who utters them, which means that they are not employed at random, nor by many. And accordingly at this time they found fault with Ateius because it was for the city's sake that he was angered at Crassus, and yet he had involved the city in curses which awakened much superstitious terror.[149]

This wonderfully dramatic story suffers only from the fact that it is not mentioned by any contemporary source, most notably Cicero. Cicero's letter which talks of Crassus' departure fails to mention any of these events and a later work of his, which harks back to Crassus' departure, only talks about Ateius reporting bad omens for Crassus' departure, which Crassus ignored.[150] Ateius was actually prosecuted for reporting these omens, but acquitted on the count that the result of the battle showed them to be true. Nowhere is there any mention of a 'dreadful and terrifying curse'. It has been argued that Plutarch and perhaps his source have mixed up this event with one that occurred in 131 BC when a tribune did use this type of curse in an incident in which an ancestor of Crassus' was involved.[151] Again we can see that the later ancient sources were all too eager to add dramatic elements to the story, especially one that made the defeat seem inevitable.

Nevertheless, despite the stories of ancient curses and domestic opposition, Crassus had much to look forward to. The Parthian empire was engulfed in a civil war, with the pro-Roman Mithradates III holding the key Mesopotamian cities of Babylon and Seleucia (which had control over the Parthian winter capital of Ctesiphon). The cities of Mesopotamia still had a large Hellenistic Greek population and, as discussed previously, had only a nominal level of Parthian loyalty or control. To the north of Parthia lay Armenia, which was allied to Rome and would be obliged by treaty to provide additional forces for any Roman campaign. To the southwest of Parthia lay various Arab territories that, whilst not part of the Roman empire, were nominally allied to Rome and would render assistance when called on.

Thus Crassus' position in 55 BC was a strong one, but we still are unclear as to his ultimate aims. One possibility was the complete annexation of Parthia, right up to the Indian frontier, as Plutarch described.[152] Yet Roman policy in relation to the states in this region had been a mixture of annexation (such as Pontus and Syria) and tributary status, such as Armenia, Judea and Egypt.

Therefore we can legitimately ask ourselves whether Crassus intended to annex the whole of the Parthian empire. Given the mixed nature of Roman policy in the region and the relatively modest Roman force at Crassus' command, it is far more reasonable to speculate that Crassus would have been aiming for the same mixed policy in relation to Parthia. Certainly, as Rome's remaining undefeated enemy and rival in this region, a clear defeat of Parthia was necessary. Following that, it made perfect sense on strategic, commercial and even ethnic grounds, for the Romans to annex Mesopotamia to their empire, giving them access to the Persian Gulf and the overseas trade routes. The rest of the Parthian empire would then remain a tributary ally of Rome, probably with a pliant client king (Mithradates III, or even a defeated Orodes II) on the throne. Thus Rome intended to defeat the Parthians, eliminating their last regional rival and annexing substantial territories to their physical empire, whilst adding the rest of Parthia to their outer ring of client states. This forms the most likely objective for Rome in their first Parthian war.

Initial Strategies: Parthia

Before we turn our attention to the first year of campaigning in 54 BC, we must first consider the issue from the Parthian perspective. All of our surviving sources and most modern commentators blindly seem to assume that the Parthians just sat there, waiting for the Roman armies to invade. In point of fact ,given that Gabinius had already invaded Parthia in 55 BC in support of Mithradates III, and given that the build up and transportation of a large Roman army would have been hard to conceal, we can rightly suppose the Parthians to have been expecting a Roman attack. However, the question of just what they could do about it is a different matter.

With regard to the Romans, it was clear that the Parthians could not go on the offensive and invade Syria. A clear violation of the terms of friendship and an invasion of Roman territory would have united all of Rome behind Crassus and made invasion a certainty. What they could do, however, was to fully mobilise their armed forces and make certain preparations. Theirs would have to be a responsive war, waiting for Rome to make the first move and then countering it.

However, two other aspects were clear to the Parthians. Firstly, their primary concern must have been to end the civil war and recover Mesopotamia. This would not only remove Rome's supposed cause for invasion, but would ensure that the Romans had no Parthian allies or bases of operation and that they would meet a united Parthian response.

Secondly, it was clear that Armenia (the third of the region's three powers) would play a role in the war and would be on Rome's side. Obviously it was possible that the Parthians would face an attack on two fronts and that preparations would need to be made to knock Armenia out of the war. Therefore, on the Parthian side as well as the Roman, preparations were being made to go to war. What is not clear is to what extent the Parthians believed that they could defeat the Romans. Clearly they were prepared to defend themselves, but we can question whether they believed that they could win a war with Rome.

54 BC – The First Year's Campaigning: Rome

As stated earlier we know that Crassus left Rome at some point in early November 55 BC. We are also told that his army boarded ship at the port of Brundisium and encountered problems with the wintry seas of the Adriatic, losing many men (a not uncommon occurrence, especially given the time of year). This had supposedly been preceded by yet another unfavourable omen which Crassus ignored, as Cicero reports:

> When Marcus Crassus was embarking his army at Brundisium, a man who was selling Caunian Figs at the harbour, repeatedly cried out 'Cauneas, Cauneas'. Let us say, if you will, that this was a warning to Crassus to tell him 'Beware of going' and that if he had obeyed the omen he would not have perished.[153]

The Latin for 'beware of going' is *cave ne eas*, very similar to *Cauneas*. How Cicero got this story, so soon after the defeat at Carrhae is unknown, but it shows the mythos that soon built up around this defeat, and the number of tall stories that soon appeared. It is possible that his story was related to Cicero by Crassus himself, as we know that the two men were in communication by letter during 54 BC (though only Cicero's letters survive). The two men had reconciled their long standing enmity at a meeting in the country a few days before Crassus' departure.[154] They also make clear that Crassus was receiving and sending a number of reports back to his family in Rome.

What also emerges from this correspondence is that the consuls of 54 BC had proposed some form of curtailment of Crassus' command (though the details are lost). It is apparent that these moves were defeated and that Cicero helped in the matter.[155] Given the resources of the triumvirate and that Pompey was still in Rome, such an attempt was always likely to fail.

After disembarkation and recovery from the storm, we know that Crassus marched his army overland to Syria, a common occurrence given the Roman dislike of sea travel. This march took him across Greece and Asia Minor. Plutarch records that he passed through the Roman client kingdom of Galatia and gives us another amusing and pointed anecdote:

> Finding that King Deiotarus, who was now a very old man, was founding a new city, he greeted him saying 'O King, you are beginning to build at the twelfth hour'. The Galatian [Deiotarus] laughed and said: 'But you yourself, Imperator, as I see, are not marching very early in the day against the Parthians'.[156]

Plutarch then goes onto remind his readers of Crassus' age, and by implication, his shortcomings as a commander. Prior to his arrival, Crassus had sent a legate ahead to co-ordinate with Gabinius, who had returned from Egypt and Judea and was awaiting the handover. Dio reports that Gabinius refused to handover power to Crassus' legate.[157] We are not told how this situation was resolved, but by mid 54 BC Crassus and his army had arrived in Syria and were preparing to invade Parthia.

It is here that Crassus faced his first major tactical decision, and it is here that the choices he made begin to come under criticism from our surviving sources. The key question he faced was which route he was going to take to invade Parthia and what campaigning he would undertake once he had invaded. In terms of routes into Parthia, there were only two obvious choices: invade from Syria across the Euphrates and into western Mesopotamia; or invade via Armenia, through the mountains and into northern Mesopotamia. Crassus chose the former and invaded Mesopotamia via the Euphrates, from Roman Syria.

There were several strong reasons for taking this direct course of action. Militarily, it was the direct route and was easier for the army to cross the Euphrates than struggle in the Armenian foothills. Secondly, the Armenian route would have meant an extra delay and given that much of the campaigning season of 54 BC had already been taken up with the journey from Italy, he would have wanted to get the campaign underway as quickly as possible. Thirdly, there was a political element, as Crassus was the governor of Syria and his whole mandate stemmed from that. Moving his army into Armenia, a Roman ally, whilst being governor of Syria, might have jeopardised his authority for a pre-emptive invasion of Parthia. The nearest Roman provinces to Armenia were Pontus and Cilicia, both with their own governors.

Added to this was the fact that an invasion across the Euphrates put him squarely in Mesopotamia, the province where the civil war was being fought and in a strong strategic position with regard to controlling the southern cities of Seleucia, Babylon and Ctesiphon, or the central routes into the eastern Parthian empire. He also had the support of the Arab rulers in the area, notably Al Chaudonius of the Rhambaei and Akbar of Edessa, securing his flank.

In 54 BC the Roman army crossed the Euphrates and the First Romano-Parthian War proper began. Crassus appears to have adopted a cautious and steady strategy. After crossing the Euphrates he sought out the Parthian satrap of the region, Silaces, and engaged him in battle. This initial encounter occurred near the town of Ichnae and was as one-sided as the Romans had expected. Silaces' forces were routed, their cavalry scattered and Silaces himself wounded (he fled the battle and made his way to the Parthian court, in order to inform King Orodes II).

With this victory having won him northern Mesopotamia, Crassus set about securing the area by garrisoning the key strategic towns of the region, notably Ichnae, Nicephorium and Carrhae. In all cases bar one, these mostly-Greek cities went over to the Romans voluntarily. Most were founded during the period of Alexander the Great and his successors and had large numbers of peoples of Greek descent, who welcomed Roman rule. Only one town resisted: Zenodotium, ruled by a tyrant named Apollonius. Rather than see his position lost to the Romans, he invited a Roman force within the city and then ambushed and massacred them. The act was a futile one and in retaliation Crassus attacked the city with his whole army. The city was soon taken and sacked, with the inhabitants sold into slavery. All Apollonius had done was to present Crassus with a wonderful opportunity to both train his men in siege tactics, provide them with an early reward for their services through booty, and give a valuable lesson to everyone in the region as to what would happen if they betrayed Rome.

Crassus had defeated the Parthian forces in the region and secured a key strategic position. The territory now under Roman control was an area of fertile land containing many of the Greek-dominated cities and towns and controlling the key communication routes of the region. In total Crassus garrisoned the region with 7,000 infantry and 1,000 cavalry and then withdrew back into Syria for the winter.[158]

This decision is one of the main points that his detractors criticise him on. Both Plutarch and Dio attack him for being too cautious and not pressing on further or remaining in the region for the winter.[159] In particular they castigate him for not pushing on to southern Mesopotamia to relieve Mithradates III and take control of the cities of Seleucia, Babylon and Ctesiphon.

For Crassus, however, the campaign of 54 BC had been a total success; northern and western Mesopotamia were firmly under Roman rule and this had been accomplished remarkably easily, as everyone had expected. The first engagement between Roman and Parthian forces had been an undoubted victory, with the Parthians routed. Only one city in the region had not gone over to Rome willingly, and a clear example had been made of it.

Yet Crassus had good reason to be cautious. His army was still composed of mostly inexperienced young recruits. Certainly they had received a taste of battle at Ichnae, but that was against a vastly outnumbered Parthian force. A lot of training was needed before his army was up to scratch, and given Crassus' experiences in the Spartacan War (see chapter three), this is something that he considered to be crucial to the success of any campaign. Furthermore, Crassus would have known that he lacked one crucial element to his army, namely cavalry. It was not until the winter of 54 BC that his son Publius arrived with a contingent of 1,000 Gallic cavalry loaned to him by Caesar (both Publius and Marcus junior had been serving in Gaul under Caesar).

Crassus would also have been concerned that the Armenian contingent had not arrived, a fact that goes uncommented upon by our surviving sources. Given that the Roman army had set off from Italy in late 55 BC, the arrival of the Armenian military assistance had been remarkably slow, not arriving until the winter of 54 BC (at the same time as the contingent from Gaul, which is interesting considering the respective distances). Therefore, a further reason for caution could have been his wish to ascertain how reliable the Armenians were going to be in this war with their former allies. Given Armenia's subjugation to Rome, a Parthian victory, or at least a stalemate, would have been in their interests. As events turned out, such a view on Crassus' part was an extremely wise one.

In addition to these purely military reasons, Crassus would have known that the winters of the region brought about heavy rainfall, which would have rendered the desert roads more treacherous. Furthermore, it appears that the province of Syria and the allied kingdom of Judea were still in some disarray and would have needed the governors' attention, and Crassus was looking for a further source of additional campaign funds.

It is with all these reasons in mind, most notably an inexperienced army lacking cavalry support, that Crassus did not continue his campaign into the autumn and winter of 54 BC. The initiative and the first blood was his. Given the presence of Surenas' forces in southern Mesopotamia, he chose not to risk giving battle by heading down the Euphrates and attempting to relieve Mithradates III. That this decision cost Mithradates his life and led to the end of the civil war probably did not disturb the Romans greatly. If he was an ally then he was an expendable one, and one who had already served his purpose, namely distracting the Parthians to allow an untroubled Roman invasion. As could be seen from Mithradates' original plea, he had no forces of his own and if the Romans had relieved him then they would have gained the headache of having to garrison the cities of the region against an aggressive Parthian force, with little help from Mithradates. His death did not really alter their plans for a Parthian puppet as a defeated Orodes would have been just as useful to them, if not more so, given Mithradates' unpopularity amongst the Parthian nobility (the reason he was overthrown in the first place).

Both Plutarch and Dio pass over the winter of 54 BC in their haste to reach the events of 53 BC. Both claim that Crassus allowed his men to grow lazy and given to plundering. However, neither source presents Crassus and his campaign in anything other than a negative light and both sources overlook the activities of Crassus in Judea. Only Josephus records the fact that during the winter of 54 BC, Crassus and a large force entered the allied kingdom of Judea and sacked the Great Temple of Jerusalem once again (Pompey had done so a decade earlier).[160] This time, there was little clear reason for this expedition, but most commentators put it down to Crassus' greed. Josephus actually states that Crassus did this in order to gain funds for his campaign. Furthermore, Josephus does not provide any background to Crassus' intervention, but given the history of Judea in the preceding decade (one of civil turmoil, exacerbated by Gabinius' intervention) it is likely that the situation called for Roman intervention and Crassus merely utilised it to gain additional funds. In addition, Crassus also confiscated the treasures from the Temple of Venus at Hierapolis.[161] He also drew up plans for the winter quartering of his men, paid for by the local rulers.

The situation that faced Crassus at the beginning of 53 BC was actually an extremely positive one. Western Mesopotamia had been secured and the Parthians defeated once already, both of which were accomplished with the minimum of effort. Despite the ease of these accomplishments, Crassus had shown restraint and preferred to winter his army in preparation for what he knew would have been at least one major set-piece battle to decide the war the following year. Over the winter he could train his army, gather additional finances and build up his cavalry contingent. Rather than get carried away with the ease of the early engagements, Crassus once again appeared to show his restraint and methodological approach as a general, ensuring that he went into battle only when it suited him.

54 BC – The First Year's Campaigning: Parthia

For the Parthians, and Orodes II in particular, it appeared that 54 BC was a year of mixed fortunes. For the first time Parthia had experienced a full-scale Roman invasion, and it appeared to be as one-sided as many expected. The cities of western Mesopotamia, which had been under Parthian control for nearly ninety years, had all defected to the Romans without a fight and his garrison in the region had been routed with apparent ease. Yet the Romans had limited themselves to western Mesopotamia and the invasion was hardly a surprise, which had allowed Orodes the time to raise two armies. He possessed the bulk of the Parthian army in Media whilst his leading nobleman had raised a second army from his own estates.

It is to the man known as Surenas that we should now turn. We know quite a lot about Parthia's foremost general in this period, with one notable exception – his name. All the surviving sources name him as coming from the noble house of Suren, and only refer to him as 'the Suren', or Surenas, with his own personal named being lost to us. Through the Suren we gain a glimpse into how the Parthian nobility had developed over the centuries of the growth of the Parthian empire. Whilst a hereditary, landowning Parthian nobility must have dated back to the creation of the new Parthian ruling order in the 240s/230s BC, it appears that the recent decades had seen them consolidate and expand their power.

It is clear from Parthian history that the absolutist monarchy of the Arsacids would not have encouraged a strong and independent nobility. Yet as the empire grew, more power had to be devolved from the Great King and more men had to be drawn into governing and fighting for the empire. By the time of the conquest of Mesopotamia we hear of generals commanding Parthian armies, most of who seem to be non-Parthian. By the 120s, however, with the death of two kings at the hands of the Saka invaders, the monarchy was in a weakened position. A weakened monarchy always allows for the growth of an ambitious nobility. Under Mithradates II such growth would have been curtailed, but the civil wars of the period 91–70 BC seem to have weakened the central monarchy considerably. We know that Mithradates III was overthrown for his unpopularity with the nobles and replaced by his younger brother. Thus the hereditary monarchy was now under the control of a group of noble families and foremost amongst them was the Suren.

As well as being one of the families on the Council of Elders, which appointed or rather confirmed the choice of king, we are told that the Suren also had the hereditary right of placing the crown on the head of the new monarch, which could easily translate itself into a veto over the choice of monarch.[162] As we can see with Orodes II, he owed his crown and his continued occupation of it to the Suren clan. Furthermore, from the events of 54 and 53 BC we know that the Suren could put an army of 10,000 men in the field, drawn from their own lands and financed at their own expenses.[163] The head of the clan was a young man in his twenties, but one who already possessed a formidable reputation. Plutarch breaks off his narrative of the campaign to detail the man:

Nor was Surenas an ordinary man at all, but in wealth, birth and consideration, he stood next to the king, while in valour and ability he was the foremost Parthian of his time, besides having no equal in stature and personal beauty. He used to travel on private business with a baggage train of a thousand camels, and was followed by two hundred wagons for his concubines[164]

Furthermore, Plutarch adds:

Moreover, he enjoyed the ancient and hereditary privilege of being first to set the crown upon the head of the Parthian King; and when this very King was driven out of Parthia, he restored him to the throne. And though at this time he was not yet thirty years of age, he had the highest reputation for prudence and sagacity.[165]

Thus, in many ways the clash that occurred at Carrhae was a clash between the two richest noblemen of their respective empires (Crassus and Surenas, a wily old dog and an ambitious young one). As usual, we have limited sources for the Parthian campaigning of 54 BC, but what we do know is that whilst Orodes was raising the main Parthian army and adopting a 'wait and see' policy, the young head of the Suren clan moved into action. Having played the decisive role in removing Mithradates III and placing Orodes on the throne, he moved decisively to end the civil war before it fatally damaged the campaign against Rome. At some point in 54 BC, Surenas (as we will to refer to him) advanced his army into southern Mesopotamia, where Mithradates was holed up in Seleucia.[166] We have no details of what route he took, but it is possible that his operations in southern Mesopotamia coincided with those of Crassus in the northwest of the region. What we do know is that both Seleucia and Babylon were placed under siege, and that both fell quickly to Surenas. Again this is highly unusual given the poor Parthian reputation for laying siege to a city, but it could also illustrate the limited control which Mithradates III had over these cities. Plutarch tells us that Surenas was the first to mount the walls of Seleucia, though this smacks of propaganda.[167] Mithradates III surrendered to Surenas, who sent him to his brother, the king, before whom he was promptly executed.

Thus the Parthians ended 54 BC on the back foot, but not without some measure of accomplishment. The civil war had been ended and the cities of Babylon, Seleucia and the winter capital of Ctesiphon had all been secured before the Romans could intervene. Thus the Parthians could face the Roman invader united and with a commander of some ability, apparently unlike Orodes himself.

53 BC – Shadows of Carrhae: Rome

The spring of 53 BC saw two significant developments occur before either army was even in the field. Crassus received two separate but important embassies, which arrived at similar times; one from the Armenian King Artavasdes and one from an emissary of Orodes II. The timing of these two visits may not have been coincidental. It has already been noted that the Armenians had been conspicuous by their absence throughout 54 BC and had taken well over six months to arrive at Crassus' camp. That they did so at around the same time as the Parthian emissary could strike a suspicious mind as having some connection.

We shall deal with the Parthian arrival first. Both Plutarch and Dio report this embassy, but Plutarch does so in far greater detail.[168] The embassy was apparently sent by Orodes to enquire about the causes of the war and to inform Crassus that the Romans had no legitimate reason for going to war with them, not that such niceties had ever bothered the Parthians themselves. Plutarch goes on to tell us that the Parthians knew that this was an unpopular war back in Rome and that Crassus was acting against the interests of the Roman people. Orodes was prepared to put this invasion down to Crassus' old age and allow him to withdraw.

It is with this analysis that we must really start to question Plutarch's account, as the chances of any Parthian envoy wishing to insult the Roman commander in such a way was remote at the least. The fact that he manages to pick on Crassus' age and the opposition to the war in Rome, both of which Plutarch has been highlighting, is too great a coincidence. Furthermore, we have to ask whether the Parthians would have thought that insulting one of the two most powerful men in the Roman Republic, and accusing him of being senile, was likely to encourage him to withdraw his invading armies and return to Rome. No Roman commander had ever committed such an act and no Roman Republican commander ever would.

A more likely reason for the embassy was a last ditch attempt by Orodes to avert the war with Rome by bargaining, perhaps with the offer of a hefty bribe. Both main sources report an interesting anecdote about the conversation between Crassus and the chief emissary, a man named Vagises. When Crassus tells them that he will give them his answer to the causes of the war from Seleucia:

> Vagises burst out laughing and said, pointing to the palm of his upturned hand: 'O Crassus, hair will grow there before you will see Seleucia'[169]

This incident raises two interesting possibilities. Firstly that Crassus is linking the origins of the war to Seleucia, until recently held by Mithradates III, who's request for assistance in securing the throne the Romans had accepted (which was possibly their '*casns belli*'). Secondly, Crassus could have been indicating his price for ending the campaign, namely Roman suzerainty of Mesopotamia. In any event, the emissaries left Crassus' camp to return to Orodes to tell him that there could be no negotiation and that a full scale war was certain. The fact that Orodes, despite having his territory occupied and his forces defeated, was still willing to negotiate shows us the relatively weak position that the Parthians, or Orodes in particular, saw themselves in.

The next arrival at Crassus' door was the king of Armenia, Artavasdes, who arrived with 6,000 armoured cavalrymen. Despite what at first seemed a welcome arrival, Artavasdes' visit brought more problems than it solved for Crassus. Despite having a year to prepare for Crassus' arrival, he only brought with him 6,000 cavalrymen, backed up by the pledge of a further 10,000 armoured cavalry and 30,000 infantry, but only on the condition that Crassus invaded Parthia via Armenia. As statements of fidelity to the Roman cause go, we can understand why Crassus was underwhelemd by such 'generosity'. Despite Plutarch stating that the meeting was a friendly one, it ended with Artavasdes returning to Armenia along with his cavalry.[170] Later, when the Armenians were attacked by Orodes, Artavasdes sent Crassus a note apologising for not sending the 40,000 cavalry and infantry and actually asking for Crassus' help in defeating the Parthians. Plutarch records that this sent Crassus into a rage and led to him promising to pay Artavasdes back for his treachery.[171]

Many commentators have criticised Crassus for not taking up Artavasdes' offer of invading Parthia via Armenia, where the foothills would have offered protection from the Parthian cavalry, as would the supporting Armenian cavalry. However, this is using both the benefit of hindsight and rose-tinted glasses at the same time. To Crassus, at the beginning of 54 BC, it seemed perfectly obvious that the Armenians could not be trusted. Artavasdes' offer was an obvious ploy to save his kingdom from Parthian invasion by having the Romans do all the fighting. In fact, Crassus could not be sure that even if he chose the Armenian route, the Armenians would help in fighting the Parthians. If anything, there was the distinct possibility of a trap, with the Armenians joining the Parthians once battle had been joined.

Given the fact that the Romans had secured a bridgehead in western Mesopotamia and that he had spent the winter training his army and having had them reinforced by Gallic cavalry, the most logical route was still a full-scale invasion through Mesopotamia. Once there he could track down the armies of Surenas and Orodes and defeat them in open battle. The downside was the loss of the Armenian cavalry, but then the Romans had seen little to fear of the Parthian cavalry and had 1,000 Gallic cavalry that they could trust, rather than 6,000 that may melt away at the first sign of trouble.

In spring 53 BC, with both the Parthian and Armenian embassies dealt with, the Roman army mobilised and crossed the Euphrates for a full-scale invasion of the Parthian empire. The place that Crassus chose to ford the Euphrates was Zeugma. Dio states this was the place that Alexander the Great had chosen to cross at, which he believed showed that Crassus was making a bold statement about his intentions.[172] Unfortunately, Dio has mixed up two different locations[173]. The town which Crassus crossed at was a trading town founded by Alexander's general, Seleucus, and was the main crossing point for the eastern trade route, more commonly known as the Silk Road.[174] It has recently been suggested that Crassus made use of the old Persian Royal Road (which ran from Asia Minor through this region) on his journey through Mesopotamia.[175] Whilst there is no direct evidence to support this theory, it raises an interesting point about Crassus' motives for taking this route and shows the accessibility of the area to a large army. Thus Crassus was merely following the most logical route into Parthia.[176]

It is at this point that Plutarch introduces no fewer than seven separate ill omens that Crassus' army supposedly encountered.[177] As the army crossed the river there was thunder and lightning and heavy winds which destroyed many of the rafts. Then two lightning bolts struck the Roman campsite. Thirdly, one of Crassus' horses was lost in the river, along with its groom. Next, the first Roman legionary eagle that crossed the river turned round of its own accord. Then came the serving of lentils and salt to his troops (traditionally a sign of mourning), followed by Crassus making a speech about burning the bridges over the river so that they might not return that way. Finally, Crassus apparently let a purificatory sacrifice drop through his hands to the ground.

To this incredible list Dio adds a legionary eagle that sticks in the ground and refuses to move, another falling into the river and, best of all, there was apparently a heavy fog on the river (which was then followed by strong winds).[178] Thus in both accounts no Roman soldier could have been unaware of the fact that they were all doomed. We should now move away from the rage of the gods and back onto military matters.

Plutarch gives us a reliable figure for the Roman army that crossed the Euphrates in such propitious circumstances: seven legions of infantry, four thousand horsemen (including the one thousand Gallic cavalry, the rest being allied horsemen), and an equivalent number of lightly-armed allied troops.[179] In total this force would number around 42,000 thousand infantry and 4,000 cavalry. One aspect which is not clear is whether Plutarch is counting the number of men with which Crassus had already garrisoned western Mesopotamia the year previously (some 7,000 infantry and 1,000 cavalry). Given the fact that we are told by the sources that these garrison troops came from the legions, then they must surely be deducted from the total.

It was after crossing the Euphrates that Crassus made another key strategic decision. He faced a choice between turning to the south and heading towards the cities of Seleucia, Babylon and Ctesiphon or keeping to an eastern course that would take him into the heart of the Parthian Empire. Crassus chose to keep an easterly course and it is this decision that the sources again castigate him for.

Before we analyse the reasons behind this and the rhetorical devices the sources employ, we should look at this situation logically. Firstly, Crassus had already garrisoned the towns along the eastern route, which was a caravan route and was well known to the Romans. The area had been visited by Roman forces under Afranius during Pompey's campaigns and would have been well scouted by the Roman garrisons. The region was crossed by many rivers and was a fertile (for the region) plain. Furthermore, Crassus' intelligence would have alerted him to the fact that the Parthian forces were in the north and the east, not the south. If he was looking for a set-piece victory over Parthian forces he would not find it in the south. Although the key Greek cities of Mesopotamia were there, what exactly would their attack and occupation achieve, aside from trophy value? By this point Mithradates had been defeated, and it was unlikely, even if the cities had gone over to the Romans, that they would have been any material use. In fact the opposite is the case, as they too would have needed garrisoning.

Furthermore, the Euphrates valley itself is fertile, but the surrounding region is not and forty thousand soldiers and four thousand horses would need a lot of provisions to keep them in the field. Added to this would be the 'bottle-neck effect', funnelling that many men either down or alongside the Euphrates River, stringing them out and leaving them vulnerable, especially when the enemy would have been behind them. For all these reasons, the most logical military position would be to keep to the eastern route, locate and destroy the Parthian armies, and then pick off the trophy cities when the campaign had been won.

Unsurprisingly, however, this is not how it is portrayed in the sources. Plutarch especially introduces two key features to his account: how Crassus is constantly being (mis)led around and influenced by treacherous Arabs; and how Cassius always advises against it.[180] As detailed elsewhere (see appendix two), we don't know the source of Plutarch's account, but it is certainly biased towards Cassius who always seems to sense the danger, advise Crassus not to do something (which is ignored) and always adopts an 'I told you so' stance.

Despite all the sound reasons for choosing the eastern route, Plutarch decides to ascribe Crassus' decision to the treacherous advice of an Arab chieftain, named Ariamnes, (Dio names him as Abgarus[181]) who, having been allied to Pompey, now worked his way into Crassus' confidence with the aim of leading Crassus to his destruction. Plutarch's account would have us believe that Crassus, a man not noted for trusting other Romans, let alone a dubious ally, now decided to believe everything this Arab chieftain was saying and was totally under his spell. The cunning plan was to apparently lure Crassus into heading directly into the path of the army of Surenas and thus ensure the Roman defeat. There are two basic problems with this view. Firstly the Romans were planning on finding and defeating the Parthians in the first place, and not simply skulking around hiding from the Parthian army, and in particular their cavalry, which seems to be Cassius' plan.[182] Secondly, no one could foresee the outcome of the encounter between the Roman army and the Parthian cavalry and there were no indicators (other than divine ones) that the Romans would be so comprehensively beaten by them.

Thus the Roman army pressed on its northeastward course in search of the Parthian army. Plutarch provides us with a dramatic description of how merciless the conditions were, with Crassus having been led into

> the midst of the plains, by a way that was suitable and easy at first, but soon became troublesome when deep sand succeeded, and plains which had no trees, no water and no limit anywhere which the eye could reach . . . For they saw no plant, no stream, no projection of sloping hill, and no growing grass, but only sea-like billows of innumerable desert sand heaps enveloping the army.[183]

In reality, Crassus and his army were heading along a main caravan route which led towards the Belikh River, a tributary of the Euphrates, which would have been swollen with waters from the Armenian mountains and the winter rains, as would the other rivers of the region. Thus the Roman army was not being misled into heading deep into a waterless desert, as the ancient sources portray. Crassus was sticking close to a major source of water and keeping to the line of fortified towns that had Roman garrisons: Nicephorium, Ichnae, Zenodotium and Carrhae. Once again the surviving sources are looking for reasons for the defeat and a chance to both excuse the disaster and blacken Crassus' name.

This march took place in May 53 BC, which was the time that Orodes attacked the Armenians and King Artavasdes sent word to Crassus that he was unable to send him any reinforcements. At a similar time the Arab chieftain Ariamnes (or Abgarus) left the Roman camp for reasons we do not know. Plutarch states that it was a desertion before the battle, but perhaps Crassus had simply got tired of him.[184] Ahead of them lay the Belikh River and on the other side lay Surenas' army. It was here that Surenas had decided to make his stand against Crassus' army. On the 9th June 53 BC Crassus' scouts ran into Surenas' force and came off worst. The survivors reported back that contact had been established with the first of the main Parthian armies.

Crassus was again faced with a key tactical decision; whether to camp by the river and wait until the following day before trying to give battle, or strike that very day. Crassus chose to strike whilst he could. Orders were given for his men to freshen up by the river and take a quick meal and then it was off in search of Surenas' army. The two armies found each other on the plains of Carrhae on the afternoon of that day. The first full scale battle between the Romans and the Parthians was about to begin.

53 BC – Shadows of Carrhae: Parthia

With the civil war ended and southern Mesopotamia recovered, the Parthians could now turn their full attention on the Roman invasion. As detailed above, Orodes made a last attempt at seeking a negotiated settlement. Given that no Roman commander had ever turned around and returned home from a campaign without fighting, and that the Romans were occupying much of western Mesopotamia, we have to ask ourselves just what was he hoping to achieve with this embassy? The main conclusion we can draw is that it was a desperate last ditch attempt to avert an outright military confrontation, which the Parthians can have had no confidence in winning. As we have seen, Rome had relentlessly marched eastwards, defeating and subsuming all of the civilisations in her path and now it must have appeared that it was Parthia's turn. Furthermore, as the Armenian war had shown, the Parthians did not consider themselves strong enough to face up to Rome militarily, added to which was Orodes' own weak position.

Whatever Orodes' intention with the embassy, perhaps including a substantial bribe to induce Crassus to withdraw, there can have been no doubt as to the result; military conflict was inevitable if the Parthians were to keep their empire intact. With that in mind, Orodes drew up an ambitious and unusual battleplan. It appears that at the failure of his embassy, Orodes ordered Surenas to attack the towns of western Mesopotamia that were under Roman control. Plutarch reports that a number of Roman soldiers returned to the main army in Syria filled with tales of how devastating the Parthians were:

> there was no escaping them, and when they fled there was no taking them; and strange missiles are the precursors of their appearance, which pierce through every obstacle before one sees who sent them.[185]

For once, even Plutarch has to admit that these men were exaggerating. However, we are not told which cities were attacked or how successful these attacks were. The problem we have with this is that as far as we can tell the Romans were still garrisoning the cities of Mesopotamia when Crassus advanced in the spring of 54 BC (we know that the town of Carrhae was still in Roman hands.) Added to this was the well-known Parthian inability to besiege towns. If

Bust of Pyrrhus of Epirus. Pyrrhus was the first enemy from the more advanced states of the eastern Mediterranean that the Romans faced. His invasion from the east in 281 BC helped to set the tone for the next two hundred years of Roman foreign policy.

The Forum in Rome, the heart of the city and of the Republic.

Bust of Gnaeus Pompeius Magnus more commonly referred to as Pompey the Great, Crassus' sometime ally and greatest rival.

Bust of Gaius Julius Caesar, the junior member of the Triumvirate.

The need to establish a military reputation to match that of his fellow triumvirs was a powerful motive in Crassus' search for glory in the East.

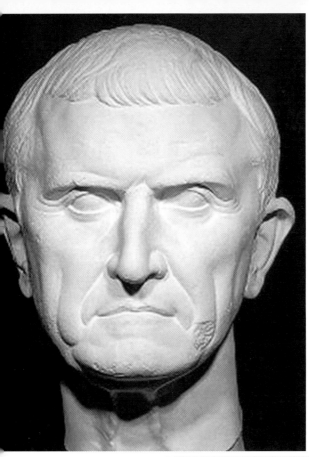

Probable bust of Marcus Licinius Crassus. The richest man in Rome and a gifted orator, Crassus had also showed military ability, most notably at the Battle of the Colline Gate in 82 BC and his defeat of Spartacus' slave rebellion in 71 BC. By 53 BC, however, these feats had long been overshadowed by Pompey and Caesar.

t of Marcus Tullius Cicero, famous orator and man of rs who was reluctantly sent ne East as governor of Cilicia 1 BC. His letters are a able source for the period.

Statue of a Parthian nobleman, possibly Surenas, architect of the victory at Carrhae; now in the National Archaeological Museum of Tehran. (© Livius.org)

A coin of Publius Crassus minted on the eve of the campaign. Ironically the reverse shows a Roman cavalryman of the type in all too short supply at Carrhae

A coin of Tigranes II whose kingdom of Armenia was one of the first points of friction between the Roman and Parthian empires. His heir, Artavasdes, proved a disappointing ally to Crassus.

Coin of Mithridates II of Parthia, under whose reign (123-88 BC) the first official contact with Rome was made.

Coin of Orodes II, king of Parthia at the time of Crassus' invasion. Faced with a war on two fronts, he sent Surenas to delay the Romans, probably with little expectation that he would win such a complete victory.

Coin of Pacorus, son of Orodes II. He was nominal commander of the Parthian counter-invasion following Carrhae but later rebelled against his father, possibly encouraged by Roman gold and machinations.

Top: The ruins of Ctesiphon, the Parthian winter capital since the reign of Mithradates II.

Above: The ruins of Carrhae (Harran). The town had been captured and garrisoned by Crassus in 54 BC and he and the remnants of his army sought refuge here during the night following the battle.

Right: Scenes from Trajan's column depicting his much later Parthian war and the capture of Ctesiphon.

Parthian horse archer armed with a ~~rt~~ but powerful composite bow.

A Parthian cataphract. Although relatively few in number, such troops played a crucial role in the battle. Even Crassus' best Gallic cavalry, veterans of Caesar's campaigns in Gaul, proved no match for them in close combat.

A Roman auxiliary cavalryman. Crassus had too few of these to counter the all-mounted Parthian force.

~~oman~~ legionary infantryman, backbone of Roman armies ~~centuries. Such troops were~~ ~~en~~ little chance to fight back ~~inst~~ their mobile opponents.

Detail of the Prima Porta statue showing Augustus' breastpla with its embossed depiction of the return of the standards los Carrhae, which he achieved by diplomacy.

The statue of Augustus found at Prima Porta, near Rome, in 1863 and now in the Vatican Museum.

A coin of Augustus, also showing the return of the standards, a major propaganda coup.

attacks were made on the Roman-controlled towns then they cannot have met with much success.

With the opening of the campaigning season, Orodes implemented his battle-plan for the war. Whilst we know the details of his plan, the motivations behind it are still unclear. Despite the Roman presence in Mesopotamia and that the full Roman attack was almost certain to come from this region, Orodes took the bulk of the Parthian army (the size of which is not given) and invaded Armenia. All he left to face the Romans were Surenas' personal army of 10,000 men, aided by the satrap of the region, Silaces (the man who Crassus had defeated the year previously). Again we must ask ourselves why he did this. On the one hand, he has been accused of wishing to avoid facing the Romans in battle himself and put Surenas in harm's way, facing what most would have thought to have been certain defeat and death. Yet there is another explanation.

We can best see the design behind this plan with relation to a modern battle-plan. Orodes appears to have implemented an ancient version of the German 'Schlieffen Plan' of the First World War period.[186] Orodes knew that he not only faced the Roman army, but also that of his neighbour Armenia. It is more than likely that he was also aware that the Armenians were prevaricating and had not yet supplied Crassus with additional forces. If he could knock Armenia out of the war before they had a chance to open up a second front, then he could wheel around and face the Romans on their own. Thus he appeared willing to sacrifice Mesopotamia to the Romans to buy him the time he needed. Surenas was deployed to try and slow the Romans and perhaps inflict heavy casualties on them. It is very unlikely that Orodes was planning on Surenas actually winning the conflict with Crassus; it was more of a case of Surenas being a necessary sacrifice (from Orodes' point of view at least).

Thus Orodes' 'Schlieffen Plan' played to Parthia's strengths and put off the moment when the key battle would occur. In Orodes' timetable, he would face the Romans without the aid of their Armenian allies, and depleted by both time and Surenas' arrows. As it happens the plan worked to perfection and not only saved Orodes' throne, but the whole Parthian Empire. We know little about the details of the Armenian campaign, only the result. When the news of Carrhae reached Orodes, he was feasting with the Armenian king, Artavasdes, in Armenia. We do not know whether Artavasdes even gave battle or simply rolled over when the Parthian army appeared. Parthia and Armenia renewed their old alliance, crowned with the marriage between Artavasdes' sister and Orodes' son Pacorus. Thus Crassus' doubts over the Armenians were borne out and they betrayed the Romans whilst Crassus' army was still in Mesopotamia. Had Crassus been victorious at the field of Carrhae, he would have faced Orodes not only without the Armenians, but with them likely lined up with the Parthians.

Thus, for Orodes the campaigning of 54 BC had been a complete success; the Armenians had been knocked out of the war and were once again under Parthia's dominance. In terms of foreign policy, Orodes had managed to turn the clock back to the days of Mithradates II, when Armenia came under Parthian suzerainty. How long this reversal would last would be down to the key battle between himself and Crassus; or so he thought. On the plain of Carrhae, the Parthian nobleman Surenas had different ideas and was unwilling to play the sacrificial role in slowing Crassus down. Confident of his own abilities and those of his personal army, he set out to confront Crassus directly. Aware of the Roman advance through western Mesopotamia he set himself in a position to intercept them. He awaited their advance on the far side of the Belikh River, having chosen the battleground. On 9 June 53 BC the Roman scouts located Surenas' army and were rewarded with a heavy defeat. Surenas now awaited the arrival of the Roman army at Carrhae. By the afternoon, two great armies, representing the superpowers of the ancient world, faced each other across the plain of Carrhae.

Chapter 6

Disaster at Carrhae (53 BC)

In order to understand the course of the battle and the tactics used by both sides, we need to first analyse the armies and assess their strengths and weaknesses.

The Roman Army at the Battle of Carrhae

The first issue we need to consider is the size of the Roman force, and here the accounts vary. Once again we are faced with the fact that we have no contemporary source for this information. Appian has by far and away the greatest figure when he quotes Crassus' army as 100,000 strong.[187] Such an army had not been seen since the days of Hannibal and would never have been raised for such a campaign. Again we must turn to Plutarch (and his unknown source) for a more realistic figure. Plutarch informs us that Crassus crossed into Mesopotamia in 53 BC with an army of seven legions of infantry, four thousand horsemen (of which 1,000 were Gallic and the rest native auxiliaries) and an equivalent number of auxiliary troops.[188] If we follow the standard estimates that each of Crassus' legions was roughly 4,800 men strong, then we have a figure of just under 34,000 legionaries.[189] Add the 4,000 cavalry and 4,000 auxiliary infantry and we have a total of some 42,000 men.[190]

There are several problems with taking this figure as an exact one. Prior to the Imperial era, the size of the legion was not an absolute and we know that Crassus had problems recruiting legionaries, so he may not have been able to fill seven whole legions. Added to this is the rough nature of Plutarch's calculation of the number of auxiliary infantry. Thus we are working with a rough estimate of 38,000 infantry (split between legionaries and auxiliaries; a difference which will be explored below) and 3,000–4,000 cavalry (of which only 1,000 were Gallic).

These numbers do not represent a homogeneous body of men. Of this figure, 34,000 were full Roman legionaries. These legionaries were the elite infantry of Crassus' army, armed with javelins (*pila*) and short sword (*gladius*), with shields, helmets and chest armour for protection. In close order combat, the Roman legionary had proved to be superior to any other infantry in the ancient world. As detailed earlier, they had defeated the Macedonian phalanx and the Armenian foot-soldier. However, this did not mean that they were without weaknesses. For the legionaries to be at their most effective, the battle would have to be fought at closequarters, where the short Roman sword would be most effective. Aside from the javelin, the standard Roman legionary had little in the way of distance weaponry. In terms of defence, the helmet, shield and chest armour were again effective defence at close quarters, but this still left much of the body undefended and vulnerable to weapons of range.

Aside from weaponry and armour, we must also examine the nature of their training and ability. On the whole it appears that the bulk of Crassus' legionaries were raw recruits in 55 BC, along with a smattering of experienced legionaries (most probably distributed in the junior NCO ranks of the legion, such as the centurions). The bulk of the men would not have seen a major battle before. Nevertheless, too much can be made of the supposed inexperience of these men. They had the autumn, winter and spring of 54–53 BC in which to be trained and they had been blooded in battle in 54 BC, when they defeated the Parthian satrap, Silaces. Given Crassus' previous focus on his men's training and an unwillingness to give battle unless he had total confidence in their abilities (as seen in the Spartacus campaign), we can safely assume that they were up to the expected Roman standard.

The other section of Crassus' infantry, however, was composed of native auxiliaries. In the case of auxiliary forces there were no strict rules as to their composition, numbers, or weaponry, as it depended entirely upon where they were raised; which in this case we don't know. It is probable that they were raised from the Roman territories in the east and the Roman allies of the region. This would give them experience of the region and local warfare, but as to their weaponry and armour, we can only speculate. It is likely that they were lightly armoured and possessed a mixture of spears, swords and light bows. We are told at one point that there were at least 500 native archers in the army.[191] Certainly they would not have been able to match the Roman legionaries in either offensive or defensive capabilities. Nevertheless, such a mixture and balance was typical for Roman armies of the period and would have mirrored the armies of Lucullus and Pompey, and thus been more than a match for the armies that they were expecting to encounter in the region.

If there was a weakness in Crassus' army, then it lay in his cavalry. Roman armies of the period rarely had large numbers of cavalry and Crassus' army was no exception. It appears that he took no cavalry with him from Italy. Of his 4,000 cavalry, just 1,000 were non-native and these were the Gallic cavalry loaned by Julius Caesar. The Gallic cavalry are described by Plutarch as being lightly equipped with short spears and having little armour.[192] This compared badly to the Parthian heavily-armoured cataphract. Of the remaining 3,000 native cavalry we are not given any detail, but the assumption is that these too were light cavalry rather than heavily-armoured ones, given the criticism of the sources. Of either group's training or experience we know nothing, though we must again assume that they would have been brought up to scratch by Crassus and his son during the winter months.

This brings us onto another topic that needs examining before we progress, namely the quality of the Roman commanders. We have already looked at Crassus himself, but one aspect that is rarely commented on is the nature and quality of his junior officers. First and foremost were his two deputies, Publius Licinius Crassus and Gaius Cassius Longinus. Publius Crassus (Crassus' youngest son) appears to us in the sources as being everything that his father was not. Cicero, eight years later, describes him to Julius Caesar thus:

> Out of all our nobility, the young man for whom I had the highest regard was Publius Crassus; and while I had entertained great hopes of him from his earliest years, I began to have quite a brilliant impression of him when the highly favourable opinions you [Caesar] had formed of him became known to me[193]

and elsewhere says:

> Publius Crassus, son of Marcus, who at an early age sought the circle of my friendship, and I exhorted him with all my power to follow that straight path to renown which his ancestors had trodden and made smooth for him. For he had enjoyed excellent upbringing and had received a thorough and complete training. His mind was good, if not brilliant, his language choice abundant, and in addition he had dignity without arrogance and modesty without sloth.[194]

These refrences of Cicero's regarding Publius Crassus are two out of just five he makes to the Battle of Carrhae in total, throughout all his extant works (the other three being comments on the supposed ill omens that occurred). As well as impressing Cicero, Publius served under Julius Caesar in Gaul, where in 57–56 BC he distinguished himself as a legionary commander in Aquitania.[195] Thus he appears to us from the sources (most of which are hostile to his father) as being a model Roman aristocrat; brave in battle, yet modest about it. In our surviving sources, and amongst the Roman aristocracy, especially Caesar and Cicero, it is his loss at Carrhae that is felt more keenly than that of his father.[196]

Yet, Publius Crassus appears to be typical of the type of officer that Marcus Crassus took on this campaign. As he had done all through his political life, and as he clearly showed during his Spartacus campaign, Crassus cultivated the best of the young Roman aristocrats; this time by giving them positions on the general staff of this supposedly glorious and profitable campaign. As well as Publius, we are given a host of names of aspiring young Roman aristocrats, such as representatives of the distinguished families of the Marcii Censorini, Octavii, Petronii, Roscii and the Vargunetii.

Added to these names is that of Gaius Cassius Longinus, who served as Crassus' quaestor (official deputy) during this campaign. Cassius was later to achieve immortality as one of the two leaders of the conspirators that assassinated Julius Caesar in the Roman Senate house in 44 BC (the other being Brutus). This campaign is the first time that we hear of young Cassius, but his role is a significant one. Plutarch's account of the whole campaign places Cassius at the centre of events, always urging Crassus not to follow what turns out to be the wrong, and often disastrous, course of action. Given the later blackening of Cassius' name (due to his role in Caesar' assassination) this is highly curious (see appendix two on the possible sources for this anomaly). Of the three main commanders, Crassus, his son, and Cassius, only the latter survived to tell the tale, which makes any account he gave, including his heroic role, questionable to say the least. Nevertheless he does appear to have been yet another young and talented Roman commander.

Therefore, we can see that Crassus, regardless of later sources' views on his own abilities as a commander, undeniably had a talented and energetic command staff surrounding him. Regarding his army, though, a closer examination of their composition does reveal a number of potential flaws and weaknesses. Nevertheless, this was still a powerful Roman army and one which, on past form, was widely expected to replicate the results of the armies of Lucullus and Pompey in fighting the armies of the east. In order to understand the reason that they failed so spectacularly we must now turn our attention to the Parthian army of Surenas.

The Parthian Army at the Battle of Carrhae

Not only do we have fewer descriptions of the Parthian army at Carrhae than of the Romans, but the issue is further clouded by some noticeable differences between Parthian armies in general and the one which Surenas fielded at Carrhae, differences that hold a key significance.

Dio (writing in the third century AD) provides us with our best general description of the Parthian military and it is with him that we should start:

> But I will describe their equipment of arms and their method of warfare;
> for the examination of these details properly concerns the present narrative, since it has come to a point where this knowledge is needed. The

Parthians make no use of a shield, but their forces consist of mounted archers and lancers, mostly in full armour. Their infantry is small, made up of the weaker men; but even these are all archers. They practise from boyhood and the climate and the land combine to aid both the horsemanship and archery.[197]

Justin, an even later Roman source, gives us the following description of the composition of the Parthian army:

They have an army, not like other nations, of free men, but chiefly consisting of slaves, the numbers of whom daily increase, the power of manumission [the freeing of slaves] being allowed to none, and all their offspring, in consequence, being born slaves. These bondsmen they bring up as carefully as their own children, and teach them, with great pains, the art of riding and shooting with the bow.[198]

He then elaborates upon their tactics:

Of engaging with the enemy in close fight, and of taking cities by siege they know nothing. They fight on horseback, either galloping forward or turning their backs. Often too they counterfeit flight that they may throw their pursuers off their guard against being wounded by their arrows. The signal for battle among them is given, not by trumpet, but by drum.[199]

And gives this detail of their armour:

Their armour, and that of their horses, is formed of plates, lapping over one another like the feathers of a bird, and covers both man and horse entirely.[200]

Lucian, a second century source tells us that the Parthians fought in units of 1,000 known as 'dragons', due to the symbol they fought under.[201]

From these later descriptions it is possible to create an image of a generic Parthian army from this period, which would be composed of three types of fighting man. The elite of the army, most probably the noble or free men, would be the heavily-armed cavalrymen, known as cataphracts. Then there would be the lightly-armed horse archers and the light infantrymen, armed with bows. Both of the latter two categories would be serfs, taken from the estates of the nobility.

Surenas awaited the Roman army at Carrhae with a force composed of just 10,000 men, which would be ten dragons (if we accept Lucian's' definition of a basic Parthian unit). Of these there were apparently 1,000 cataphracts, 9,000 horse archers and no infantry. All of these men came from Surenas' own estates. In addition, Plutarch furnishes us with one crucial detail, namely that there were 1,000 baggage camels laden with spare arrows.[202] It is these last two facts that mark Surenas' army out from a standard Parthian army of the era, and we need to understand both their cause and their effect.

The lack of infantry has rarely been commented upon and, when it is, it is usually dismissed as being a side effect of Orodes taking the bulk of the army into Armenia.[203] Yet the Parthians had no single standing army as such. Each landowner was responsible for raising troops and supplying them to the king. In Surenas' case, he raised and fought with his own army, manned from his own family estates in eastern Parthia. It is unlikely that he would have split this army and even if he had, then why would the king take all of his infantry? To my mind the lack of infantry is not a passing detail or a side effect of the army's division. It is far more logical to see that the army that Surenas put into the field to fight Crassus in 53 BCwas deliberately created without any role for infantry.

Surenas had a year to study the Roman method of warfare and could consult Silaces, the defeated satrap of Mesopotamia, for first hand experience of how they fought. As the Romans had demonstrated time and again, in close order fighting they were virtually invincible. The Armenians, who fought in a similar style to the standard Parthian manner, had met with heavy defeat in 69 BC. Given everything we know about Surenas, it is clear that he would have been well aware that Orodes was intending to sacrifice him to slow down the Romans by letting him face them first, and it is equally clear that he would not meekly wait for his supposedly 'inevitable' destruction. It is obvious that Surenas did not meet the Romans in battle blindly, but had worked out a strategy that he hoped would bring him victory. To accomplish this he needed to avoid playing to the Roman strengths, whilst utilising those of his own army. In this case, the Roman strength was close-quarter infantry fighting, whilst his army's were speed and long-range weapons.

Therefore, it appears that Surenas spent the winter months modifying the standard Parthian army and way of fighting into a force capable of defeating a Roman army. One key element of this plan would be the complete lack of infantry, with his whole army being composed of nothing but cavalry. Thus his army would be able to engage the Romans at speed and avoid getting entangled with the legionaries on the ground.

However, whilst the lack of footsoldiers would allow him to avoid getting entangled in a close-quarter battle, this alone would not bring him victory. Disposing of the infantry element of his army was nothing more than removing a negative aspect from his force. Of his remaining force of 10,000 the majority were lightly-armoured horse archers, who on the face of it would never be able to defeat an infantry army on their own, as they traditionally had one key flaw; once they had emptied their quiver of arrows then they would be useless at a distance and would have to attack the Romans at close quarters, for which they were not armed or armoured. It is here that Surenas introduced the key element of his battleplan and one which (as far as we can tell) was unique to him. This is of course the addition of the baggage train of 1,000 camels laden with tens of thousands of additional arrows. In addition, this baggage train would be at the front line, or just behind it, allowing the horse archers to re-arm at the battlefront, rather than having to ride to the back of the army, dismount, re-arm and then return. The whole process could be done whilst still mounted, near the battle-line and would therefore take far less time.

There is one further element that was crucial to the success of this plan, namely the quality of the arrows themselves and the bows used to fire them. Here we are operating in the near-complete absence of any evidence for the type of arrow used at Carrhae. All we know is that they were barbed and completely penetrated the Roman shields and armour. Now this cannot be a coincidence, and raises two interesting aspects. The Parthians and Romans had never fought before, yet Surenas had total faith that his arrows would penetrate Roman armour. Furthermore the Romans had fought eastern armies before (the Seleucids, Pontines and Armenians), and never encountered the same problems with arrows that they did at Carrhae. The first issue can be answered with reference to Surenas' attacks on the Roman garrisons during the winter of 54–53 BC, which would have had more to do with the Parthians testing of their arrows' abilities on Roman armour, than a serious attempt to retake the towns. We might recall that Plutarch relayed the Roman soldiers' claims that 'strange missiles are the precursors of their appearance, which pierce through every obstacle'.[204] The strangeness of these arrows may be more than Plutarch's dramatic turn of phrase and may well illustrate that the Romans had never encountered that particular type of arrow before. Certainly Surenas went into the battle well aware of the devastating capabilities of his arrows against Roman armour. However, we must not discount the contribution made by the Parthian compound bows either. As seen in the illustration of the horse archer (figure 15), the Parthians used a short compound bow, which must have given the arrows a tremendous velocity. We have little exact evidence for the bows, other than descriptions, and shorter bows were common throughout eastern armies. Nevertheless, it is clear that the combination of this short compound bow and the barbed arrows produced devastating results on this occasion and may well have been aunique combination.

Surenas' army was fronted by one thousand cataphracts fully clad in heavy armour and armed with long lances, superficially resembling medieval knights and far superior to the Roman cavalry. These shock troops formed an advance guard for the 9,000 horse archers armed with the armour-penetrating arrows and supported by a thousand baggage camels, allowing for near instantaneous re-arming on the move. Therefore, we can see that it was an army designed for fighting a battle at speed and at distance, which was just the type of fighting that did not suit the Romans.

Furthermore, Surenas' tactics played to the strengths of his men in terms of upbringing. The horse archers were all serfs from his estate and would have all been trained in horseback archery from childhood. They would have been used to following and obeying their feudal lord from birth and would have had the winter to practise the new tactics that they had been given. In short, they were the perfect body of men to learn these new tactics and carry out their master's modified version of Parthian warfare.

Thus the army that the Romans faced at Carrhae was not there as a consequence of chance, but had been designed with fighting them specifically in mind. It was not designed to fight a long campaign, but to defeat this particular Roman army in a battle. This army reflected the genius of its commander and showed the Parthian system of private armies and devolved commanders at its best. It is clear that Orodes would not have thought out or executed these tactics. The uniqueness of this force and its difference to the standard Parthian method of fighting gave Surenas another major edge in that Crassus was not expecting it. Surenas had taken the opportunity to study the Roman army and how it fought and had been given the time to modify his own force accordingly. As far as Crassus was concerned, the army that he would soon be facing would fight in exactly the same way as had the one the year before, and as the Armenians had a decade before (who after all had comprehensively defeated the Parthians themselves, a generation earlier). What he did not know is that Surenas had created a new and unique method of warfare, designed specifically to win the upcoming battle.

It is highly unlikely that Crassus would have been able to discover Surenas' new tactics before it was too late. Even his scouts would not have been able to see much difference in Surenas' army at a glance. They could report seeing little in the way of infantry, but not know that there were in fact none at all. They could report a baggage train, but then such things were common in armies; they would not have been able to tell that it contained nothing but arrows. To all intents and purposes it would have looked like the army that Crassus was expecting to face. The only warning sign he had were the soldiers' stories of strange arrows raining down on them during the winter clashes, but whether he would have given any greater significance is doubtful. When battle was joined, he would have been unaware of how truly unique a Parthian force he faced. Thus Surenas went into the battle knowing his enemies tactics, but not vice versa.

The Dio Variation of the Battle

Of the battle itself, we have two detailed descriptions from Plutarch and Dio; neither is contemporaneous and they differ in some important ways. Of the two, the more detailed and knowledgeable is Plutarch's (see appendix two for the possible reasons why). In order to gain the full picture of events though, we must look at both accounts and the best place to start is with the shorter variant of Dio.

Dio's version has Crassus' army being led directly into the path of Surenas' by the Arab traitor Abgarus (though Plutarch states that he had left Crassus' army by this point[205]). In effect it is a classic ambush, with the Parthian army being concealed, awaiting the arrival of the Romans (though this account ignores any presence of Roman scouts). Dio states that this was accomplished by the Parthians hiding in dips and woods, despite the fact that there was no woodland in this area.

Nonetheless, when the Romans were led into this trap, the Parthian army revealed themselves, at which point Publius Crassus suddenly broke ranks and led his cavalry at the Parthian ranks, which then appeared to break, with Publius giving chase. This however was a feint (which was an old tactic even in this century) and when they had led Publius away from the main army, the Parthians turned, surrounded and annihilated him.

This concluded Dio's first phase of the battle. The second phase commenced with what is described as an almost suicidal charge by the Roman infantry who did so, according to Dio, 'to avenge his [Publius Crassus'] death'.[206] The Roman infantry were then devastated by the Parthian cataphracts, whose heavy lances broke the Roman ranks. Again Dio takes a scathing line on the Roman troops when he states that 'many died from fright at the very charge of the lancers'.[207] With their lines broken, the Roman soldiers were then slaughtered by the Parthian archers.

The final defeat came in the third phase, which began with the final treachery of Abgarus, who not only led the Romans into this ambush, but at the appropriate point apparently turned his allied forces (which are presumed, but not mentioned prior to this point) against the Roman lines, attacking them from the rear. The Romans, apparently unable to face two enemies at once, then turned their line around and exposed themselves to a Parthian attack from the rear.

> for Abgarus did not immediately make his attempt upon them. But when he too attacked, thereupon the Osroeni themselves assailed the Romans on their exposed rear, since they were facing the other way, and also rendered them easier for the others to slaughter.[208]

Dio then concludes this brisk battle description with a wonderfully dramatic picture of the Roman plight:

And the Romans would have perished utterly, but for the fact that some of the lances of the barbarians were bent and others were broken, while the bowstrings snapped under the constant shooting, the missiles were exhausted, the swords all blunted and most of all, that the men themselves grew weary of the slaughter.[209]

Dio would therefore ask us to believe that the Parthians ran out of weapons and ammunition (in his account there is no mention of Surenas' ammunition train) and then decided to take it easy and have mercy on the Romans, who they had grown tired of killing. It is not this aspect of his account that we find hard to believe. Dio's account is a catalogue of staggering incompetence and failures on the Roman part.

Firstly, Marcus Crassus walks the Roman army into an ambush, led along by Abgarus. Then Publius Crassus breaks with all known Roman discipline, not to mention common sense, and races off to attack the Parthians on his own and is slaughtered. Third, we have the Roman infantry rushing headlong into attacking the Parthian army, seemingly for no better reason than revenge. Fourth, we have the Romans being taken completely unawares by the treacherous attack of Abgarus' allied soldiers. Fifth, the Romans were seemingly unable to fight on two fronts and managed to get themselves twisted and turned around until they did not know which way they were facing. Marcus Crassus' role in this sequence of errors is unclear, for we hear nothing more of him once he has led his men into the trap.

Aside from the catalogue of Roman failings, Dio' account is short, devoid of any clear detail, and introduces a number of new elements which we do not find in any earlier source. They range from the significant (the treachery of the Arab allied contingent), to the bizarre (Surenas hiding his army in the woods – on a dusty north Mesopotamian plain).[210] From start to finish, this battle narrative was designed to show the incompetence of the Roman army and especially it's leadership, in the form of the Crassi. Actually, the Parthians do not come out of this narrative particularly well either. It seems that they won through a mixture of underhand tactics, treachery, ambushes and feints, combined with Roman ineptitude. Given the poor state of the Parthian Empire in his own day (third century AD), this is not perhaps surprising, but as an historical record it leaves much to be desired.

If we are to find out how the Roman Republic met such a catastrophic defeat in the east, then we need to turn to Plutarch, who presents us with a more detailed and logical sequence of events, which appear to have been based on a source with first-hand experience of the battle itself.

The Initial Clash

Throughout his account, Plutarch presents us with a far more realistic depiction of the Battle of Carrhae, and it is this one that we must accept as being the closest to the true sequence of events, as far as can be determined.

Rather than walking into a trap, Plutarch tells us that Crassus had sent his scouts out looking for Surenas' army. By mid-afternoon, just beyond the river Belikh, they found what they were looking for. Given that Surenas' battleplan was based on a significant element of misinformation, not in terms of location, but in terms of his army's unusual formation and potential method of attack, it is no surprise that his own advance guard inflicted heavy casualties on the Roman scouts.[211] The fact that some survived to report their presence is also not a surprise as Surenas' plan involved the Romans advancing onto his chosen ground.

Here we can see both the brilliance of Surenas as a tactician, and where Dio gets at least one of his oddest pieces of information from. Plutarch reports that Surenas had concealed the bulk of his army behind an advance guard. Therefore, an approaching force would only see the front of the army, in its width, rather than its depth. Thus Surenas concealed the bulk of his army from Crassus until battle was engaged, but not in the bizarre method that Dio states. Plutarch tells us that;

> the enemy came in sight, who, to the surprise of the Romans, appeared to be neither numerous nor formidable.[212]

Furthermore, Surenas had ordered his heavily-armoured cataphracts to wear concealing robes and skins over their armour, in order to disguise their true nature. To an observer they would appear to be ordinary cavalrymen, rather than cataphracts. Surenas' plan was obviously to lure Crassus into battle before he knew the number and type of force he was truly facing. It is at this point that Crassus made a decision that with hindsight may have proved to be a mistake. Plutarch reports that when the Parthians were located nearby, the Roman officers wanted to camp and give battle at day break. It is possible that this break would have allowed the Romans time to scout out the Parthians more thoroughly and therefore discover that the army which they were about to face was not a typical Parthian one. Crassus, however, wanted to push on immediately and Plutarch states that he was urged on by his son Publius, who was eager for battle.[213] It is obviously this statement that led Dio into making his claim that Publius Crassus broke away from the army at the beginning of the battle and launched himself at the Parthians.

Even if Crassus had camped for the night and attempted to scout the Parthian army, there is nothing to indicate that they would have been any more successful than their predecessors, who had been dispatched with heavy casualties (a process made easier by the massed Parthian archers). All that a further scouting mission would have been able to tell Crassus is a rough estimate of the numbers, which would give the Romans a clear four to one advantage, and that the majority of them were mounted. They would not have been able to tell him how many were cataphracts (he would have been expecting a number of them anyway), nor that the baggage train of camels actually contained a large number of spare arrows, nor that there were no infantry. When Crassus advanced upon the waiting Parthians, he did so in full confidence that his army would easily outmatch the supposedly-inferior Parthian army (both in numbers and type). He had no reason to believe that he was in fact playing right into the hands of Surenas, who had chosen his ground – mostly flat with little cover, ideal for a fully mobile attack – and had concealed his true tactics.

Plutarch also gives us the Roman formation as they advanced upon the Parthians. At first Crassus adopted a linear formation with his army strung out across the plain in a long line and his cavalry divided between the two wings. Crassus commanded this formation from the centre, with the two wings commanded by Cassius and Publius Crassus. Plutarch tells us that he did this in order to avoid being surrounded by the enemy and that it was Cassius' idea; the implication here being that if Crassus had stuck to this formation then the Parthians would not have been able to ride around the army and attack them from many sides. [214] Quite why he was expecting them to do this at such an early stage we are not told.

However, Plutarch then tells us that Crassus altered this formation and advanced upon the Parthians in a square formation:

> Then he changed his mind and concentrated his men, forming them in a hollow square of four fronts, with twelve cohorts on each side.[215] With each cohort he placed a squadron of horse, that no part of the line might lack cavalry support, but that the whole body might advance to the attack with equal protection everywhere.[216]

Plutarch does not give us the reasons why Crassus changed his tactics. In fact the whole passage is an odd one. Plutarch (or his sources) is attempting to alert us to the fact that he believed that Cassius' formation was the best one and that by changing it Crassus made a mistake. We are told that Cassius' formation would have prevented the Parthians from surrounding the army, but given that the Romans only had 4,000 cavalry, compared to the Parthians' 10,000, this is an ambitious statement to say the least. Furthermore, Plutarch or his source are using hindsight here as prior to the battle no-one knew that the Parthians were going to surround the Roman army, as the Romans did not know the size of Surenas' cavalry force or his tactics.

In fact there is nothing at all wrong with Crassus' chosen formation, which as Plutarch states gave the Romans strength on all sides and would prevent an enemy from exploiting a weak area.[217] As for why Crassus chose to ignore the advice of his vastly less-experienced junior officer (Cassius), we will probably never know, but it does perhaps show a greater degree of caution, for which he was known. The battle commenced with a thunderous wall of noise from the Parthians. Plutarch describes the scene well:

> the signal was raised by their commander, first of all they filled the plain with the sound of a deep and terrifying roar. For the Parthians do not incite themselves to battle with horns or trumpets, but they have hollow drums of distended hide, covered with bronze bells, and on these they beat all at once in many quarters, and the instruments give forth a low and dismal tone, a blend of wild beast's roar and harsh thunder peal. They had rightly judged that, of all the senses, hearing is the one most as to confound the soul, soonest rouses its emotions, and most effectively unseats the judgement.[218]

Utilising this battle cry to full effect, Surenas opted to begin the battle with a full-scale cavalry charge at the Roman army, with the cataphracts at the front, followed by his archers. Leading the charge himself, he then had his cataphracts remove the coverings which had been hiding their armour as they were galloping.

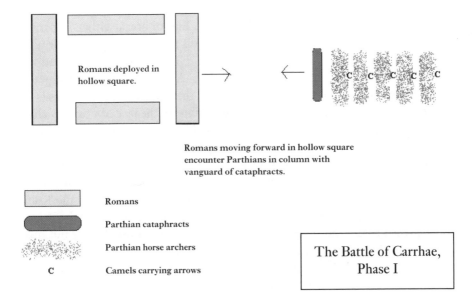

Romans deployed in hollow square.

Romans moving forward in hollow square encounter Parthians in column with vanguard of cataphracts.

Romans

Parthian cataphracts

Parthian horse archers

c   Camels carrying arrows

The Battle of Carrhae, Phase I

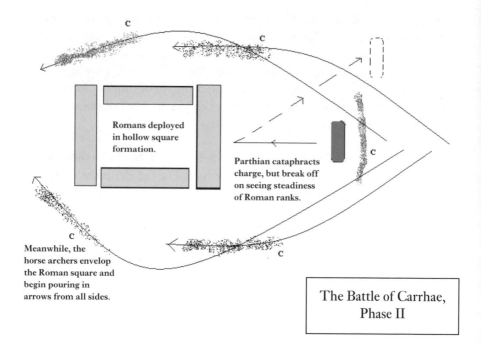

c

c

Romans deployed
in hollow square
formation.

Parthian cataphracts
charge, but break off
on seeing steadiness
of Roman ranks.

c

c

Meanwhile, the
horse archers envelop
the Roman square and
begin pouring in
arrows from all sides.

c

The Battle of Carrhae,
Phase II

This would have added to the dramatic effect of the charge, as their highly-polished bronze and steel armour would have caught the sun. The Romans would suddenly have realised that they were facing a full charge by heavily-armoured cavalry. Surenas was clearly using every psychological trick he could to unnerve the enemy.

However, if he was hoping for the Roman line to break, either in panic or under the force of his heavy cavalry, then he was to be disappointed. For unlike in Dio's account of the battle, the Roman line held strong. As they had been trained to do, the Romans soldiers locked their shields together and maintained their discipline and composure. We can see that in this respect Crassus had trained his army well. To maintain your discipline in the face of a cavalry charge was one thing, but given the added drama that Surenas had brought to this charge, it is a testament to the Roman discipline that they stood their ground.

This was incidental to Surenas' plan; if the Roman line had broken then all the better, but it is doubtful that he ever believed it would do so. Rather than charge into the Roman line, Surenas actually diverted his cavalry around the Roman square, on both sides, until they had the Romans surrounded, taking the Romans by surprise. Crassus, however, soon recovered from this unusual tactic and, aware that he was being surrounded, ordered his auxiliary troops to charge at the Parthians and break their flanking manoeuvre. But they were met with a hail of arrows that forced them back into the square, taking heavy casualties in the process.

We can see that Surenas' battleplan had worked beautifully thus far. Rather than attack the Romans head on and get involved in a static mêlée, which would have favoured his enemy, he encircled them at speed and deployed the bulk of his force, his 9,000 horse archers, to devastating effect. Now the Parthian archers began to unleash a barrage of arrows at the Romans from all sides. Given the penetrative capabilities of the arrows the Parthians were using, the Roman army was soon being slaughtered. Plutarch again captures the scene well,

> But the Parthians now stood at long intervals from one another and began to shoot their arrows from all sides at once, not with any accurate aim, for the dense formation of the Romans would not suffer an archer to miss his man even if he wished it, but making vigorous and powerful shots from bows which were large and mighty and curved so as to discharge their missiles with great force. At once the plight of the Romans was a grievous one; for if they kept their ranks, they were wounded in great numbers, and if they tried to come to close quarters with the enemy they suffered just as much. For the Parthians shot as they fled and it is a very clever thing to seek safety while still fighting and to take away the shame of flight.[219]

Thus the Roman army, despite its numerical superiority, was trapped, huddled in a square and coming under a constant barrage of arrows. If the Romans moved to engage the archers, they would turn and retreat whilst still firing. The Roman soldiers could not get near enough to the archers to engage them in close combat. This tactic became known as the 'Parthian shot', the ability to still attack your opponents whilst retreating. Once Crassus had recovered from the initial shock of the Parthian tactics, however, he still had several reasons to be hopeful. Although his army was taking casualties, he must have sensed that if this was the best the Parthians could do, then he could still carry the day. The Parthian army seemed to be composed of nothing but horse archers, supported by a relatively low number of cataphracts. The Romans had already shown that they could withstand a full cavalry charge, the Parthians had no infantry, and once the archers ran out of arrows then the Romans could advance and force their retreat.

In this regard Crassus would normally have been quite correct. Under the usual terms of battle, the horse archers would soon have emptied their quivers and the Parthian cavalry would then have had to attack the Romans legions at close quarters (or withdraw). However, it is at this point that the true master-stroke of Surenas' plan was brought into play – namely mobile re-arming. Having surrounded the Romans, Surenas deployed his camel train to replenish the archers. Thus the Parthian archers would only need a short break to ride up to one of the camels, take a fresh quiver of arrows, return to their positions and continue shooting. So long as the archers did this at slightly different times, and as long as the camels were well spaced amongst the surrounding archers, then the barrage would continue indefinitely.

It appears that Crassus soon became aware of this development. Perhaps he observed it actually happening, or he simply deduced that the rain of arrows was not weakening. Once he was aware of it though, he realised that his only hope now lay in breaking the encirclement. To that end, he sent a message to his son, out on one of the wings (we do not know which), ordering him to lead a breakout and engage the enemy at close quarters with his cavalry. If the Roman cavalry could drive off the Parthians, even in one area, then it would give the main army time to regroup. This breakout and the engagement that followed would determine the outcome of the whole battle.

The Breakout and the 'Battle within a Battle'

Publius Crassus gathered together as many troops as he could muster on his wing. Plutarch tells us that he had 1,300 cavalry (including his own 1,000 Gauls), 500 auxiliary archers and eight cohorts of legionaries (just under 4,000 men).[220] Publius then led this force and charged the Parthian cavalry ahead of him. Plutarch also records that with him leading the charge were two young aristocratic friends of his, Censorinus and Megabacchus.[221] At first it appeared that the plan had worked successfully as the Parthians appeared to break, turn and retreat. Not wanting to lose the initiative and sensing victory, Publius chased after the enemy, with both cavalry and infantry, hoping to finish the Parthians off.

Whether the Parthians on Publius' wing did genuinely break or not, we will never know. Plutarch certainly raises it as a possibility.[222] Publius' charge would certainly have taken them by surprise and it was conducted with a large number of Roman and allied cavalry, backed up by archers and legionaries. Such a force was a formidable combination of speed, firepower and close-order infantry. However, the retreating Parthians wheeled their horses away from the main Roman army and towards their cataphracts. At that point the retreating Parthians turned, were joined by the cataphracts and attacked the oncoming Romans.

Whilst it appeared that the Romans still had the numerical advantage, and had a good mix of cavalry and foot, once again the Parthians adhered to the battle-plan of their master and placed the cataphracts between the Romans and their archers. This would have allowed the archers to continue to fire at the Romans as the two cavalry forces engaged each other, in the first, and only, close-order clash of the battle.

Although the Romans had the numerical advantage in this encounter, the Parthians had by far and away the advantage in terms of weaponry. The Roman cavalry were lightly armoured and only had short spears, whilst the Parthian cataphracts were heavily armoured and carried long lances. They were supported by mounted archers, whilst the Roman archers were on foot and would not have been able to keep up with the mounted clash. The same goes for the 4,000 Roman legionaries present. Nevertheless it is said that Publius Crassus led the charge into the Parthian cataphracts with great bravery and determination, backed up by his Gallic cavalry.

Plutarch gives a testimony to the bravery of the Gallic cavalry:

> with these [the Gauls] he did indeed work wonders. For they laid hold of the long spears of the Parthians, and grappling with the men, pushed them from their horses, hard as it was to move them owing to the weight of their armour; and many of the Gauls forsook their own horses, and crawling under those of the enemy, stabbed them up in the belly. These would rear up in their anguish, and die trampling on riders and enemy indiscriminately mingled.[223]

Thus Plutarch paints a harrowing picture of the chaos that was a battle within a battle. Strategy went out of the window, replaced by a mêlée where it came down to hand-to-hand fighting between Gauls and Parthians. When the dust had literally settled, despite their bravery and savagery, it was clear that the Gallic cavalry had been well beaten. Those that remained were all wounded, including Publius Crassus himself, and they retreated to the relative protection of the Roman legionaries that had accompanied them. This force then moved to a nearby hillock to make a determined last stand, with the horses in the centre and a ring of legionaries, with locked shields, on the outside to protect the wounded. This, of course, did not save them from a fresh barrage of arrows from the Parthian horse archers.

Plutarch reports that despite being advised to either flee or surrender, Publius Crassus was determined not to desert his command.[224] Seeing that they were surrounded on that hillock and that defeat was inevitable, and unwilling to be taken alive, he resolved to choose a more dignified exit. Being unable to pick up a sword due to an arrow wound to the hand, he ordered a soldier to strike a sword into his side, killing him instantaneously. Plutarch also tells us that Censorinus did likewise, whilst Megabacchus still had the strength to take his own life, as did the other surviving officers.[225] The rest of the men fought on until the Parthian cataphracts charged the hillock, butchering them with their long lances. Of a force of around 5,500, less than 500 were taken alive[226]. The Romans had lost over a quarter of their cavalry (including all of their best Gallic cavalry), and a good number of their archers, along with a number of the key junior officers. It was a defeat that sounded the end for Roman hopes at Carrhae. With this force

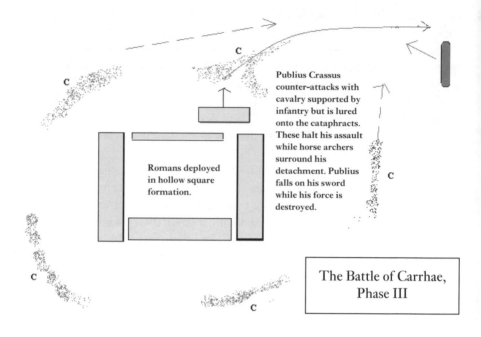

Publius Crassus counter-attacks with cavalry supported by infantry but is lured onto the cataphracts. These halt his assault while horse archers surround his detachment. Publius falls on his sword while his force is destroyed.

Romans deployed in hollow square formation.

The Battle of Carrhae, Phase III

defeated, the Parthians chopped off Publius' head, stuck it on top of a lance, and returned to the main battle. Before we return to the battle though, we need to dwell on this most important encounter within the Battle of Carrhae, as ultimately it decided the fate of the battle.

This episode has often been explained as being nothing more than Publius Crassus falling for one of the oldest traps in existence: a faked retreat to draw him away from the main body of the army, leading him into heavier Parthian forces, which then turned on him and cut him down. Yet this view overlooks a number of key elements. Firstly, the Romans had to attempt a breakout or they would have faced total annihilation. Secondly, the Parthian cavalry surrounding the Roman army was mostly horse archers; they had only 1,000 cataphracts to protect 9,000 horse archers from 40,000 Romans. Publius took with him all of Rome's best cavalry (the Gauls) as well as a number of archers and legionaries in support.

The question of whether it was an intended trap depends on what orders Surenas had given. He must have expected the Romans to attempt to break out of his encirclement and we must ask ourselves what strategy he had prepared for this eventuality. Given the appearance of a large force of cataphracts, it is more than likely that Surenas had held them in reserve, following the initial charge and encirclement, so that they could be deployed against any breakout. With careful observation the cataphracts could be sent to wherever the Romans broke out of. All the horse archers had to then do was retreat, whilst still firing, and lead the Roman force towards where they knew the reserve force of cataphracts would be. The trap would then close in on them.

Again, this shows the brilliance of Surenas. Not only did he have an initial strategy, but he had a counter strategy to deal with any Roman breakout. It also demonstrates the severe threat that the Parthians still faced from the Romans, despite the successful encirclement and the barrage of arrows. Had the Roman cavalry successfully broken out of Surenas' trap, then they could have put the horse archers to flight and allowed the army to extricate themselves. It is unlikely that it would have brought them victory, but it would have given them time to retreat and regroup.

The aim of Surenas' plan must have been a clear and total victory on the day. Anything less than the destruction of the Roman army would have allowed them to withdraw and fight another day, and Surenas was only ever going to fool them with his modified way of fighting once. For Surenas it was all or nothing; winning the day would not be enough, he had to win the war in one battle. Without total victory at Carrhae, the Romans would return, stronger than before.

Even though the breakout had been planned for, the fighting itself was still going to be close. The Romans broke out with 1,300 cavalry and over 4,000 foot. Given that Surenas only had 1,000 cataphracts in total (and we do not know how many were deployed against Publius) the result was never going to be a foregone conclusion. As it was, the superior Parthian cataphracts carried the day, which meant that the key encounter of the battle was lost due to the poorer quality of the Roman cavalry. For all the tactical planning and innovations, in the end it came down to that one factor. The Romans were not lacking in courage, on the part of Publius or his Gauls; they simply were outmatched in terms of weaponry.

The Final Stage

Initially at least, the breakout that Crassus ordered appeared to have worked. A large part of the Parthian army encircling the main Roman force was drawn away, either fleeing from Publius or riding hard to catch up with him. Crassus used this let-up wisely and staged a withdrawal, whilst still under intermittent arrow fire. The Roman army, laden with casualties, regrouped on nearby sloping ground, which would at least give them some protection from the Parthian cavalry. Here Crassus was faced with a difficult decision, exacerbated by a lack of information, as he needed to know how his son was doing. If Publius had routed the Parthians opposed to him, then he could have possibly advanced and cleared the rest of the Parthian cavalry away, or at least retreated back to the safety of one of the garrisoned towns and regrouped. However, he was not able to come to any decision until he had this information, to which ends he sent messengers out, to try to reach Publius' position.

Plutarch records that the first one was intercepted and killed, but that the second messenger not only reached Publius' position, but was able to assess the situation and mange to return to the main army. When he did so, he informed Crassus that his son was surrounded and being cut to pieces.[227] To say that this left Crassus with a dilemma would be an understatement. On a military basis, he knew that the breakout would fail unless he took the main army to link up with Publius. However, this meant gambling with his army and putting them back into the mess that they had only just managed to extricate themselves from. Even if they got there in time, there was no reason to assume that they would be victorious, as the rest of the Parthian army would also converge there.

On the other hand, if he turned and retreated he was not only condemning his son to death – a death that would have been his responsibility – but as the majority of the Roman army was on foot and the Parthians were mounted, there was no reason to believe that they would reach safety in time. Given the number of casualties that they had already sustained, their progress would not have been swift. Furthermore, if the main body of the Parthians did catch them up, they would be strung out in columns and with their backs to them. For whatever reason, military or personal (or both), Crassus resolved that the only move open to them was to advance and meet up with Publius' beleaguered force.

But, before they had advanced far, they were met with the sight and sound that told them that the encounter between Publius and the Parthians was over. Coming towards them was a cloud of dust accompanied by the beating of war drums. When the Parthians did come into view, they were preceded by the severed head of Publius Crassus. Plutarch tells us that Roman morale sank.[228] Not only had a large number of their colleagues been slaughtered, depriving them of most of their cavalry support, but they knew that the battle was about to be rejoined. Despite his grief, it was at this point that Crassus showed his qualities as a general and tried to rouse his men with an impassioned speech:

> Mine, O Romans, is the sorrow, and mine alone; but the great fortune and glory of Rome abide unbroken and unconquered in you who are alive and safe. And now if you have any pity for me, thus bereft of the noblest of sons, show it by your wrath against the enemy. Rob them of their joy; avenge their cruelty; be not cast down at what has happened, for it must needs be that those whose aim at great deeds should also suffer greatly. It was not without bloody losses that even Lucullus overthrew Tigranes, or Scipio overthrew Antiochus; and our fathers of old lost a thousand ships off Sicily; and in Italy many imperators and

generals, not one of whom, by his defeat, prevented them from afterwards mastering his conquerors. For it was not by good fortune merely
that the Roman state reached its present position of power, but by
patient endurance and the valour of those who faced dangers on its
behalf.[229]

Now, whilst we have to admit that it is highly unlikely that anyone had the time
or the materials to note the speech down word for word, there were enough
survivors to have noted the general contents of the speech. Furthermore, as it is
reported by Plutarch, who takes a fairly hostile line on Crassus over Carrhae, we
can have some confidence that the speech is a fairly accurate representation of
what Crassus said.

Nevertheless it was going to take something greater than a stirring speech to
save the Romans from the impending slaughter. True to his plan, Surenas (and
we are not told whether he was directly involved in the defeat of Publius)
employed his tried and tested tactics. The cataphracts again charged the Roman
army, forcing them to form closely together, and then the horse archers were
brought back into the fray. The Roman army was subject to a constant barrage
of arrows and lances, slowly whittling down their numbers.

Only one thing saved the Roman army from total annihilation that day at
Carrhae, and that was the arrival of dusk, whereupon the Parthians withdrew for

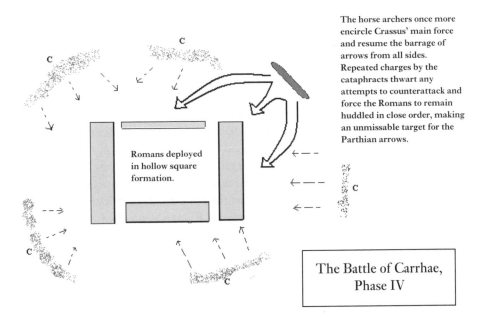

The horse archers once more
encircle Crassus' main force
and resume the barrage of
arrows from all sides.
Repeated charges by the
cataphracts thwart any
attempts to counterattack and
force the Romans to remain
huddled in close order, making
an unmissable target for the
Parthian arrows.

Romans deployed
in hollow square
formation.

The Battle of Carrhae,
Phase IV

the night. Even though they had the Romans surrounded, the Parthians were unwilling to risk fighting at night. Aside from the traditional reluctance they had of fighting after dark, the conditions made continuing highly risky. They were in the middle of a plain with little natural light and the danger of getting too close to the Romans, or even of friendly fire, was too great.

Thus despite the slaughter and the total defeat they had suffered, the Romans still had a glimmer of hope. The Parthians withdrew and camped nearby, and made no attempt to block their escape. This may seem odd to us today, especially given that the Romans still numbered some 20,000 men (including their wounded) and Crassus himself was still alive and unwounded (in the physical sense anyway). Surenas knew that he had won a spectacular victory, the likes of which no one but he had thought possible, yet he still faced problems. Although the Romans had been comprehensively defeated, a large number of them yet remained, who, if they made for the safety of Roman-held territory, would have been able to recover and regroup. Furthermore, Crassus, the architect and driving force of the Roman invasion, was likely to be more determined than ever to avenge the death of his son. As long as Crassus remained free, the danger to Parthia was not over. Plutarch hints that the Parthians sent an embassy to the Roman army when night fell, to discuss terms of surrender. All he actually says is that:

> they would grant Crassus one night in which to bewail his son, unless, with a better regard for his own interests, he should consent to go to Arsaces (Orodes II) instead of being carried there.[230]

Taking Crassus alive would have been a major prize for Surenas. Yet, due to the Parthian inability or unwillingness to fight at night, the prize could still have eluded Surenas and if Crassus escaped then it would tarnish the remarkable achievements of that day. Ironically, Crassus' decision to fight immediately in the afternoon, rather than next morning, actually saved the Roman army from utter annihilation, though the Romans had clearly suffered a devastating defeat. Half of their army was dead, and they had been comprehensively outfought. Yet all was not lost. As Crassus himself had pointed out in his rousing speech, Rome had been defeated many times in battle and yet had always emerged victorious in the end. Half the army lay dead on the field of Carrhae, but half yet remained. If they could get safely back to the series of Roman-controlled Mesopotamian towns and then ultimately back into Syria itself, they could re-group for the winter.

It was still possible for Crassus to turn the clock back a year. Rome still held the bridgehead of garrisoned towns in northwestern Mesopotamia. If Crassus wintered in Syria, he could allow his injured soldiers time to heal, raise fresh troops (he was still one of the three men who dominated the Roman Republic after all) and rebuild his army. Certainly his reputation would have taken a battering, but his powerbase was secure. His command extended until 50 BC so there was plenty of time for a fresh campaign in 52 BC. Furthermore, Surenas could only play his masterstroke once. Crassus was not going to fall for that trick twice and could send to Rome for fresh forces, especially additional cavalry. He could plan a new route of invasion, perhaps taking the cities of Babylon, Seleucia and Ctesiphon, which would rebuild shattered Roman morale and then tackle Surenas in his own time and fashion. Thus, as night fell on the battlefield of Carrhae, the Romans had lost the battle, but not the war; the whole campaign was still in the balance, dependant upon the Romans making it to safety.

Before we commence an analysis of the Roman retreat we must pause and comment on the one major discrepancy between the accounts of Plutarch and Dio, that is the treacherous attack of the Osroene leader, Abgarus. Plutarch, writing a century earlier than Dio and seemingly using a first hand account of the campaign, had no such attack take place. Crassus was accompanied for a time in Mesopotamia by an Arab chieftain, whom he names as Ariamnes.[231] Even allowing for confusion over names, there is the fundamental point that Plutarch records the Arab chieftain left Crassus' army before the Battle of Carrhae.[232] Furthermore, in what is a very detailed account of the battle itself, at no point does Plutarch mention that a native allied contingent betrayed the Romans and attacked them, which we must expect to find if it actually happened. Given its absence from this, our best source for the battle, we must assume that this treacherous attack did not occur. Where Dio got this from we will never know, but, as far as is possible to do so when dealing with ancient sources, we must clearly note that this treacherous attack by Abgarus in the Roman rear did not take place and was a later fiction copied by Dio into his account.

The Retreat to Carrhae

Again, Plutarch and Dio disagree on the finer details of the retreat. Nevertheless, the first stage of the Roman retreat was to get safely back to the town of Carrhae itself and the security of its walls and Roman garrison. Plutarch tells us that the Romans looked to Crassus for leadership, but that he was lying on the ground in despair, which meant that the escape had to be organised by the two most senior surviving Roman officers: Cassius and Octavius.[233] Dio omits this and states that Crassus led the survivors on the retreat.[234]

It is clear that the journey itself was a perilous one. In the dead of a cold Mesopotamian night, 15,000–20,000 men, a good many of them injured, had to walk the route back to Carrhae. In fact it was no mean feat that they were still able to navigate their way back to the town in darkness and following the hardship of the day's battle. A hard decision had to be taken that night, in regard to what was to be done with those men who were too seriously wounded to walk. Given that time was of the essence and that they had to be at the walls of Carrhae before dawn, the brutal decision was made to leave the seriously wounded behind. Plutarch provides us with a dramatic description of their journey;

> Then the sick and wounded perceived that their comrades were abandoning them, and dreadful disorder and confusion, accompanied by groans and shouts filled the camp. And after this, as they tried to advance, disorder and panic seized upon them, for they felt sure that the enemy was coming against them. Frequently they would change their course, frequently they would form in order of battle, some of the wounded who followed them had to be taken up, and others laid down, and so all were delayed[235]

Not only were a number of men left behind, numbering some 4,000 it is estimated, but a number would have died on route to Carrhae, from untreated wounds and fatigue.[236] For many it was a march of death. The first Romans to reach the town of Carrhae were the remnants of the Roman auxiliary cavalry, about 300 in number. They were led by a Roman nobleman by the name of Egnatius. However, when they reached the town an event occurred that was to set the tone for the whole Roman retreat. Upon reaching the walls of Carrhae, Egnatius gained the attention of the Roman guards on the walls, shouting to them to tell their commander (a Roman officer by the name of Coponius) that a great battle had taken place between Crassus and the Parthians. At that point he and his men promptly rode off and headed towards Zeugma and the crossing back into Roman Syria, without even identifying who he was.

This was an ominous sign: a Roman officer deserting his commander and the whole campaign and riding as fast as possible for the safety of a Roman province. Plutarch tells us that Egnatius was forever tainted by this act of cowardice and we can find no further trace of him in subsequent Roman political or military life.[237] Nevertheless, despite its brevity, the message actually had the desired effect and Coponius, realising that something catastrophic had occurred, immediately led an expedition out from Carrhae, located the column of Roman survivors and escorted them back into the town.

For Crassus at least, the first stage of the retreat had been accomplished and the bulk of the Roman survivors had reached safety. Exactly how many men reached the relative safety of Carrhae is difficult to estimate, as we are not given a clear figure by Plutarch. However, it does seem, judging from some of the later figures that Plutarch gives us, that between 15,000–20,000 men reached the town. Actually, this raises one of the most surprising and neglected aspects of the whole Carrhae campaign, namely how many Romans were killed during the battle and how many were killed during the aftermath. As we shall see the balance between the two is actually quite surprising.

When dawn broke, the Parthians advanced upon the site of the Roman army's last stand, and as they expected found that the bulk of the army had fled. What they also found were the 4,000 seriously wounded Roman soldiers, who had been left behind. Surenas, unwilling to show any more mercy to them than their comrades had, promptly had these men slaughtered. He then set upon the task of locating the bulk of the Roman army. During this day his cavalry came across a number of Roman stragglers, who had either been separated from, or fallen behind, the main group (an easy thing to do given the state of the retreat at night). In all but one case they too were easily dispatched.

There was, however, one notable exception, which Plutarch chooses to high-light and so should we. One of Crassus' legates was an officer by the name of Vargunteius, who hailed from a minor senatorial family. During the retreat he was in command of four cohorts, less than 2,000 men (especially given the losses of the previous day), but became separated from the main group. When day broke and the Parthian cavalry located them, they decided to make a last stand on a small hillock. Given the overwhelming odds there was only ever going to be one outcome, yet they fought and died hard to such an extent that the Parthians noted them for their bravery, not something that had been in great supply from the Romans during the retreat. As they were down to the last twenty men (not including Vargunteius, who had already fallen) they charged the Parthians in a last defiant gesture. So impressed were the Parthians with their defiant stand that they parted and allowed them to continue to Carrhae unmolested.[238] Such tales of heroism in this retreat were few and far between.

As stated earlier, we therefore have recorded incidents of over 6,000 Roman soldiers surviving the battle, but dying the next day. Given that these are only two such incidents (many more not being recorded due to the absence of any surviving witnesses) we can begin to appreciate the scale of the Roman losses that occurred in the days after the battle.

The Retreat to Syria

At this point, both Crassus and Surenas were locked in an odd game of cat and mouse. Surenas was not exactly sure of where Crassus was, whilst Crassus and his army had to evade the Parthians and seek the refuge of either Armenia or Syria. Although Carrhae was the most logical place for Crassus to make for, Surenas could not be certain. Added to this, Plutarch states that Surenas received a report (from whom we are never told, nor are we told how Plutarch's source got to know of this) that Crassus was not in Carrhae and was in fact heading for the border.[239] This would have left Surenas in something of a dilemma. However, he soon came up with a plan to resolve it by sending a man up to the walls of Carrhae and requesting a peace conference between himself and Crassus, to organise a truce and a safe withdrawal of the Roman forces from the towns and cities of Mesopotamia. Whilst the evacuation of the occupying Roman garrisons was a necessary move for the Parthians, Surenas needed to locate Crassus, dead or alive, even more. Plutarch reports that Cassius took the bait and reported back to Surenas' emissary that Crassus would be willing to meet with him, which only served to confirm Crassus' presence within the town.[240] By this simple ruse and by Cassius' short-sightedness, the Parthians now knew where to end this war and Surenas moved his entire army towards the town of Carrhae.

For Crassus, Cassius' stupidity had left him with an even bigger headache. Given the strength of the Roman forces in Carrhae (a garrison, plus 15,000–20,000 survivors) he would have been able to resist a Parthian siege, not that Surenas' army was equipped for storming a city. The problem was that although the Parthians could not get in, soon the Romans would not have been able to get out and they did not know how long the food and water would last, given the size of the Roman forces within. Crassus could have adopted a policy of waiting it out if he knew help was going to arrive to alleviate a siege, but where would this help come from? Assistance would not soon be forthcoming from Roman Syria, given the few forces that remained there, which only left Armenia. However, as Crassus was not able to rely on the Armenians to help him when he was in a position of power, it was highly unlikely that he could do so now in such a weakened one. Although he was never to know it, this assessment proved to be a highly perceptive one, as only a few days later King Artavasdes would meet with King Orodes to discuss a peace treaty between Armenia and Parthia.

This left Crassus with only one viable option; he would have to break out of Carrhae, evade the waiting Parthians and make for Syria or the Armenian foothills. It appears that the Roman army was divided up into groups, each led by one of the senior surviving commanders. We know of groups led by Crassus, Octavius and Cassius, but there must have been more. It is probable that each group had a different destination and different route, to divide and distract the Parthian pursuers. The move had to be made at night, so as to slip past the Parthians and had to be done when there was no full moon, in order to keep as much cover as possible.

Although we know what happened next, why it happened is the subject of much conjecture. The facts, ultimately are that whilst Cassius' group made it to Syria, Octavius' and Crassus' did not. Plutarch ascribes this to Crassus once again relying on, and being betrayed by, a native guide, this time a man known as Andromachus. According to Plutarch, Andromachus offered to guide Crassus and Cassius from Carrhae, but planned to lead them on a circuitous route and delay them, so that the Parthians would be able to find them by daybreak.[241]

Plutarch's version of the event also has Cassius realising that they were being led into a trap, then breaking away and returning to Carrhae without telling Crassus[242]. If this was true then it was desertion of the highest order. It would seem to be either a daring double bluff or foolish in the extreme to return to the town of Carrhae, past the Parthians once more and hope that they rode off after the other groups. Dio, naturally, has none of this detail. He has Crassus making for the Armenian foothills and Cassius safely reaching Syria independently.[243] When day broke and the Parthians realised that the Romans had evacuated Carrhae, they set off after them once more. Again Dio reports that many groups did not escape the Parthian cavalry, though it seems that on this day a number of them were taken prisoner (perhaps this was due to Surenas wanting Crassus alive or at least to confirm that they had killed the right man).[244]

Of the three main groups, we know that Crassus' got bogged down in a marsh, whether at the hand of a treacherous guide or by simple misfortune, and thus when day broke he was still out in the open and some way off safety. Octavius and the 5,000 men he commanded had reached the relative safety of the mountains at Sinnaca before daybreak. Cassius it seems disappears from the picture and only turns up again safe and sound in Roman Syria, the only one of the key Roman commanders to do so.

By now the Parthians, led by Surenas, had spotted Crassus' group and were moving in on them. However, he was saved by the intervention of Octavius, who could see the relative position of both groups from his high position. Unlike many of the Roman officers in that retreat, he appears not to have thought of his own safety, but his duty to his commander and led his force of 5,000 men (some of them unwillingly) to rescue Crassus from the advancing Parthians, who were far less in number than the Romans. Thus Crassus finally reached the safety of the foothills, where the Parthian cavalry were far less potent and where Roman numbers would count.

For Surenas, the situation was serious. Certainly he had defeated the Roman army at Carrhae and he had inflicted further heavy casualties on them during the retreat, but if Crassus should escape, even with a force of 10,000 men back into Syria, then the war would continue. In desperation, he tried one last stratagem. He either sent an embassy to the Romans in the hills, or went himself, stating that he wanted a peace conference to offer the Romans the opportunity to evacuate all territories east of the Euphrates. The details of this treaty were to be worked out at this meeting between the two men, along with a few officers from either side, on neutral ground between the two forces. Plutarch reports that he went and delivered this offer himself and reports his words:

I have put your valour and power to the test against the wishes of the king, who now of his own accord shows you the mildness and friendliness of his feelings by offering to make a truce with you if you will withdraw and by affording you the means of safety.[245]

Now, Dio and Plutarch report very different reactions by Crassus to this offer. Dio reports that:

Crassus, without hesitation, trusted him. For he was in the very extremity of fear, and was distraught by the terror of the calamity that had befallen both himself and the state.[246]

According to Dio, therefore, Crassus was eager to meet Surenas and accept whatever deal he offered, and so walked right into his trap. Dio's account would have us believe that the experienced general and the cynical political manipulator that Crassus was, fell for this ruse due to the pressures he had been under during the last few days. Plutarch however reports a very different Crassus and one more in keeping with the man we know. He reports that:

Crassus, who's every discomfiture at the hands of the barbarians had been due to fraud, and who thought the suddenness of their change a strange thing, would not reply, but took the matter into consideration.[247]

This description fits the cunning and cynical Crassus that is more familiar to us. Even after all that had happened to him, he was still very much in control of his faculties. He would have been well aware that he had lost the battle, but not the war. However, he was not prepared for what happened next. Although he and his officers saw through Surenas' ruse, the surviving legionaries, trapped on a desolate Mesopotamian hilltop, and with the Parthian force below, apparently did not. In yet another example of the lack of discipline that had plagued the retreat from the start, the troops mutinied and demanded that Crassus attend the peace negotiations. They had survived the calamitous day at Carrhae and the two near-disastrous retreats and now it appeared that their officers wanted more hardship for them, rather than a negotiated settlement. Plutarch reports that Crassus once again attempted to reason with them, arguing that they could make good their escape into the hills, but to no avail.[248] In all fairness he had led them on what turned out to be a disastrous campaign and we could hardly blame the legionaries for having little faith left in his abilities or judgement. Thus Crassus was forced to meet Surenas, for what he believed would be his death, rather than his soldiers' salvation.

Plutarch reports that before he descended to meet Surenas, he made one final and prophetic speech to his two senior surviving commanders:

> Octavius and Petronius and you other commanders of Rome here present, you see that I go because I must and you are witnesses of the shameful violence I suffer; but tell the world, if you get safely home, that Crassus perished because he was deceived by his enemies, and not because he was delivered up to them by his countrymen.[249]

With that he descended to meet Surenas. Once again though, Octavius did not let him down and he and Petronius and some other of the officers went with Crassus, in order to protect him. When Crassus sent two legates ahead of him to meet with Surenas and see what protocol was to be observed, neither returned. Plutarch names them as the two Roscius brothers.[250] Nevertheless, Crassus and his retinue continued onwards. When Surenas and his officers met with Crassus they noted that they were on horses whilst he was on foot and offered him the use of a spare horse, which they had brought along. When Crassus mounted the horse, the Parthian grooms attempted to gallop the horse away towards the Parthian lines, with Crassus still on top of it. At once Octavius stepped in and killed one of the grooms, but was in turn struck down by the other one. Petronius too entered the fight and was killed by his commander's side. It is reported that Crassus was the last to fall in this unedifying struggle, killed by a Parthian soldier named by the sources as either Promaxathres or Exathres.[251]

Upon the death of Crassus and most of his senior officers, Surenas sent word to the Romans up in the hills, who had witnessed this assassination (which they had greatly been responsible for), and called for their surrender, pledging that they would not be ill treated. Amazingly, a number of them actually believed Surenas' offer, despite what happened to Crassus, and did surrender. They were added to the growing tally of Roman prisoners. Understandably a number of the remaining soldiers did not accept Surenas' offer and made away under the cover of night. Plutarch reports that the majority of them were hunted down and killed, whilst Dio states that the majority escaped through the mountains and reached safety in Roman territory.[252]

Thus died Marcus Licinius Crassus, one of the three leading men of Rome; assassinated in an ignominious scramble over a horse. Within a decade he was joined by the other two members of the triumvirate: Pompey, assassinated on an Egyptian beach in 48 BC and Caesar, four years later, assassinated in the Roman Senate House by a group of his so-called supporters (who incidentally were jointly led by Cassius, the man who had let Crassus down on so many occasions).

It was here, in the hills of Sinnaca, that Surenas finally completed his victory. With Crassus dead the Roman campaign was over and the war had been won.

Surenas seized the chance to celebrate and did so in a vindictive style. He had Crassus' head cut off (as he had done with Publius') as well as his hand, and sent Silaces (the satrap of Mesopotamia, whom Crassus had defeated in 54 BC and who was at the Battle of Carrhae) to convey both trophies to King Orodes. Before doing so it is alleged that he poured molten gold into the mouth of Crassus' head, mocking his great wealth.[253] Crassus' body was then apparently left to rot on a heap of Roman corpses.[254]

Before the head reached the king he arranged a victory parade in the city of Seleucia (which he had retaken the previous year from the rebel Mithradates III and which was known to harbour pro-Roman sympathies). He paraded the Roman captives through the streets of Seleucia in a mockery of a Roman triumph. At the head of the procession he placed a Roman prisoner who was said to resemble Crassus and had him dressed in a woman's robe and forced him to pretend to be Crassus.[255] Behind him he had men carrying Crassus' *fasces* (the ceremonial bundle of rods and axes which symbolised a consul's authority), but now they were crowned with freshly-severed Roman heads. Next came the captured Roman legionary eagles, the symbol of Roman military might, which were then distributed amongst unnamed Parthian temples and hung there as trophies for the next thirty years.[256] Following the prisoners were a number of Seleucid musicians who sang songs ridiculing Crassus for his cowardice and effeminacy. Surenas even brandished a number of parchments of the *Milesiaca*, a noted erotic work, found amongst the possessions of one of the Roscius brothers, to ridicule the Romans' weaknesses.

In Armenia, Silaces arrived with his special delivery just as King Orodes and King Artavasdes of Armenia were conducting a treaty of alliance. There are no reports of whether any fighting actually took place between the Armenians and the Parthians. Given this silence and Artavasdes' vacillating mood earlier in 53 BC, it is most probable that the Armenians gave in without a fight. It is possible that Artavasdes was hoping that this would only be a temporary treaty and that he could break it when Crassus defeated Orodes and then try to explain away his actions.

As it turned out, both kings at the meeting were in for a shock. Under the terms of the treaty with Parthia, Armenia would return to the vassal status that it occupied in the time of Mithradates II, with Parthia acknowledged as the stronger, but Armenia retaining its territorial integrity. Once again the treaty was sealed with a marriage alliance, with Artavasdes' sister being married to Orodes' eldest son, Pacorus. Ultimately Crassus' invasion had allowed Orodes to turn the clock back on Parthian-Armenian relations and restore the old balance of power. It was at the feast to celebrate this alliance that Silaces arrived with Crassus' head; to be more precise, it was during a theatrical performance of the *Bacchae*, by the famous Greek playwright Euripides (both the Parthian and Armenian kings had developed a taste for the mainstream Hellenistic culture). During a pause in the singing, it is reported, Silaces entered and, after making his bow to the king, cast Crassus' head into the space where the singer stood. At which point the singer, named as Jason of Tralles, picked the head up and recited the verse from the play:

> We bring from the mountain, a freshly cut twist of ivy to the palace, a prosperous spoil.[257]

To the Parthians it seemed fitting; for Crassus it was the final humiliation, his head being use as a theatrical prop in a Greek drama.[258] However, when the rejoicing was over, both kings would have realised that they now had growing problems. For Artavasdes, rather than playing the Romans off against the Parthians and thereby maintaining an independent Armenia, now found himself with Rome defeated and Parthia in the ascendant. What he must have hoped would be a temporary treaty to avoid the Parthian army had now turned into a permanent position of vassalage to a resurgent Parthia. The Parthian heir now had a clear claim to his throne and he had clearly miscalculated when he did not provide Crassus with the cavalry he needed.

For Orodes, the utter surprise and joy at the news must have soon soured when he realised just how the invasion had been defeated. On the one hand, not only had Armenia been brought back under the Parthian wing (as it was prior to 87 BC), but the looming threat of Rome had been met and comprehensively defeated, with the ultimate Parthian prize of Syria (which they had quested after for nearly one hundred years) now lying open and defenceless. On the other hand, however, he will have soon realised just how this had been accomplished and that, although he had eliminated one threat to his throne, he had just greatly increased another.

It is probable that Orodes sent Surenas to meet the Roman invasion purely in order to slow it down, and it is highly unlikely that he was expecting Surenas to win such a decisive victory. Prior to Carrhae, Surenas was already the second most powerful man in Parthia; his family was the strongest of the noble houses outside of the Arsacids themselves. Furthermore, Surenas had been responsible for putting Orodes on the throne in preference to his brother, and then responsible for ending the ensuing civil war by defeating said brother. Now, if that were not enough, Surenas had actually managed to comprehensively defeat the Romans in battle (in their worst defeat for 150 years), kill one of Rome's leading men and single-handedly not only end the Roman invasion, but stop the juggernaut that was the Roman Republic. The acclaim that Surenas would receive from all non-Roman quarters, never mind the Parthian people, army and nobility was going to be immense. No king could stand such acclaim for another and certainly not one as weak as Orodes.

For Orodes, if he was to keep his throne and stop the House of Suren replacing the House of Arsaces on the Parthian throne, there was only one possible answer. Within a year, Surenas, the man who had done what no other had done for generations (defeat a Roman invasion), was put to death on the orders of the king. We do not know the details of how he managed to do this, but the charge used was treason. Possibly he lured Surenas away from his forces with the promise of more honours and then had him swiftly executed. In any event, the man who had accomplished so much was murdered by an undeserving monarch who would soon regret the disposal of his best general.

In the end, therefore, there was only one winner to emerge from the Carrhae campaign. It was neither Crassus, nor Surenas; both had met ignoble ends, rather than death on the battlefield. The only clear winner was Orodes II, who began this war as a weak monarch in charge of a weak empire and ended it as the unquestioned ruler of the region's leading superpower. All that lay ahead was the resumption of Parthian westward expansion and the accomplishment of the long term Parthian goal of reaching the Mediterranean.

Summary – The Battle and the Retreat

We can now see the full scale of the disaster that befell Rome during the Carrhae campaign. The Romans had lost battles before, but never one in such a comprehensive manner and followed by such a comprehensive rout. At the end they were literally chased out of Parthian territory in abject disarray, with their vaunted Roman discipline abandoned and with an 'every man for himself' attitude being the order of the day. The retreat from Carrhae was as disastrous as the battle itself and must count as one of the great disastrous retreats in history. The only clear estimates we have for Roman casualties are from Plutarch, who puts the Roman dead at 20,000, with 10,000 captured (see appendix one) and Appian, who merely reports that less than 10,000 escaped to Syria.[259]

One aspect that is rarely noticed is just how many of these dead and captured resulted from the retreat, rather than the battle itself (at least 6,000 were killed on the day following the battle). This is not as surprising as it sounds, as there was little hand-to-hand fighting during the battle; it was mostly a barrage of arrows, most of which disabled rather than killed outright. The only close-quarter fighting occurred during Publius Crassus' breakout, during which less than 6,000 Romans died. For the rest of the battle, the Roman casualties were from arrow strikes. Given the prolonged nature of the Roman resistance and the random barrage of the Parthian arrows, it appears that a great many of the Roman casualties were not immediate fatalities, but men who suffered multiple wounds of varying degrees. Many of these would have succumbed to their injures after the battle, due to the fatigue and blood loss, rather than during the battle itself.

Of the Parthian casualties we have no word, though again the only close-quarter combat which the Parthians took part in was during Publius' breakout. Given that the bulk of this fighting was done by the Parthian cataphracts and the ferocious nature of the battle, even with their heavy armour we can expect them to have taken a considerable number of casualties. The difference here is that Surenas would have taken the bulk of his casualties from amongst his 1,000 cataphracts, rather than across the army evenly. This still gave him more than enough horse archers available to hunt down fleeing Romans, but may explain his apparent inability to tackle the force that assembled around Crassus at the end.

What can be learnt from the battle itself? It certainly would appear that whilst the Romans had the overall numbers they lacked depth in certain areas, most notably the cavalry. This, however, was not an intrinsic flaw of Crassus' preparations. As the wait until 53 BC showed, Crassus knew that his army was weak in cavalry. This shortage only became the crucial issue because Surenas choose to exploit a known Roman weakness. For the battle he was expecting, Crassus had enough cavalry to keep the Parthian cataphracts occupied. Yet for the battle that Surenas engineered; a highly mobile and missile-based one, he was hopelessly outclassed.

Nevertheless, it must be pointed out that the Roman loss at Carrhae was down to one man. Unlike traditional views of the battle, it was not lost because of Crassus' incompetence, but because of Surenas' brilliance. Surenas realised that he could not defeat Rome over the length of a campaign; past history had taught him that. He did realise, however, that Rome could be defeated in a single battle, if he prepared for it properly. If that defeat was a heavy one, both in terms of the psychological damage and the number of casualties, then the war would be over. Added to this was his realisation that the Roman Republican system had mutated to such an extent that it began to resemble Parthia, in so much as the whole campaign was reliant on a single commander. If he captured or killed Crassus then the invasion would be over. Certainly there would be likely to be another dynast along at some point in the future (most likely to be either Pompey or Caesar), but that would be a different war.

Crassus and the Romans were undone at Carrhae by Surenas' tactics of turning the battle into a fast-paced cavalry engagement, with no infantry and a total reliance on missile fire. Had the Romans got close enough to the Parthians in sufficient numbers, then their numerical and military superiority at close quarters would have shown. Surenas' genius lay in stopping the Romans from doing this. Nevertheless, for the Romans the battle itself was not as catastrophic as many would believe. This was not a typical Parthian army that they faced, but one that very much reflected the genius of its commander. As Publius' breakout had shown, at close quarters the Romans were still a force to be reckoned with, and there must have been points when the outcome of the 'battle within a battle' was still in the balance. Furthermore, Surenas' tactics could only be used once, after which the Romans would be ready for them. It is interesting to note that when Caesar was preparing for his Parthian campaign (which was abandoned following his assassination) the sources note that his proposed force was heavy in cavalry.[260]

What really did the damage for the Romans, and what turned a terrible defeat into a catastrophic one, was the retreat, or as we should say the retreats. These shambolic manoeuvres doubled the numbers of men lost, either killed or captured. The Roman general was killed, along with the majority of his young aristocratic officers. Both retreats were plagued by a complete breakdown of discipline. During the first retreat, to Carrhae, Crassus' advance guard did not stay to provide cover, which could have allowed the stragglers to catch up, or to find the groups that had become detached from the main force (such as the force led by Vargunteius). Instead, they deserted their post and fled back to Roman Syria. Of the two officers who are known to have survived, both could be, and indeed were, accused of desertion. Furthermore, there are excellent comparisons to their contemporaries who died. Whilst Vargunteius died fighting a brave last stand, Egnatius fled Parthia and survived in ignominy. Whilst Cassius betrayed Crassus and reached Syria safely, Octavius died fighting to defend him, when he too could have put his own life first. On too many occasions the Roman army was beset by indiscipline from both officers and men. This was an ominous sign for the Roman Republic.

The combination of the defeat and the retreat made the Parthian campaign a total disaster for Rome, the likes of which had not been seen since Hannibal crossed the Alps into Italy during the Second Punic War. Of an army of 40,000 plus, barely a quarter of them returned back to Syria. The seemingly unstoppable Roman juggernaut had come off the road altogether. Thus in the first battle and the first war between the two great superpowers of the east, Rome was the clear loser. Given that their rapidly-expanding empire had been built on an almost legendary invincibility, this defeat had serious implications. Not only had the Roman Empire been prevented from advancing, but it was now in clear danger of retreating.

Chapter 7

Storm Over the East (53–50 BC)

Though the events of 53 BC had seen the comprehensive failure of the Carrhae campaign, the First Romano-Parthian War was far from over. We must therefore look at the aftermath of the campaign and the other years of the war before we can draw any overall conclusions about this period of history.

Rome after Carrhae

For Roman power in the east, the disastrous Carrhae campaign had a number of effects. In the first place, the Roman province of Syria (a long term Parthian target) now lay virtually defenceless. The legions stationed there had been taken by Crassus on his invasion of Parthia and had died along with him. Thus the province of Syria had neither governor, nor garrison. All it did have was around 10,000 legionaries (from across the seven destroyed legions) who had made it back from Carrhae. In terms of officers, the most senior man in Roman Syria was Gaius Cassius Longinus, who only held the rank of pro-quaestor and whose military capabilities had been seriously called into question during the Carrhae campaign.

If this was not enough, then we need to consider the state of the Roman Empire in the east as a whole. The Pompeian settlement which had established Roman hegemony in the east was based on the power, image and threat of Rome, rather than a present physical force. The only territories that were Roman provinces were Asia, Bithynia & Pontus, Cilicia and Syria. Outside of Syria the only one of these with more than garrison strength was Cilicia, and that had less than 15,000 men stationed there. Most of the region was composed of client kingdoms who owed their allegiance to Rome due to a combination of past obligations and Rome's overwhelming military superiority; and in matters of statecraft, past obligations tended to count for little. These kingdoms remained allied to Rome through the fear and respect that the Roman army had instilled in them. Thus the defeat at Carrhae had done more than simply cost the Romans a commander and his men; it had devastated their military reputation in the region at the expense of their neighbour and rival.

Of these client kingdoms, the greatest of them, Armenia, had already moved from the Roman sphere of influence back into the Parthian one. In the region of the northern Euphrates lay two minor client kingdoms: Osroene and Commagene. Abgarus, the ruler of Osroene, wasted no time in affirming his allegiance to Orodes and dismissing any talk of him aiding Crassus (as seen earlier) as being nothing more than a double bluff. He probably attempted to claim some of the credit for leading Crassus into defeat at Carrhae. The Kingdom of Commagene appears to have remained loyal to Rome in the short term, but could do little about the Parthians crossing the Euphrates and invading them, other than warn the Romans. Should the Parthians do so, then Commagene would have to swear allegiance to Orodes. Cappadocia had just gained a new young king, whose grip on the throne was tenuous at best and so was of little use to Rome and actually gave them another source of concern.[261] This left the kingdom of Judea in the south, which had been a perpetual source of revolt for the Seleucids and had already twice required Roman intervention in the past decade (Pompey in 63 and Gabinius in 55). Given their past reputation and perpetual internal chaos, it is not surprising that when the news of the Roman defeat at Carrhae reached them, yet another anti-Roman insurrection broke out.[262] Even within Syria itself, anti-Roman elements were agitating against the Romans. All in all, the situation that Rome faced in the east was grave. Leadership and decisive action would be needed by the Senate, and Rome's two surviving triumvirs, if the situation was to be salvaged.

Unfortunately for the Romans in the east and the Republic as a whole, the Senate and Rome's leading men were apparently too busy with domestic politics to bother about a catastrophic situation on the edges of their empire. For much of 53 BC the Republic was without formal government. It was not until July that consuls for that year were elected (rather than during the previous year). This situation was symptomatic of the chaos that had broken out in Rome. Following Crassus' departure for the east, Caesar became bogged down in Gaul and an abortive invasion of Britain, leaving Pompey to manage affairs in Rome. Furthermore, a bribery scandal had broken out during the elections for the consuls of 53 BC, which resulted first in political deadlock and then outright chaos, as the elections were continually prevented from being held. Old political scores were being settled both in the courts (Gabinius was tried twice for his actions in Egypt and finally convicted[263]) and ultimately on the streets, with Clodius and Milo both re-arming their gangs and bringing armed fighting onto Rome's thoroughfares once more. Pompey had to absent himself from Rome to see if the chaos died down. By the time he returned and used his authority and political power to get the elections held for the consuls of 53 BC, attention immediately turned to the elections for the consuls of 52 BC, and thus the whole cycle of political chaos was sparked off once more. It was into this chaos that news of the disaster at Carrhae arrived.

It appears that few tears were shed by the Senate and people of Rome over the loss of Crassus. It also appears that both groups failed to appreciate the gravity of the situation in the east. As for Crassus' former colleagues, Caesar was still fighting for his life suppressing rebellions that had broken out all over Gaul and even striking out across the Rhine to stabilise his new conquests, and Pompey was trying to hold the situation in Rome together and hoping to profit by it. Therefore neither man had time to worry about the eastern frontier.

In the midst of this turmoil we are unsure how the news of the disaster at Carrhae was received. It came on the heels of a reversal for Caesar in Gaul (a rebellion had broken out, which resulted in the loss of a legionary camp and a whole legion with it). Thus it was possible that Carrhae was seen as one disaster amongst many, which could have lessened its impact on the minds of the people in Rome. It was only after the chaos of 53 and 52 BC had subsided that people had time to assess the defeat, and Crassus' part in it. However the situation in Rome at this time is difficult to judge because there are large gaps in the surviving collections of Cicero's letters (our best source for the period), which affect 53 BC in particular. There is no doubt that Cicero would have recorded the news of Carrhae, but regrettably those letters have not survived (appendix two will deal with possible other sources for the Battle of Carrhae).

The year 52 BC opened up with the by-now-familiar sight of election chaos and no fresh consuls elected. The situation got markedly worse when a battle between the gangs of Clodius and Milo ended with the murder of Clodius. In anger his supporters built a funeral pyre inside the Senate House and set light to it, resulting not only in the cremation of Clodius' body, but also the destruction of the building. This crisis resulted in a proposal being made for an emergency government in the form of a sole consul. The man proposed was Pompey himself, and with the Senate's backing the Republic chose to have a sole consul for the first time.[264] Pompey cemented his power within Rome and the Senate by hastily arranging to marry the newly-widowed wife of Publius Crassus, which even the Roman elite found somewhat distasteful but which again showed his political acumen by taking advantage of a crisis.[265] One of the emergency laws which Pompey passed specified that there should be a five year gap between a consul holding office and gaining a provincial command. Naturally, Pompey himself was exempted from this law. It was only as a consequence of this law, and the resultant shortage of provincial governors that it led to, that finally in 51 BC the Senate turned to the issue of the east and its governance.

In what was little more than a provincial house-keeping exercise, the Senate appointed new governors of Cilicia and Syria. In accordance with this new five year rule, they had to appoint men who had been consuls some years before. For

Cilicia they chose Marcus Tullius Cicero himself (the consul of 63 BC), who had spent the years following his consulship in writing numerous legal, political and philosophical tracts and working in the courts. For Syria they chose Marcus Calpurnius Bibulus (the former Consul of 59 BC) who had spent most of his consulate closeted in his own house looking for ill-omens with which to veto the legislation of his colleague, Julius Caesar. Neither man therefore inspired any confidence in their ability to handle a military crisis. To show just how little the Senate understood of the situation in the east, Cicero's proposal that fresh legions should be levied in Italy in order to strengthen the forces on the borders of Syria and Cilicia was vetoed by the consul Sulpicius.[266] Though the Romans may not have thought it, we are fortunate that Cicero was one of the men chosen to go to the east, as his numerous surviving letters give us a first-hand testimony of events there.

Thus the reaction in Rome to the catastrophic Carrhae campaign, and its perilous position in the east as a whole, was one of almost complete disinterest. As always happened in Roman Republican politics, the affairs of Rome itself took precedence over the affairs of their empire. Those men who did realise the threat, and Cicero must count amongst them, especially once he had been sent out to the east, did not have sufficient political weight to do anything about it. The only men with enough political power in the 50s BC were Crassus' colleagues, Pompey and Caesar, and both men were too busy with their own problems and affairs, and with each other's, to turn their attention to the crisis in the east. The death of Crassus may have been a disaster for Rome, but it was also an oppor- tunity for Pompey. His old rival of over twenty years had been removed and it is no surprise that Pompey's third consulship was a sole one (the first two having been with his equal, Crassus, in 70 and 55 BC). Pompey now saw himself as a man without equals.

Thus the Romans showed total disregard for the east and the potential Parthian threat. The defence of Syria, and Rome's whole position in the east, fell upon the shoulders of one man, Gaius Cassius, who had less than two legions of Carrhae survivors with which to accomplish this.

Parthia after Carrhae

Parthia, however, after the victorious Carrhae campaign, had just the opposite problem: how to build on the successes of 53 BC? Once again we suffer from a lack of non-Roman sources here. For the remainder of 53 BC the Parthians did not appear to cross the Euphrates, and Dio tells us that, quite logically, they spent the rest of the year reasserting control of the territories east of the Euphrates. The Roman garrisons may have fled along with Crassus, but Parthian control needed to be reinforced in these towns considering how easily they had gone over to the Romans. The same would have been true of the cities of Babylon and Seleucia, which were known to harbour pro-Roman sympathies and which had gone over to Mithradates III during the civil war of 55/54 BC.

A full-scale invasion of Syria would take some time to plan, especially since the bulk of the army was with Orodes in Armenia and they had not been expected to mount an offensive operation so soon, if at all. Orodes had another headache: who would lead this invasion? The obvious choice would have been Surenas, but Orodes had already had him murdered to secure his own throne. Whilst this brutal and treacherous action may have been in Orodes' own best interests, it certainly was not in Parthia's, for it robbed the Parthians of one of the most talented generals they ever possessed. Not only that, but it is unlikely that the Suren clan (Parthia's most powerful, after the Arsacids), would have taken the murder of their chief easily. So the murder of Surenas may have stirred up trouble within Parthia, which would need to be dealt with before offensive action could be taken.

Whilst this internal reorganisation was going on, however, there were certain measures the Parthians could take to strengthen their position against Rome. Firstly, the Parthians could secure their alliances with some of the smaller states of the region. Certainly the area of Osroene quickly came back into the Parthian fold, and it is probable that a number of the other semi-autonomous Arab tribes that bordered the Roman and Parthian empires would have switched their loyalties to Parthia. Secondly, Parthia could encourage pro-Parthian elements in both Syria and Judea to overthrow Roman rule and destabilise the region prior to a Parthian invasion; ironically just as Rome had done to the Mesopotamian region in 55 BC (by sending Mithradates III back to stir up a civil war). In Judea, little such encouragement was needed and the result was perfect for Parthia – a full-scale insurrection against Roman rule.

52 BC – The Calm before the Storm

The year following Carrhae was an unusually quite one in terms of the war between Rome and Parthia. Rome was still too busy with domestic politics to bother about the east and Parthia was still going through an internal re-organisation. For one man, however, it was a year that would be a highly active one, and one that would go some way to restoring his reputation. That man was Gaius Cassius Longinus. We know little of Cassius prior to the Carrhae campaign. He came from a consular family which had a steady, but unspectacular, lineage in Republican terms.[267] Given the later offices which he held, we can estimate a date of birth of somewhere in the late 80s BC for Cassius.[268] Thus he was still a young man in his late twenties or early thirties when he was taken under Marcus Crassus' wing, as had been done with many young ambitious aristocrats (including Julius Caesar). By the autumn of 53 BC he found himself, by process of elimination, as the governor of Syria and the man in charge of defending Roman interests in the whole region in the face of an impending Parthian invasion. Given his track record during the Carrhae campaign (he had fallen for Surenas' ruse and deserted his commander), the omens were not looking good. However, when put in this high pressure situation at such a young age, he appears to have come into his own.

For the events of 52 BC, Josephus is again our best source; Cicero had not yet been appointed and thus he largely ignored the situation. Josephus states that the Parthians pursued the Romans across the Euphrates, which does contradict Dio's account [269]. However, it would have been a good Parthian tactic to send raiding parties across the Euphrates whilst they were preparing for a full scale invasion. Meanwhile, Cassius formed the survivors of Carrhae, including at least 800 cavalry, into two legions and set about repelling the incursions, which he did with some considerable success.[270] Once the Parthian raids of early 52 BC had been repulsed, Cassius set about securing the region by tackling the growing problem of the Jewish insurrection. This rebellion was led by a man called Peitholaus, who was attempting to revive the rebellion led by King Aristobulus, which had been crushed by Pompey in 63 BC. Cassius dealt with this fresh rebellion in similarly brutal fashion. With only two legions he stormed the city of Taricheae and enslaved over thirty thousand inhabitants who had been supporting the rebellion; Peitholaus was executed. In crushing this rebellion, Cassius had the friendship and support of an influential Judean Arab by the name of Antipater, who was to become the father of the infamous King Herod the Great. When he was confident that Judea had been pacified, Cassius returned to the Euphrates region to deal with further Parthian incursions. Once again it is reported that he did so successfully.[271]

Thus for Cassius and ultimately Rome, 52 BC had brought some much-needed stability and some limited successes. Roman Syria was no longer leaderless or undefended. Cassius had formed the survivors of Carrhae into two efficient legions, had routed a number of Parthian border incursions and had successfully crushed an insurrection in Judea. He had done so with a ferocity that would have made any other anti-Roman elements in the region think twice. All in all it had been a good year for Cassius, who had restored both his own and Rome's reputation. Even so, some of the responsibility for these Roman successes must be laid at the door of the Parthians, who wasted a whole year's campaigning in internal re-organisation and planning. This year-long respite allowed Cassius to regroup and forge an effective defence force in Syria to secure the border and restore Roman authority over the region. Again we can see the indecisive hand of Orodes behind this delay. Had Surenas still been alive then it is highly unlikely that the Romans would have had the luxury of eighteen months to await the Parthian invasion. Nevertheless, repulsing border raids was one thing, repulsing a full-scale invasion was another.

51 BC – The Parthian Invasion of Roman Syria

On 14 June 51 BC, as he was on his way from Italy to take up his command in Cilicia, Cicero wrote to his friend Atticus expressing the sentiment 'Only let the Parthians keep quiet and luck be on my side'.[272] He was soon to be disappointed.

At some point during 52 BC, Orodes finally made the decision to invade and conquer Roman Syria. He also came to a decision on who was to lead the expedition, naturally not wanting to take the risk himself. He opted for a joint command and a blend of youth and experience. Nominally in command of the invasion was one of his own sons, Pacorus, who appears to have been Orodes' favourite son and his heir. Aiding him was a veteran Parthian noble general, Osaces.[273] Thus Orodes appears to have opted for a 'safety first' mentality to the campaign. Clearly he did not want another Surenas, but recognised the need to temper his son's youthfulness with an experienced soldier.

We can track the prelude to the first Parthian invasion of the Roman Empire through Cicero's letters as he crossed the Mediterranean en route to Cilicia. From Athens on 6 July 51 BC he wrote:

> Of the Parthian, there is no whisper. As for the future, heaven be my help.[274]

Then on 27 July, from Asia Minor:

> Meanwhile certain welcome reports are coming in, first of quiet from the Parthian region.[275]

Having reached Cilicia he wrote on 3rd August:

> I reached Laodicea on 31st July. My arrival was most eagerly anticipated and widely acclaimed.[276]

We can also see how little Cicero was looking forward to his military duties from this:

Contrary to my inclination and quite unexpectedly, I find myself under the necessity of setting out to govern a province.[277]

And, with growing desperation, this:

For mercy's sake, as you are staying in Rome, do pray first and foremost build up a powerful defensive position to ensure that my term remains only one year.[278]

How inadequate he thought his resources is also made plain:

And to think that while our friend [Pompey] has his huge army, I have a nominal force of two skeleton legions. But I'll stick it out as best I can so long as it's only for a year.[279]

By 14 August, rumours were beginning to reach Cicero which made him think that it was not going to be his year:

Of the Parthian there is no whisper, but travellers say that some of our cavalry have been cut to pieces by the barbarians. Bibulus [the new governor of Syria] is not so much thinking of getting to his province even now.[280]

By 28 August Cicero received the news that he had been dreading:

Ambassadors sent to me by Antiochus of Commagene have arrived at my camp near Iconium on the 28th August, and having reported to me that the son of the Parthian King, whom the sister of the Armenian King had married, had reached the banks of the Euphrates with a large Parthian force and a large army of many other nations besides, and that it was said that the Armenian King intended an attack upon Cappadocia.[281]

By 20 September Cicero gave a further grim assessment of the situation:

the Parthians have crossed the Euphrates under Pacorus, son of King Orodes of Parthia, with almost their entire force. There is no word of Bibulus being in Syria. Cassius is in the town of Antioch with his entire army[282].

Despite this, his major concern is still for his own governorship:

but first and foremost (ensure) that nothing is added to my responsibil-
ities or my tenure twixt the slaughter and the offering [twixt cup and lip]
as they say[283]

He then gives a brutally honest summary of his own position:

> For with an army as feeble as mine and so little in the way of allies, loyal
> ones particularly, my best resource is winter. If that comes without the
> enemy invading my province first, my only fear is that the Senate will
> not want to let Pompey go in view of the dangers at home. But if they
> send someone else by the spring I shall not worry, as long as my own
> term is not extended.[284]

Thus we have Cicero's strategy for dealing with the first full-blown Parthian
invasion of the Roman empire: pray winter arrives before the Parthians do and
hope that the Senate either sends Pompey out to deal with the Parthians, or a
replacement for Cicero as governor of Cilicia. Fortunately for the Romans, the
Parthians did not invade Cilicia, but made straight for the jugular of Roman Syria.

Cicero's letter of 28 August gives us a fair idea of the Parthian plan and the
nature of their attack, though he does not provide us with an overall figure for
the Parthian numbers, which he probably did not have himself at the time.
Fortunately, we do possess Cicero's report to the Senate, sent at some point in
the autumn of 51 BC, which outlines the whole situation and provides us with
invaluable information:

> I received a dispatch from Tarcondimotus, who is regarded as our most
> loyal ally, beyond Mount Taurus, and the best friend of the Roman
> people. He reported that Pacorus, son of Orodes, the Parthian king, had
> crossed the Euphrates with a very large force of Parthian cavalry, and
> pitched his camp at Tyba, and that a serious uprising had been stirred
> up in the province of Syria. On the same day I received a dispatch
> dealing with the same incidents from Jamblichus, the leading tribesman
> of the Arabs, a man who is generally considered to be loyally disposed
> and friendly to our Republic. On the receipt of this information, I fully
> understood that our allies had no firmly established opinions, and were
> wavering in their expectation of a revolution.[285]

From these two pieces of testimony we are able to piece together the Parthian
battleplan for their invasion of Syria. Pacorus and Osaces crossed the Euphrates
and headed deep into Syria with a large army. This force was mostly composed
of cavalry, thus copying Surenas' tactics, as well a large contingent of allied

forces, most likely to be from the tributary Arab territories. Some commentators have criticised this force as being nothing more than a large raid, rather than an army of conquest, because of the preponderance of cavalry.[286] However, this view fails to understand the subtle nature of the Parthian plan. The invasion force was not there to take every city in the province by storm, but to defeat the remaining Roman forces, and then be invited in by the inhabitants of the Syrian cities, who would want to overthrow Roman rule. In many ways this appears to have been a copy of their highly successful invasion of Mesopotamia in the 140s BC, where, after the Seleucid forces were defeated, the Parthians appear to have been welcomed into the cities by the inhabitants.

To ensure the success of this strategy, the Parthians had engineered a general uprising throughout Syria, through use of agents and pro-Parthian forces. There would have been many inhabitants of Syria, who believed that they had more in common with Mesopotamia and the east than with the inhabitants of Italy, and would have seen their being part of an eastern empire as the more logical. If nothing else, the defeat of Rome at Carrhae had shown that it was Parthia, rather than Rome, which appeared to be the ascendant power. This plan also explains the predominant cavalry element of the Parthian army; they were copying Surenas' tactics and had designed this force not to storm cities, but simply to defeat and destroy the remaining Roman forces in the region.

It remains to be seen whether the second arm of this invasion, a full-scale attack by Armenia on the Roman ally of Cappadocia was ever a real possibility, or merely wild rumour. Certainly in his report to the Senate, Cicero at one point states that 'there were certain persons who did not consider the king altogether to be trusted'.[287] Therefore the impending Armenian invasion may have been nothing more than worried speculation. Given the vacillating nature of King Artavasdes of Armenia and his desire to keep on the good side of both Rome and Parthia, such a rash move on his part would have been out of character. It is possible that he promised Orodes that he would invade Cappadocia (to keep the Romans in Cilicia occupied), and then stalled to see how the invasion of Syria went. In either event, Cicero's dithering more than kept the Cilician legions out of the war, without Armenian intervention.

Despite our focus on Cicero's testimony we must not forget that it was Cassius who was at the centre stage of this war; in command of two under-strength legions in Syria and expected to deal with a full-blown Parthian invasion at the same time as a full-scale Syrian revolt. Cassius was left with an unenviable choice of actions. He had less than 10,000 men, which must have been outnumbered by the Parthian cavalry under Pacorus and Osaces. If seven legions could not deal with the Parthian cavalry at Carrhae, then it was unlikely that two legions would fare any better in open battle. It was at this point that Cassius appeared to look back into Roman history and come up with a tactic that a Roman general had not had to use in over one hundred and sixty years; that is, when faced with an undefeatable enemy, don't fight them. Thus 'Fabian strategy' was re-introduced into Roman warfare (so named after Quintus Fabius Maximus, the Roman general who so successfully negated Hannibal after his victory at the Battle of Cannae by refusing to fight him, allowing Rome vital time to rebuild her shattered armies).

Thus Cassius retreated to the heavily fortified port of Antioch with his two legions and waited for the Parthians. Incidentally, given that Cassius was able to do this, it provides us with evidence that the Syrian revolt was not as widespread as Cicero and his sources had assumed. It appears that the Parthians soon discovered Cassius' location and brought their whole force to bear on the city, ravaging the suburbs, but failing to trouble the Romans protected behind the city walls. Despite the usual charge thrown at the Parthians (about them not being able to lay siege to a city), the Parthian army under Pacorus and Osaces was designed to fight the Romans in open battle as they had done at Carrhae.

Whilst the Parthians were attempting to lure Cassius out, a detachment of Parthians and their Arab allies had made an exploratory raid into Cilicia, where they were promptly slaughtered by a detachment of Roman cavalry, technically under the command of Cicero. He reports it with some surprise:

> Meanwhile I was informed by written and oral messages from many quarters that strong forces of Parthians and Arabs had approached the town of Antioch, and that a large body of their cavalry, which had crossed into Cilicia, had been cut to pieces by some squadrons of my horse and a praetorian cohort, which was on garrison duty at Epiphanea.[288]

Thus for the Parthians things were not going according to plan. The Roman legions of Syria refused to give battle and were happy to allow the Parthians to ravage the countryside. This, incidentally, would not have helped the Parthian cause with the rebels and the rebellion itself seemed to have run out of steam. Aside from Cicero's reports there are no further mentions of it, and it certainly did not seem to be affecting Cassius' control of Antioch. Added to that, a raid into Cilicia had been destroyed and there was no sign of any of the other client kings throwing their lot in with Parthia, or of an army from Armenia. As Cicero quite rightly surmised earlier, the majority of the semi-autonomous kingdoms in the region were waiting to see which way events turned.[289] The victory at Carrhae may have been a spectacular one, but the Parthians were now on Roman territory and would need to repeat the feat if the locals were going to throw their lot in with them, especially given Rome's brutal record at repaying treachery (of which Cassius' handling of the Judean insurrection was an apt reminder).

Cassius handling of the situation, however, seems to have been perfect. The Parthian wave crashed into Syria, but then broke on the walls of Antioch. Whilst a strong Roman presence remained in Syria, the bulk of the region would not turn to Parthia. After a short period of time, the Parthian army abandoned the attack on Antioch and moved further into Syria. Cicero, with typical modesty attempts to claim the credit for this when he boldly asserted that 'the rumour of my advent encouraged Cassius'.[290] However, once the Parthians had moved away from Antioch, heading towards the town of Antigonea, Cassius and his legions left the safety of Antioch and followed them, hoping to inflict some damage on them as they went, but without engaging in a set piece battle.[291] The Parthian army made its way through Syria, with Cassius' legions harrying them as they went.

The decisive encounter came on 7 October as the Parthians turned away from the city of Antigonea, apparently due to the city's heavily-forested environs making it impossible for their cavalry to operate with any cohesion. As they set about their return journey, Cassius gambled everything on an ambush. He confronted the Parthians with just a small part of his army and, eager for the battle which had been denied them so far, the Parthians took the bait. In a move reminiscent of the one that had been used against him at Carrhae, Cassius had his men fake a retreat, which led the Parthians into an ambush (the exact nature of which is not detailed). The Parthians were then surrounded suddenly by the emergence of the main Roman force and defeated.

Cicero mentions the encounter, but gives us no details, beyond the extra-ordinary claim that as a result of this battle 'My name stood high in Syria', which amply shows just how self-aggrandising he could be at times. Though the details are hazy, the result was not. The Parthian army was heavily defeated and forced to retreat and the Parthian general Osaces was killed as a result of the battle. Dio states that he was killed in the battle itself, whilst Cicero, with the advantage of being contemporary, reports that he died during the retreat of a wound he received during the battle.[292] Neither source records any wider casualty figures.[293] Pacorus and the rest of the Parthian army retreated back across the Euphrates to spend the winter regrouping for a fresh campaign in 50 BC, whilst maintaining a bridgehead over the Euphrates, as can be seen from Cicero's letters of 14 November 51 BC:

> our friend Cassius had driven the enemy back from Antioch in a successful action.[294]

And 17 November:

> Cassius has written announcing that the Parthian forces are this side of the Euphrates[295]

For the Parthians, the campaign of 51 BC, which everyone had been expecting for the two years following their stunning victory at Carrhae, turned into a spectacular anti-climax. The first Parthian army to invade the Roman empire arrived in a flourish, wandered about a bit, walked into a basic trap, and limped back into Mesopotamia with its tail between its legs. For the Parthians, the whole sorry episode could be put down to one factor: abysmal leadership. Not only did it take the Parthians two years to invade Syria, thus allowing the Romans time to regroup, but the invasion was led by a joint command, designed more to negate any threat to Orodes than to defeat the Romans. The Parthian army arrived with only one plan in mind and when that failed (due to the Roman unwillingness to oblige them with a fresh victory) they lost impetus and walked into an ambush. By any standard of military conduct, this campaign was a shambles, especially given such a stunning springboard.

For the Romans, however, the campaign of 51 BC had shown them at their best. Despite the total indifference of the Republic's leadership back in Rome, Cassius had forged the wretched survivors of Carrhae into a force that was able to defeat the Parthians and rout their invasion of that year. Cassius had obviously learnt the lessons of the Carrhae campaign well; in particular that it was up to the invading army to force the pace. In 53 BC the Parthians defeated the Roman invader because Surenas was confident that he could defeat the Romans in battle. In 51 BC, the Romans defeated the Parthian invader because they knew that they could not. By adopting the old Roman 'Fabian tactics', Cassius denied the Parthians the crucial victory in Syria that they needed to conquer the province. He frustrated and totally disrupted their plans, forced them into making mistakes and then led them into an ambush. What had worked against Hannibal, now worked against the Parthians. By the end of 51 BC, the whole momentum of the First Parthian War had swung back in Rome's favour.

No sooner had Cassius written his victorious report to the Senate than the new governor of Syria, Marcus Calpurnius Bibulus, finally deigned to arrive in his war-torn province, some two months behind Cicero (despite their leaving at similar times). What he would have found was a province that was firmly in Roman hands, that had defeated a Parthian invasion and that had restored some martial pride back into Rome's reputation in the region. Furthermore, it was clear that the onus had shifted back to the Parthian court, in the form of Orodes II, to respond in order to recover the impetus that had been gained after Carrhae and lost during this year. It had soon become clear that the turning point in the war for the Parthians had been Orodes' murder of Surenas. With Surenas still leading their armies we can imagine that the two year wait, the aimless wandering around Syria and the walking into an ambush would never have happened. The question that Orodes faced over the winter of 51–50 BC was whether the Parthians could regain their momentum without him.

50 BC – Storm abated

Certainly the Romans thought that the Parthian threat for 50 BC would be a more severe test than that of the previous year. Again we can turn to the letters of Cicero from early 50 BC, which indicated that the Romans were awaiting the Parthian storm. In his letter of 13 February 50 BC he wrote:

> The son of King Orodes of Parthia is in our province, and Deiotarus, whose son is to marry the daughter of Artavasdes, a good source of information, has no doubt that the King himself will cross the Euphrates with his whole power as soon as summer comes.[296]

And in similar vein on 20 February:

> A Parthian War is threatening. The Parthians are wintering in our province and Orodes in person is expected.[297]

Thus Cicero was merely voicing the widely-held view that the Parthian king himself would lead a fresh invasion in 50 BC. In fact, it was hard to see how he could do otherwise. Surenas and Osaces were dead and Pacorus had not only been deemed too young for full command of the campaign of 51 BC, but had made such a mess of it that he was unlikely to be given sole charge any time soon. Yet the Romans were overlooking the fact that Orodes, as far as we can tell, had only limited military experience himself. In the civil war and the Roman invasion it was Surenas who commanded the Parthian armies in battle. All that Orodes had in terms of experience was leading an invasion of Armenia, whose king had promptly capitulated. In fact, we have little evidence for any Parthian king since Mithradates II leading his troops into battle, the practise having seemingly fallen out of favour. The question was whether Orodes felt confident enough in his abilities to fight the Romans, or even had enough confidence in the security of his throne to leave Parthia.

One other interesting aspect that emerges from Cicero's letters concerns the figure of Deiotarus, whom Cicero mentions. He was the king of the Roman client kingdom of Galatia, whose territories had been enlarged by Pompey the previous decade. During Cicero's governorship of Cilicia, the two men had become good friends and by early 50 BC he had raised '30 cohorts of 400 men armed in the Roman style (equivalent to 12,000 legionaries) and 2,000 horse', which he placed at Cicero's disposal for the coming war.[298] Not only was this a sign that Rome's allies were beginning to shift back towards supporting Rome against Parthia, but as Cicero informed us earlier, Deiotarus' son was to marry the daughter of Artavasdes, the king of Armenia. Such timing cannot have been a coincidence.

Not only had Artavasdes surrendered to the Parthians and negotiated a treaty of alliance, but his brother-in-law was the Parthian prince, Pacorus himself. Suddenly it appeared that Artavasdes was attempting to tie himself to a staunch Roman ally. As Cicero's comment about this alliance being 'a good source of information' reveals, it appears that Artavasdes was feeding the Romans information about the coming campaign via the back door, in order to get himself back into Roman good books.[299] More than anything else, this shows that the kingdoms of the regions believed that Romans had weathered the storm.

At Rome, it appears that both Cassius and Cicero's reports of the campaigning in 51 BC had galvanised the Senate, as well as Pompey and Caesar.[300] In fact, the Senate saw an excellent opportunity to aid the east and defuse the tensions between Pompey and Caesar at the same time. To this end they recommended that both men give up a legion each and send them to reinforce Syria (a proposal that they both agreed on, though Pompey did still try to gain an advantage by nominating a legion that he had already lent to Caesar in Gaul, thus depriving Caesar of two legions in reality).

Thus Rome's leaders were finally taking the war with Parthia seriously; both the governors of Cilicia (Cicero) and Syria (Bibulus) were ready for the Parthians and had won back a number of their regional allies. The only thing missing was the Parthians, and as we can see from Cicero's letters, the events of 50 BC are somewhat confusing. In April 50 BC he wrote:

> For a major war is threatening with Parthia.[301]

In late May or early June 50 BC:

> There is thought to be a major war in Syria, which looks as though it will erupt into this province[302]

By mid-June 50 BC his fears seemed confirmed:

> There I found much to disquiet me; a great war in Syria[303]

Yet by 3 August 50 BC he was able to write:

> None the less as long as the Parthians appeared to be coming down on us, I had decided to leave my brother, or even for my country's sake to stay on myself . . . But when by an incredible stroke of luck they disappeared, my doubts were removed.[304]

In his letter of 1st October 50 BC the danger has clearly passed and Cicero is able to pass judgement on his colleague's performance:

> If it were not that Bibulus is exerting himself to get one [a Triumph], who so long as there were a single Parthian in Syria did not stir a step from the city [Antioch] gates[305]

This latter point is confirmed by a remark by Julius Caesar in his own civil war commentaries which tells us the following:

> [The] Parthian enemy, who a little before had slain the commander Marcus Crassus, and had kept Marcus Bibulus closely invested.[306]

A surviving précis of Livy also records that Livy's book 108 (now lost) 'also includes the achievements of Marcus Bibulus in Syria'.[307] Cicero finishes commenting on the Parthian campaign with the following, penned on 25 November 50 BC:

> However, when I think of how the Parthians all of a sudden left Bibulus half dead [they did not finish the job].[308]

What can we conclude from this about the events and the campaign of 50 BC? It is clear that the long-expected second Parthian invasion did indeed take place during the summer of 50 BC, but we are unsure who was leading it. None of our contemporary accounts throws light on this. Given the absence of any named individual, we must assume that Orodes refused the opportunity to lead the invasion himself, and also denied Pacorus the chance as punishment for the debacle of the previous year. We can therefore only assume that Orodes gave the command to either another (unnamed) son, or a noble general (a probability that will be discussed below).

In any event, the campaign of 50 BC mirrored that of the previous year. The new governor, Calpurnius Bibulus, still had only the two under-strength legions, and had even less military experience than the young Cassius. Wisely, however, he too decided to emulate Cassius in his Fabian tactics and stayed shut up behind the walls of Antioch, whilst the Parthian army tried in vain to get the Romans out in the open and fight them in battle. After failing once again to take Antioch, however, the Parthians suddenly disappeared and withdrew from Syria altogether, not to return for a decade. This action struck contemporary Romans such as Cicero as mysterious. Fortunately, two later sources give us the reason why the Parthians chose to end the war with a complete withdrawal. Justin presents us with this passage:

His son Pacorus, who was sent to pursue what remained of the Roman forces, after achieving great actions in Syria, incurred some jealousy on the part of his father, and was recalled into Parthia; and during his absence the Parthian army left in Syria was cut off, with all its commanders, by Cassius the quaestor of Crassus.[309]

Dio tells us that Bibulus

turned the Parthians against one another. For after winning the friend-ship of Ornodapates, a satrap who had a grudge against Orodes, he persuaded him through messengers to set up Pacorus as king, and with him to conduct a campaign against the other.[310]

Whilst both sources contain some inaccuracies (Justin, in that this occurred before the defeat at the hands of Cassius, and even before Pacorus' 'great actions in Syria'; and Dio with their being no military action that year), both contain the same basic story. This is that during the campaign of 50 BC, Orodes and his eldest son fell out, with Pacorus making a bid for the throne. We have no direct evidence that the Parthians fell into a civil war once more, but there are some interesting indicators. Whilst technically Orodes remained king until his murder in 37 BC (at the hands of another of his sons) there is room to speculate upon the nature of the struggle between him and Pacorus, and upon Pacorus' consti-tutional role within Parthia during the next decade.

One implication that arises from reading Dio's account is that the invading army of 50 BC was used by Ornodapates in an attempt to place Pacorus on the throne. One aspect that has been little commented on before is that Dio's account surely implies that Ornodapates himself was the commander of the invasion of 50 BC and that he turned his army around and invaded Parthia with it. Justin merely has it as Pacorus being recalled, with no fighting, yet that would not account for the removal of the invading army. If there was an armed conflict, then it is hard to determine the result. Although Orodes retained his throne, we know that coins were minted in the name of Pacorus (see plate 12), an action which was usually only reserved for kings and pretenders.[311] Yet, within a decade both Pacorus and Orodes were working hand-in-hand during a renewed invasion of Syria, during the Second Romano-Parthian War.

Thus it appears that Parthia did degenerate into another civil war (only four years after the end of the previous one). Given the nature of Orodes' rule and his actions, this is hardly surprising. He had come to the throne following the usurpation and murder of both his father and brother. He then compounded these actions by murdering the greatest Parthian general of his age, Surenas, the man who had masterminded the stunning victory over the Romans at Carrhae.

This action had led to Parthia squandering the considerable advantages that they had over Rome, with two years of dithering and a failed campaign in 51 BC. Therefore, it is no wonder that there were elements within Parthia who wanted rid of this vacillating and murderous monarch, and his replacement by someone more vigorous. Certainly the Suren clan would have had little time for Orodes and would have looked forward to his removal. Whilst we have no account of the ensuing civil war, it is clear that a compromise was reached between father and son and that some form of co-rule was established. Orodes kept his throne, and his life, whilst Pacorus gained control of the armies and most probably possessed the bulk of the power.

It only remains to be determined what role Rome played in this process. Cicero appears to have no knowledge of Roman involvement, but then as the tone of his letters showed, he and Bibulus had little regard for each other. Cicero describes Bibulus' emulation of Cassius' Fabian tactics as nothing more than 'not stirring a step whenever there were Parthians in Syria', so we cannot read much into his ignorance here. Justin assigns no role for the Romans in the squabble, but Dio clearly believes that Bibulus was at the forefront of this scheme. The epitome of Livy is interesting, as Livy clearly devoted a section to Bibulus' actions in Syria. We can rightly ask ourselves whether this simply referred to the holding of Antioch, or whether they did include fomenting civil war in Parthia.[312]

If Bibulus did have a large part to play in this rebellion then he is to be congratulated indeed. Such a policy had overtones of Gabinius' earlier use of Mithradates III, (including possibly being responsible for sending him back into Parthia armed with Roman gold). It is also possible that Bibulus included a hefty contribution to Pacorus' campaign; at the very least he could have assured him of Rome's support against Orodes and their strict neutrality in the affair. Given the testament of Dio and the remarkably fortuitous timing of the Parthian withdrawal, then it is more than likely that the Romans did have a hand in generating this third Parthian civil war, as they had done with the second one. What the Romans could not achieve by force of arms, they managed by cunning. Thus, the First Romano-Parthian war ended in a stalemate, with the Parthian Empire turning in on itself once more, nicely mirroring the prelude to the war. After five long years, peace broke out between the two great empires, though an unofficial and uneasy one at that. From the depths of disaster the Romans had dug deep and managed to hold onto Syria and maintain their empire's territorial integrity, though, as we have seen, they were greatly aided by Parthian indecisiveness and incompetence, all of which stemmed from the figure of Orodes II.

Postscript

Whilst the outbreak of yet another Parthian civil war brought the First Romano-Parthian war to a conclusion, many expected that Rome's retaliation for the setbacks and humiliations which they had suffered would be swift and decisive. Rome still possessed two great generals, in the form of Pompey and Caesar, and now the Parthians had challenged Roman might by inflicting a heavy defeat on them. In fact it looked as though Cicero's wish was going to come true, when he reported on 20 February 50 BC that Pompey had written to him stating that 'this [Parthian War] is going to be his concern'.[313]

It appears that Pompey had decided that the Parthians were fitting opponents for him to campaign against and restore lost Roman pride in the east. A machiavellian mind might argue that the events as they transpired had worked out very well for Pompey in the end. In 56 BC it was difficult to see why Pompey had allowed Crassus the glory of the Parthian war, as opposed to his lieutenant Gabinius, or even himself. Yet in 56 BC there was little appetite amongst the Senate or the Roman people for such a war. However, by 50 BC much had changed. Crassus' campaign may not have had public support, but no Roman would allow the defeat at Carrhae to stand. Roman honour dictated that the Parthians should be made to pay for their humbling of a Roman army and the invasion of one of their provinces. Thus by 50 BC a Parthian war did have full public support, and it would be to Pompey that the Senate and people would turn.

Furthermore, Crassus had proved to be no match for the Parthians, though as it turned out he was only outwitted by one Parthian of genius, Surenas, who was now dead himself. Parthia had lost their best general and had now collapsed into a civil war and looked weaker than they did in 56 BC. At this point we should remember Orodes' plan for dealing with the Romans, namely sacrifice Surenas to slow the Romans down, weakening them, and then come in for the kill himself. In what may just be a coincidence, as events turned out, the same plan could be applied to Pompey and Parthia – send an expendable general (who you really want out of the way anyway) to fight the Parthians in order to weaken them and then move in for the kill yourself. No two men knew each other so well as Pompey and Crassus. The two had been rivals for nearly thirty years when Pompey agreed to Crassus leading the Parthian campaign. Certainly Pompey knew that Crassus was a good general, but did he foresee that Crassus would fail but weaken the Parthians in doing so?

By 53 BC, the plan (if there was one), looked like it had misfired. The Parthians had not only defeated Crassus, but seemed to be on the verge of over-running the Roman East, though this again would only fuel calls for Pompey, as Cicero alludes to on many an occasion. In fact, if we are pursuing a machiavellian line for Pompey here, this would also explain Rome's apparently blasé approach to defending the East following Carrhae, including the seemingly incredible decision of the consul Sulpicius (in 51 BC) to prevent any fresh troops being sent to the east. It could be argued that the whole scenario looks as though someone wanted the situation to get worse, and who would want that, other than someone hoping to restore his military dominance in Rome by coming to their aid when all others had failed? In the murky world of politics in the late Roman Republic, it is entirely possible.

Yet even the best machiavellian scheme can be undone by circumstance or by another schemer. With the death of Crassus (planned or otherwise), Pompey clearly believed that he had no equal. This position appeared to have been confirmed by the Senate's decision (in 52 BC), to make him sole consul. There was only one other man left in the Republic who might one day threaten his position: Gaius Julius Caesar, Crassus' former protégé. At the meeting of the triumvirate in Luca in 56 BC, both Crassus and Caesar had received substantial military commands. Crassus had already fallen, and for much of the years 54–52 BC it looked as though Caesar would join him, with the conquest of Gaul floundering upon reversals and rebellions, perhaps as Pompey had foreseen. What he hadn't foreseen was that Caesar would come through these reversals and by 50 BC would have added a substantial amount of territory to the Roman empire, taking it up to the German (English) Channel, and enhancing his reputation considerably. By 50 BC, Caesar was looking like he could rival Pompey and that clearly was not in Pompey's plan. However, help was at hand in the form of the termination date of Caesar's five year extension to his command in Gaul. All Pompey had to do was ensure that this was not renewed and Caesar would have to return home empty-handed, possibly to prosecution (for real or alleged crimes), whilst Pompey could command a triumphant campaign against the Parthians to avenge Roman honour.

Unfortunately for Pompey, he had not reckoned on Caesar having plans of his own. In an outrageous example of blatant self-interest, Caesar chose not to emulate the generation of Pompey and Crassus, but the one before it. Copying the example of Sulla, he led his army in an invasion of Italy and caused the outbreak of the Second Roman Civil War.[314] Thus, once again, Rome and Parthia appeared to emulate each other in their rise and fall, with both collapsing into civil war. Pompey was denied his great Parthian war and was defeated by Caesar at the Battle of Pharsalus in 48 BC. His eastern connections came back to haunt him when he was assassinated on an Egyptian beach by his supposed allies as they attempted to ingratiate themselves with the rising power of Caesar.

By virtue of his victory Caesar inherited the war against Parthia and was in the final preparations for a renewed invasion of the East when, in the Senate House in Rome, he too fell to the knives of assassins, one of which belonged to a certain Gaius Cassius, who had now betrayed both the master and pupil. Caesar's death sparked off a fresh round of civil war which spread to the east and even involved Parthia. Whichever empire came out of civil war first would have the initiative, and in Rome's case all the planning of Pompey and Caesar came to nought when Parthia stabilised first and unleashed a second war on Rome (which at one point found the whole east up to and including Asia Minor under Parthian control). Though the Second Romano–Parthian War was as epic as the first, we must leave our narrative here and look back upon this first momentous clash of ancient civilisations and see what it meant to the development of the ancient world.

Chapter 8

Epilogue – The Consequences of Carrhae

How can we sum up the Battle of Carrhae and the whole First Roman-Parthian War? Clearly it was a defining battle in the history of both the late Roman Republic and the Parthian Empire. But, aside from it being the decisive encounter of the First Romano-Parthian War, what was the battle's wider significance? In order to fully answer this most important question we need to assess the various areas that it impacted on. The most logical place to start is with the Roman Republic, and here we must analyse the effects on both the Republic's territories in the east and on domestic politics back in Rome.

Consequences for the Roman Republic in the East

In the short term, the most obvious consequence for the Romans was the disastrous loss of life at the Battle of Carrhae. Out of an invading army of over 40,000 men, barely 10,000 managed to return to Roman territory. Of the others, around 20,000 were killed and 10,000 taken captive and held as prisoners for over two decades (see appendix 1). Thus the Romans lost three quarters of their army, along with their commander and most of his aristocratic command staff, nearly all young nobles from senatorial families. In total, seven legions were destroyed and their standards paraded as war trophies by the Parthians; which would remain a contentious issue in Roman minds until their recovery in 20 BC.

The war had been launched as a war of conquest, but had ended with the Romans desperately defending their own territory, shut up in the cities, with the Parthians ravaging their province. Although they had managed to salvage some pride out of their defence of Syria (which came mostly as a result of Parthian failings) and from the fact that the situation did not deteriorate as badly as they had thought it would after Carrhae, there is no hiding from the fact that they had comprehensively lost this first war with Parthia.

We can see that the Battle of Carrhae itself had been won by the better general, but this does not mean that we can perpetuate the blackening of Crassus' reputation. Crassus was a fine Roman commander, who possessed sound judgement, clear tactical planning and the quality of never seeking battle unless he was sure of his own army's abilities. It could be said that perhaps he lacked the flair of a Pompey or a Caesar, but then few men possessed that. He had earned his place in the pantheon of great Roman commanders on account of his defeat of Spartacus and saving Rome from the slave army, and must be judged as a good, if not a great, Roman general. The spectacular loss at Carrhae was the result of a good Roman general running into a truly great Parthian one. History has been as unkind to Surenas' reputation as it has to Crassus' (at least in the Christian West). Surenas turned an almost inevitable defeat into a spectacular victory and his accomplishments must surely rank him as one of history's great generals.

Nevertheless, Surenas had accomplished this great victory as a result of deficiencies in the Roman method of warfare, namely their reliance on a slow moving infantry-based battle. It is true that they had faced cavalry before, in numerous battles, and been successful, but they had never faced an entirely-mounted army and this was the cause of their undoing. However hard a lesson it was, it was one that could only be taught once, and the Romans never again went into a battle in the East with such a light cavalry contingent.

If the battle was a disaster for the Romans, then the retreat was worse. As we saw earlier the Romans lost as many casualties (dead and captured) on the retreat as they did in the battle. Had the Romans retreated in a more orderly manner from Carrhae, then probably up to 20,000 men would have reached the safety of Syria (twice as many as actually did). Here Crassus does deserve censure for allowing the retreat to turn into a full-blown rout. Just because the battle had been lost, it did not mean that the war would be. His ineffectual leadership during the retreat turned the disaster at Carrhae into a complete catastrophe, though he was greatly aided by the incompetence and poor discipline of many of his officers and men. Thus all sections of the Roman army at Carrhae must stand accused of contributing to such a catastrophic defeat. Even so, in the short term, troops could be replaced, standards could be recovered, properties repaired and crops re-grown. It is the long term factors that reveal the greater impact which the Battle of Carrhae had.

As the surviving ancient sources show us, the Battle of Carrhae loomed far larger in the popular consciousness than the rest of the campaign itself (a view which most modern historiography appears to copy). Carrhae must go down as the worst defeat that the Romans suffered in the century and a half since Hannibal had ravaged Italy, defeating Roman armies with impunity. Certainly there had been setbacks in the intervening period, most notably those inflicted upon them by Mithridates of Pontus, and the loss of troops was not the greatest that they ever suffered; but Carrhae was an outright comprehensive defeat, on all scales.[315] Previous setbacks in the intervening years had been at the hands of an invading enemy and when the Romans were on the defensive. They had not lost a battle of this nature, when they had been on the offensive, in a very long time (certainly never during their expansion throughout the Mediterranean). That is the reason why this defeat did so much damage to Rome's military and imperial reputation. Rome had launched an aggressive war of conquest and for the first time had failed, and had done so spectacularly.

This was not a quiet disaster either, for the peoples of the Parthian empire were able to see the captured Roman prisoners in their thousands, along with the captured legionary eagles (which were then placed in Parthian temples). Thousands of Roman corpses must have littered northern Mesopotamia, not only at the battle site, but on the route between there and Syria, where the fleeing Romans had been caught and slaughtered. At the Parthian court, it is likely that the head of Marcus Crassus became a permanent trophy, a witness to the Roman defeat (though the sources do not record any mention of it after its use in the play). All these very public displays of the Roman failure would have been transmitted throughout the East, not just the Parthian territories, by the various economic and social networks that existed between the cities and peoples of the East and which overrode any distinction between Roman and Parthian.

Thus Rome's military reputation was shattered at Carrhae and the seemingly inexorable annexation of the eastern civilisations was brought to a shuddering halt. Inevitability was replaced by uncertainty as Parthia emerged as a credible threat to Rome's hegemony in the East, not merely stopping Rome's progress but raising the possibility that they might even reverse it.

The other major long term consequence was the establishment of a lasting enmity between Rome and Parthia over domination of the East. Although a clash between the two was inevitable, the crushing nature of Rome's defeat and, as they saw it, humiliation meant that the Romans would never rest until this loss was avenged. This humiliation was worsened by the outcome of the Second Parthian War (40–36 BC) which saw the Parthians invade and temporarily annex all of Rome's territories in the East. Although the Romans ultimately recovered these lands, a second Roman invasion of Parthia, led by Mark Antony, then the foremost Roman general of his day, met with a similar disaster to the first and again led to a retreat in chaos and ignominy. Thus Rome now had a permanent rival in the East. This permanence was entrenched by Caesar's son, Octavian (who became the sole ruler of Rome under the name Augustus), when in 20 BC he chose not to confront the Parthians, but to engage them in diplomacy. In return for the Parthians returning Crassus' and Antony's captured legionary eagles, a formal peace treaty was drawn up between the two great empires. Thus, for the first time, Rome formally acknowledged the limits of their empire in the East. This treaty was renewed in AD 2 by Augustus' adoptive son and heir, Gaius.[316] Given the end of the republican system and the advent of emperors in Rome, Roman expansion ground to a halt, perpetuated by most subsequent emperors aping Augustus' passivity in the East (the most notable exception being Trajan).

Thus the spread of Roman civilisation came to a halt in the East, caused by the failure of the Romans at Carrhae; an outcome that was formalised by Augustus. We will examine the wider implications of the division of the East below. For now, in mentioning Rome's transition from Republic to Empire, we must examine the contributory role that the Carrhae campaign had in this phenomenon, by assessing its effects on domestic Roman politics.

Domestic Consequences for the Roman Republic

If the consequences of this war for Rome's empire were bad enough, then the effects back in Rome were even greater. As stated earlier, Crassus' death did not cause the triumvirate to become a duumvirate, but spelt the end of the alliance altogether. Crassus and Pompey had worked together on several occasions as they were contemporaries, but Pompey and Caesar had not. The only other strong link between the two men was Pompey's wife, Julia, who was Caesar's daughter, but she had died in childbirth in 54 BC. Pompey soon found a new wife, the widow of Publius Crassus, who was a Metellus by birth. This new marriage alliance tied Pompey closer to the traditional senatorial families. Not only did Crassus' death remove the link between Pompey and Caesar, but it also probably left Pompey thinking that he now had no rival, a view which was seemingly confirmed when he was chosen by the Senate to be the sole consul of 52 BC.

Although they were of similar age[317], Pompey had been a dominant figure in Rome for some three decades, whilst Caesar was a relatively new figure on the scene (he gained the consulship in 59 BC and only did so with the backing of Pompey and Crassus). Thus Pompey dismissed Caesar as a junior, who was not on his level. However, when he and the Senate attempted to deal with Caesar, late in 50 BC (by not renewing his Gallic command, nor allowing him to stand for the consulship *in absentia*), they fatally underestimated the ambition of the man. Caesar took a huge gamble to save his career by invading Italy, crossing the Rubicon River early in 49 BC (thereby violating the law that forbade him to cross from his province into Italy whilst still at the head of his army). As he is famously reported to have said at the time; *'alea jacta est'* (let the die be cast).[318] For Caesar and the Republic there was no turning back and Rome fell into a second civil war.

The early stages of the war culminated at the Battle of Pharsalus (in Greece) in 48 BC, when Pompey and Caesar met on the battlefield for the first and last time. By the end of the day Pompey had been comprehensively defeated. He fled, vowing to fight on, but was assassinated as he landed in Egypt by the authorities there. Caesar went on to establish a firm control of Rome, finally taking the office of Dictator for Life early in 44 BC. A conspiracy of twenty or more senators determined to ensure that both his life, and thereby his dictatorship, would be short. This culminated in his assassination in the Senate House on the Ides of March 44 BC. One of the two ringleaders was none other than Gaius Cassius (thus betraying a second triumvir).

However, Caesar's death did not restore the Republic as they hoped and a further war broke out between the 'Caesarian' faction, now led by Mark Antony and Octavian, and the 'Conspirators' led by Brutus and Cassius. Having won this war, Antony and Octavian inevitably turned on each other, which led to the Battle of Actium in 31 BC. Octavian defeated Antony and Cleopatra and established himself as *princeps* of the Roman Republic. More commonly historians label him as the first Roman Emperor and name 31 BC as the date upon which the Roman Republic ended and the Roman Empire began (though this is a simplistic view of events).

Thus we can see that Crassus' death at Carrhae did more than cost Rome a general. It was a contributing factor leading to the outbreak of the Second Civil War at Rome and the ultimate collapse of the Roman Republic. It can be argued that tensions between Caesar and Pompey could have resulted in open warfare anyway, given that Crassus was out in the East and would have continued to be so had he been successful. We might ask, however, if either man would have gone to war with Crassus still a powerful figure at the head of a large and successful army. Had Crassus lived then it is far more likely that some form of compromise deal would have been worked out between the three men, each with their own spheres of influence. It may have been that Crassus and Pompey would have united to see off Caesar, and they might have been no more successful than Pompey was on his own. In any event, whilst the removal of Crassus at such a key moment in the late Republic did not make civil war inevitable, it certainly made it more likely and for that fact alone, it renders Crassus' death of even greater importance to history.

Consequences for Marcus Licinius Crassus

This title sounds rather obvious at first, as the immediate consequences for Crassus were the severest possible, namely death and decapitation at the hands of his enemies. However, the abuse of Crassus did not end with his mortal remains, but has continued throughout the centuries. When Crassus fell in the aftermath of Carrhae, he was one of the three leading men in Rome, had rivalled Pompey throughout the latter's entire career and was a major force in the politics and history of the late Roman Republic. However, as seen throughout this work, upon his death Crassus' reputation was torn to shreds by his contemporaries and by commentators ever since. Rather than admit that Rome had seemingly met its match in the Parthians, the defeat at Carrhae was all too easily exorcised by blaming it squarely on Crassus' shoulders. Across the centuries he has been labelled as being too old, too gullible, too easily led or too hasty. As detailed earlier, Crassus was not a member of the triumvirate by accident, or to make up the numbers; he was one of Rome's two foremost statesmen and gene-rals (at the creation of the triumvirate), a man who had saved his state from the seemingly-invincible Spartacus and who was well versed in the arts of war.

The defeat at Carrhae was indeed the result of one man's abilities, but that one man was Surenas. On the day, Crassus, as any Roman general could have done, simply ran into a better general and tactician. Some would argue that had it been Pompey or Caesar then they would not have made the same choices and that is certainly possible, but it neglects the genius of the man who crafted the Parthian army into a force capable of beating any Roman army. Carrhae is a testa-ment to Surenas' genius, rather than to Crassus' incompetence and his reputation needs to be salvaged and restored to its rightful place as one of the key figures in the history of the Roman Republic.

Plutarch, in his comparison of Crassus and Nicias (the Athenian general with whom he paired Crassus' biography), actually presented a balanced judgement on Crassus, something he had failed to do in his main biography:[319]

> What then would have been their feelings, and for how many days would they have sacrificed to the gods, if Crassus had written to them from Babylon that he was victorious and had overrun Media, Persia, Hyrcania, Susa and Bactria, and declared them Roman provinces.[320]

He then concludes:

> Those who have praise for Alexander's expedition, but blame for that of Crassus, unfairly judge of a beginning by its end.[321]

In the end Crassus' reputation fell from its deserved heights for committing the ultimate sin in the eyes of the Romans, namely failure on the battlefield. Hopefully we will not fall into the same pitfall and judge him so harshly. Crassus the Roman needs to be judged, rather than Crassus the defeated.

On a wider note, this particular branch of the Licinii Crassi had seen a father and son killed together for the second generation running. The surviving son, Marcus Licinius Crassus, who had been serving with Caesar in Gaul, overnight became Rome's richest man and sole heir to a great dynasty. His father's decision to have him serve with Caesar, rather than go with him to the East appears to reflect Crassus' cautiousness and desire to ensure the dynasty's survival should anything go wrong. Such caution had served the family well in the previous generation, where one son stayed in Rome and was killed, whilst another went to Spain and survived. Given the wealth and accumulated political power that Marcus received at such a young age, (around thirty years old), he appears to have kept a remarkably low profile during the civil wars that followed.[322] Aside from finding him still in Caesar's army in 49 BC, we hear no more about him.[323] It appears that, given the recent history of his family and the tragedies that their prominence had caused them, he kept a deliberately low profile in the wars and slaughter that followed, marking him as a truly insightful Roman aristocrat.[324]

This low profile appears to have done his family no harm, in fact just the reverse. We find a Marcus Licinius Crassus as consul of 30 BC serving alongside Octavian, who was a late, but welcome supporter of the new order. He had in fact opposed Octavian not once, but twice, by siding first with Sextus Pompeius (son of Pompey the Great) and then with Mark Antony.[325] Yet, despite this, he became consul (which shows that Octavian was making a clear statement about reconciling Republican nobles to his new regime) and subsequently had an illustrious military career.[326] Perhaps we can see his father's hand in the background.

Further generations of the Licinii Crassi were to be found as supporters of the Julio-Claudian emperors, with the grandson of the younger Marcus becoming consul in 14 BC.[327] Further consulships can be found in AD 27 (under the emperor Tiberius) and in AD 64 (under Nero), by which time the family had further intermarried with the descendants of Pompey and now posed a credible threat to the throne.[328] The last recognisable descendant was executed by the emperor Hadrian, when he came to the throne in AD 117, in order to eliminate a potential rival claimant. Thus, despite the tragedy at Carrhae, the family remained a powerful force in the Roman Empire for the next 150 years.

Consequences for the Parthian Empire

For the Parthian empire, the consequences of Carrhae, and the First Romano-Parthian War in general, were mixed and can again be broken down into short- and long-term effects. In the short term the stunning victory at Carrhae not only propelled the Parthian empire back into the position which it had occupied upon on the death of Mithradates II in 87 BC, but actually seemed to surpass it. For the thirty years prior to Carrhae, Parthia had clearly been on the decline and had been supplanted in the East, not merely by Rome, but by her former vassal Armenia as well. As a result of Carrhae, the Romans had been defeated militarily and the Armenians had been reduced to the status of junior partner once again.

It is also probable that the peace treaty which Orodes negotiated with Artavasdes (which in the latter's case was only ever intended to be temporary) included a return of the Parthian lands taken by Armenia in the 70s BC and not returned when Armenia was defeated by Rome. In 53 BC the Parthian empire was once again the foremost power in the region and looked poised to resume her seemingly unstoppable sweep from the east.

By 50 BC the situation had changed and held out some inkling of Parthia's long-term future. The invasions of Syria in 51 and 50 BC were not only failures as campaigns in themselves, but undid the wonderful position that the Parthians had found themselves in following Carrhae. The execution of their best commander in 53 BC had led to a delay in the invasion and when it did occur it was marked by dithering and incompetence. The Parthia of old had made spectacular territorial advances when its armies were commanded by kings who possessed tactical brilliance. By the mid 50s BC Parthia looked as though it was evolving into a system where the kings could take a back seat, if they so chose, and allow the growth of professional military commanders from the noble houses, thus separating the military command structure from the monarchy.

This had been the one key weakness of the Parthian Empire in the past, when a monarch with no military ability took the throne. Carrhae should have been a lesson to Parthia that this new system was the way of the future. Instead Orodes' insecurity over his throne led him to murder his best general and give command of his armies to a hybrid system which saw a noble general partnering a royal prince. This led almost inevitably to the disastrous campaign of 51 BC when, instead of sweeping the last of the Romans out of Syria, the Parthian army wasted its time in attempting to force the Romans into battle, then appeared to wander about the region with no clear strategy (probably the result of a dual command) and finally fell into a Roman ambush. The obvious move for the Parthians would have been for Orodes to take command of the invasion and stamp some royal authority on it. In 50 BC, however, he once again failed to do so and the latest invasion fell to a combination of Roman intrigue and Orodes' unpopularity, sparking off the second civil war within the decade.

Thus the Parthian Empire had restored its military reputation and its dominance of the east, but its one key flaw remained – the monarchy. A weak monarch could still undermine the empire and in the short term had reduced what should have been a clear victory in the East into an uneasy stalemate. Without a strong monarch on the throne Parthia was vulnerable, unless military command could be safely separated from the monarchy itself (which proved to be the case in the Second Romano-Parthian War).

Nevertheless, despite these shortcomings, Parthia emerged from the First Roman War as the clear victor. The Roman eastward advance had been comprehensively halted and the Romans defeated militarily. As a result Parthia appeared to have overcome her weaknesses of the years 87–55 BC and was once again the dominant non-Roman power of the region. In the long term it was clear that Parthia and Rome were locked into a bitter feud, which would mirror Rome's rivalry with Carthage for the western Mediterranean during the previous two centuries. Until one of the two powers fell, as had eventually happened to Carthage, neither could claim dominance in the region.

There was one further consequence for the Parthian empire that came about partly as a result of the deadlock with Rome to the west, namely expansion to the east. Following the first two Roman wars, the Parthian empire started making significant inroads in conquering the Afghan and Indus regions, and established what became known as the Indo-Parthian Kingdom.[329] This took place late in the first century BC and seems to coincide with the deadlock in the west of the Parthian Empire.

Consequences for Surenas

Again, as with Crassus, this at first appears to be an odd heading. However, Surenas has been neglected for far too long in Western historiography for us to repeat this omission. In the short term, his victory made Surenas a national hero and he became a 'scourge of Rome' comparable to Hannibal or Mithridates of Pontus. Unfortunately for Surenas, it also made him a prime target for an extremely insecure king, who promptly had him charged with treason and murdered in a most cowardly, and ultimately costly, act.

In the long term, his stunning victory at Carrhae made him one of the ancient world's greatest generals. Few men could boast of a decisive battlefield victory against Rome, the most recent of them being Hannibal (Mithridates of Pontus never achieving such a set-piece victory). At Carrhae, we saw a wonderfully conceived and executed battle-strategy. He had analysed the Roman military machine and saw their strength as being close-order combat and engineered his army in such a way that the Romans would never engage in this type of fighting. The twin pillars of this scheme, having a totally mobile army composed of nothing but two complementary types of cavalry (cataphract and archer), combined with a near-endless supply of arrows, were masterstrokes and showed the true genius of the Parthian art of war (when handled well). Such a tactic was the ultimate refinement of Parthian warfare and foreshadowed the devastating Mongol armies of over a thousand years later.

Yet, whilst the exploits of Hannibal are well known and he is deservedly lauded as being one of history's great generals, Surenas (at least in the Western world), has been largely ignored. There are three clear reasons for this. The first one is that the Battle of Carrhae has always been written off as being a Roman loss (due to Crassus' incompetence), rather than a Parthian victory.[330] The Romans always liked to treat it as such, in order to keep the moral and military high ground. This fits in with the second factor, which is the West's inheritance of this historical tradition and the ability to see this battle as being a loss for Rome, rather than a victory for the Parthians. At best this is an accidental standpoint that hopefully has been challenged in this work. The third reason is that Surenas, as a figure, is more obscure in the surviving ancient sources; we merely have a few lines here and there and none of the narrative that accompanied the other great ancient generals, such as Hannibal. We do not even know his own name, just that of his family. This was all exacerbated by his sudden execution which robbed him of further campaigns against the Romans, which if Carrhae was anything to go by, would have cemented his reputation once and for all.

Again, we can see that like the Licinii Crassi, the Suren clan survived the loss of their leader and continued to prosper, though given the scarcity of the surviving Parthian sources (see appendix three), this is much harder to document. We find a Suren heavily involved in another Parthian civil war during the 30s AD, crowning one of the claimants to the throne.[331] In fact, the Suren continued to be central to the Parthian Empire throughout the next three centuries and we even have inscriptions that record the Suren as one of the leading noble families supporting the new Sassanid Persian dynasty, which displaced Parthian rule in the region, in the 220s AD and beyond. Having outlasted the Arsacids, they clearly remained an important noble family in the region and only lost power when the Muslim invasion of Persia took place, during which it appears the clan became scattered. A funeral inscription of the 9th century AD in China records a member of the Suren clan, so it appears that the clan remained recognisable for many centuries more.[332]

Consequences for the Ancient World in the East

Having looked at Rome and Parthia individually, we must finally consider the significance of the Battle of Carrhae and the First Romano–Parthian War in the wider context of the history of the ancient world as a whole. The war was the inevitable conclusion of the process that had seen two new powers rise on the fringes of the Hellenistic world. Both Rome and Parthia took advantage of the instabilities amongst the existing Hellenistic kingdoms and created fresh empires that inexorably ate away at the more established states, from both ends (east and west). This process continued until they inevitably met in the middle, in Syria as it turned out. War between the two was expected to determine which civilisation would be the one to reunify what was considered (in the West) to be the known world (from Italy to India) and succeed both the First Persian Empire and that of Alexander the Great. At the outset of the war it was Rome who was considered to be the stronger and thus the more likely to re-unify the ancient world.

In the end, and as a result of this first war (whose result was ratified by Augustus), the states of the ancient world were permanently divided between East and West, with the Euphrates as the dividing line. The Romans, under the Republic, only fought one more war with Parthia (40–36 BC), the eventual outcome of which resulted in the same dividing line as the one established after Carrhae. Augustus' peace led to the formalisation of the Euphrates as the natural limit to Rome's empire; something that no Republican general would ever have tolerated. Rome's relations with Parthia then became subject to the whims of the emperor, much as Parthia's had done (thus Rome inadvertently appeared to copy a failing system). In the centuries that followed, another five Romano-Parthian wars broke out, many of them centred on the struggle for control of Armenia.

The third war broke out in the reign of Nero and again ended with a dismal stalemate. The fourth war, under the emperor Trajan, broke the mould and resulted in spectacular Roman successes, with Trajan annexing both Armenia and Mesopotamia, and giving Rome access to the Persian Gulf for the first time. However, this lasted only from AD 115 to 117, as on Trajan's death his successor Hadrian abandoned Mesopotamia to the Parthians and returned to a Euphrates border.[333] The fifth war broke out in AD 161 under the co-emperors Marcus Aurelius and Lucius Verus, and saw Rome again successfully defeat the Parthians in Mesopotamia, and resulted in the sacking of the cities of Seleucia and Ctesiphon. Once again, however, the Romans withdrew from the majority of Mesopotamia, but they did annex some of the lands on the Euphrates border.

The sixth war broke out in AD 197 and was led by the emperor Septimius Severus, who again successfully overran Mesopotamia, and even burnt Ctesiphon. Ultimately Severus again withdrew from many of the territories which he had conquered, but on this occasion he annexed a large swathe of northern Mesopotamia and turned it into a Roman province. As a consequence, the town and battle site of Carrhae finally became Roman territory, over 140 years after Crassus' death. A final war broke out under the emperor Caracalla in AD 217, but ended in another stalemate when Caracalla was assassinated and his successor defeated and forced to pay a huge war indemnity.

In AD 224–226 the Arsacid kings were overthrown by a noble revolt led by a man named Ardashir, who founded a new dynasty, the Sassanids. Once in power he attempted to erase the Arsacid and Parthian past by claiming that this new dynasty was a restoration of the old Persian empire, rather than a Scythian-originated and thoroughly-Hellenised Parthian one. This resulted in a policy of the deliberate destruction of all traces of the Parthian past in an effort to portray this 'new' empire as a continuation of the first great Persian empire. This partly accounts for how little original Parthian material we have left today (see appendix three).

In terms of external relations, little had changed, as the new Persian empire had exactly the same boundary with Rome and the two empires continued to struggle for dominance in the East. For the next four hundred years the empires of Rome and Persia continue to war with each other, and for the same period the dividing line between East and West barely moved. During this time the Roman Empire itself became divided in two, between east and west (in AD 395), with the Western Empire and the city of Rome falling to a barbarian invasion less than a hundred years later (in AD 476). Yet throughout these momentous events, the Eastern Roman Empire (usually referred to as the Byzantine Empire by historians) continued its long struggle with Persia.[334]

We cannot predict how long this war between Rome and Persia would have continued, but by the beginning of the seventh century, when both empires were exhausted from yet another long and brutal war (which lasted from AD 603–630, and during which both capitals of Constantinople and Ctesiphon were attacked), a third force emerged, which was to exploit this centuries long conflict and sweep away the ancient world. Whilst this war devastated the region, a new monotheistic religion had sprung up in Arabia, and used the inattention of the region's two great powers to gain control of the whole peninsula. Fired up with a religious zeal, this new force swiftly invaded both the Byzantine and Persian empires.

Persia met its first defeat at the hands of the invaders in AD 636 at the Battle of Qādisiyya, and a further defeat at Nihāvand in AD 642 ended Persian resistance. By the murder of the last Persian emperor in AD 651, the whole Persian empire was in the hands of this new power. Thus this second Persian empire lasted just under 450 years, which was slightly less than the Parthian empire (c.247 BC to AD 226).

The Byzantine Empire faired little better and by the end of the 640s had lost North Africa, Egypt, Judea and Syria and was left with only Asia Minor in the east. Finally, the eastern ancient world had been united under one empire, but it was neither Roman/Byzantine nor Parthian/Persian; it was the empire of this new religion, Islam.

Thus the failure of Crassus at Carrhae sparked off a near seven hundred year period of warfare between the two great empires for control of the East. Incredibly, after seven hundred years the border between the two, which became the border between the Eastern and Western civilisations in the ancient world, barely moved from the Euphrates. In some wars the Romans/Byzantines advanced to the Persian Gulf, in others the Parthians/Persians advanced into Asia Minor. In the end they so exhausted each other that their armies became easy prey for a third power. Furthermore, after the devastation that the two had caused each other's territories in these endless years of warfare, the peoples of the region were receptive and eager for a new power to rule and one that would unite them in internal peace. Thus was born the empire of Islam and so ended the ancient world.

Appendix I

The Fate of the Roman Prisoners

Some comment must be made upon the fate of the 10,000 Roman soldiers captured at the Battle of Carrhae and during the subsequent retreat. This was unprecedented, as never before had so many Roman soldiers been taken into captivity. Along with the captured legionary standards, these legionaries were a visible symbol of Parthia's dominance. As was detailed earlier (chapter six), we know that the prisoners were paraded through the streets of Seleucia by Surenas, in a victory parade that made a mockery of the fabled Roman triumph, but what became of them afterwards?

We only have one explicit testimony as to what happened to these Roman prisoners. Pliny records that these 10,000 men were transported across Parthia into captivity at the city of Merv, which was near to the River Oxus (now the Amu Darya, which forms the Turkmenistan/Afghanistan border), on the easternmost fringes of the Parthian empire. This is a brief note by Pliny, mentioned in passing whilst discussing the geography of the region.[335] We have no accounts of the journey, which must have been a harrowing march of some 1,500 miles across the Middle East and Central Asia to their captivity, and thus we have no way of knowing how many of the 10,000 actually made it there alive. We have no details as to what they did during their captivity in Merv (we must remember that a majority of them were young men freshly recruited into Crassus' legions).

Mark Antony appears to have been the first Roman figure to raise the issue of the Roman prisoners. On two occasions we are told that Antony demanded both the return of Crassus' legionary eagles and the surviving captives, as part of his conditions for peace with Parthia, during the Second Parthian War, but to no avail.[336] The Augustan poet Horace composed a work on 'martial courage' and in the second and third stanza's speculated on the fate of these Roman prisoners:

> Did Crassus' soldiers live in base wedlock with barbarian wives and grow old
> in the service of the enemies whose daughters they had wedded, alas our sunken
> Senate and our altered ways.
>   Marsian and Apulian submissive to a Parthian King, forgetful of the sacred
> shields, the Roman name, the toga, and eternal Vesta, while Jove's temples and
> the city of Rome remained unharmed?[337]

Here Horace speculated that the Roman captives married into the peoples of the eastern Parthian empire and served in their armies. As the reader may recall, in the 120s

BC the Parthian king had incorporated captured Greek soldiers into his army, following his victory over the Seleucids (though they did betray him in battle at the first chance they got). We have one piece of evidence that appears to support this opinion however. Florus, in his work on Roman history, records an incident that occurred during Antony's invasion of Parthia, during the Second Parthian War:

> No disaster had ever occurred comparable with that which threatened the Romans on the following day, if the gods in pity had not intervened. A survivor from the disaster of Crassus dressed in Parthian costume rode up to the camp, and having uttered a salutation in Latin and thus inspired trust by speaking their language, informed them of the danger that was threatening them.[338]

Thus we have explicit testimony that the Parthian army did indeed contain an element of Roman soldiers from Crassus' lost legions. However, we must be careful here, as not only is this source not contemporary, but this incident is not recorded in any other source that deals with Antony's campaign. In fact in other accounts, notably Plutarch, the Romans are indeed warned of an impending trap, but are done so by locals, not by captive Roman soldiers.[339] The other question that Florus' reference raises is why the Parthians would bring the Romans back from the east to fight against their own kind, when they knew that the dangers of betrayal and treachery were high? We must also ask ourselves why, in Florus' account, did only one former Roman soldier defect back to the Roman side? The balance of the evidence suggests that the Parthians would have kept the survivors of Crassus' legions on the eastern side of the empire, where they could not return to Roman territory. In the end, Antony's disastrous invasion of Parthia in 36 BC actually increased the number of Roman prisoners that the Parthians had. We can assume that they too were shipped off to the eastern front.

Nothing more is heard of them until 20 BC when Augustus decided to negotiate with the Parthians, rather than engage them in a third war. Famously, as a result of this peace treaty Augustus recovered the legionary eagles that had been lost during the first two Parthian wars[340]. He commemorated the event in coins (see figure 21) and with a triumphal arch (more than a little disingenuous given the absence of any fighting).[341] This is Augustus' own testimony:

> I compelled the Parthians to return to me the spoils and standards of three Roman armies, and as suppliants to seek the friendship of the Roman people. Furthermore I placed those standards in the sanctuary of the temple of Mars Ultor.[342]

Whilst most attention has been given to the return of the legionary standards, Dio also records the following

> Meanwhile Phraates had become anxious that Augustus might lead an expedition against him, because he had not yet fulfilled any of the agreements concluded

earlier with Rome. So he now returned the standards and all the prisoners of war, except for a few who had taken their own lives out of shame, or else had managed to escape detection and had hidden in the country. Augustus received them as if he had conquered the Parthian in a war; for he took great pride in the achievement, declaring that he had recovered without a struggle what had formerly been lost in battle. Indeed, in honour of this success he commanded that sacrifices be decreed and likewise a temple to Mars Ultor on the Capitol, in imitation of that of Jupiter Feretrius, in which to dedicate the standards; and he himself carried out both decrees. Moreover he rode into the city on horseback and was honoured with a triumphal arch. [Dio. 54.8]

So, it it appears that the Parthian king sent all of the Roman prisoners (that he could find) back to Rome. For the survivors of Antony's invasion this would have ended an absence of sixteen years, but for those of Crassus' legions it would have been thirty-three years. Again we have no testimony of how they fitted back into Roman society, but given Horace's poem, it is possible that they returned to Rome along with their Parthian wives and it would have been intriguing to see where they settled in Italy. Interestingly there is no mention of Crassus' head being returned, and it is entirely possible that it was kept in the Parthian court.

This issue does not end here, as a radical theory has sprung up concerning the fate of some of Crassus' legionaries, who fall into the category of those who 'managed to escape detection'. This highly unorthodox theory has it that a group of these Roman prisoners ended up creating a settlement in ancient China, the descendants of which are still alive today.

The basis of this seemingly incredible theory lies with the work of Homer Dubs, a scholar of Chinese at Oxford in the 1940s and 1950s.[343] Over several works, he advanced the theory that a group of Carrhae survivors fled from the city of Merv and, finding that they could not cross the Parthian Empire westwards, turned east and engaged in mercenary work in Central Asia. By 36 BC they were apparently in the employ of King Jzh-jzh of the Huns, whose empire stretched across Central Asia, and went to battle against the armies of the Han Dynasty of China. The Chinese subsequently defeated the Huns and accepted the surrender of the Roman mercenaries and settled them in the border town of Li-jien, now Liqian, in western China.

This remarkable theory is based on just a few pieces of evidence. Firstly a Chinese Imperial register of AD 5 records a town with the name of Li-jien, which was also one of the words that the Chinese of the period used to describe the Romans.[344] From this small piece of evidence Dubs advanced the theory that this must have been a settlement of Romans and then went back through Chinese history to see how this could have occurred. From the chronicles of the battle in 36 BC, between the Chinese and the Huns, the following passage occurs:

> More than a hundred foot-soldiers, lined up on either side of the gate in a fish-scale formation, were practising military drill. The men on the wall challenged the Chinese army, saying 'Come and fight'.[345]

It is this 'fish-scale formation' that Dubs argues must be a Roman legionary *testudo*, or 'tortoise'. Apparently Dubs had discounted this theory on the grounds that there could not possibly have been any Roman legionaries in Central Asia, but was informed by William Tarn, the eminent Hellenistic historian of this region, of the survivors of Carrhae in the city of Merv. From this the two of them concluded that some of the survivors from Carrhae fled Merv to take up mercenary work and, seventeen years after Carrhae, found themselves fighting for the Huns against the Chinese.

As can be seen, the gaps in Dub's evidence and between his leaps of logic are quite large. Firstly, he makes no mention anywhere in his works of the return of Roman prisoners in AD 20, as recorded by Dio. Secondly, not only is there nothing to link the two separate pieces of evidence (the town in AD 5 which may be named similarly to Rome, and the 'fish-scale' warriors), but there is nothing to link either of them to the Roman prisoners at Carrhae. As noted in chapter two, the region between Parthia and China had been home to the kingdom of Bactria, which was a Greek/native mixed civilisation, until its conquest by Asian tribes.[346] Therefore, it is perfectly possible that these 'fish-scale' soldiers, if they were not Huns, and there is nothing to say that they were Caucasian at all, were some remnant of the Bactrian civilisation. There is absolutely nothing to link them to the Romans; they could have been any body of known or unknown fighting men from the region. As for the name of the town, there is no conclusive proof that it was named after the Romans; it could easily have some other unknown meaning. Furthermore, despite all the contacts Rome had with China, through trade, there is no mention of a Roman colony living in China.

Therefore, there is no real evidence that a contingent of Crassus' men fled from their captivity, became mercenaries in Central Asia, and settled in western China. Nevertheless that has not stopped the inhabitants of the modern village of Liqian in western China from claiming descent from Crassus' legionaries. Their claim surfaced as recently as February 2007, when a national newspaper ran their story and Dubs' theory once again, complete with the claim that scientists are taking blood samples from the inhabitants.[347] They are apparently intending to check them against the DNA of modern Italians (which after the migrations and ethnic shifts in the last 2,000 years, in both regions, is a mighty tall order). The inhabitants have even built a mock Roman portico, hoping to cash in on their surprise ancestry. This has to be the wildest possible modern consequence of the Battle of Carrhae, but one that in all truth holds little validity.

It is the case that the survivors of Carrhae suffered a horrendous march across the Parthian empire, probably being shown off at every major city along the way, until they reached a city at the edge of the Asian steppes, where they would have spent a wretched thirty-three year existence, until their repatriation. How many of the original 10,000 actually survived the march and this length of captivity are unknown, but in reality it can't have been many. For these men the consequences of Carrhae were all too real.

Appendix II

Sources for the Battle of Carrhae

It will be useful to briefly detail both the existing ancient sources that relate the Battle of Carrhae, as well as the First Romano-Parthian War as a whole, in order to gain a fuller understanding of the campaign. Furthermore we can examine the question of what the original sources were and how this affects our understanding of the events that transpired.

Surviving Original Sources for the Battle

As we have seen, there are two substantive surviving accounts that detail the campaign and the battle itself.

Plutarch – *Life of Crassus* (first century AD)

The best account comes from the Romano-Greek historian Plutarch, who wrote a series of biographies of the leading Greek and Roman figures of the ancient world. He was born in Boeotia in Greece around AD 45, and grew up under the Roman emperors of the Julio-Claudian and Flavian dynasties. He wrote several works, of which his *Parallel Lives* are the most famous. These are a series of biographies of the most famous Greek and Roman figures, with one Greek and one Roman figure paired together. He wrote them late in his life, either at the end of the first century, or the beginning of the second century AD. We know that he died at some point in the 120s AD.

Plutarch's biography of Marcus Crassus, paired up with that of Nicias, the Athenian politician and general of the fifth century BC, provides the bulk of the details for Crassus' life. Out of the thirty-three chapters of Crassus' biography, chapters sixteen onwards are devoted to his Parthian campaign, and provide a highly detailed narrative of the events. The number of details has led many scholars to accuse him of inventing some of them, such as the story involving Crassus' severed head.[348] We have no direct attestation for his sources for Crassus' life, but we do know from his *Life of Mark Antony* that he used Dellius' history of the Parthian Wars (see below). His version of the Carrhae campaign is highly critical towards Crassus and notably biased in favour of Cassius, suggesting that he used a pro-Cassius source. Nevertheless, Plutarch's narrative contains the finest second hand eye-witness reports of the battle that we have.

Cassius Dio – *History of Rome* (third century AD)

Cassius Dio provides us with the second substantive account of the battle and the campaign. Dio was a Roman senator of Greek birth, who served under the Severan dynasty of the late second and early third centuries. He wrote a history of Rome from its origins to AD 229 in eighty books, many of which survive intact, including the period from 68 BC to AD 46. Book thirty-nine deals with the build-up to the campaign, whilst book forty deals with the campaign itself, the battle, and the aftermath.

We have no clear idea of his sources for the period, which probably included Livy, and this is reflected in the briefer narrative and less-detailed account of the battle. Even so, it remains the second-best account we have.

Cicero – letters and other works (106–43 BC)

The works of Marcus Tullius Cicero, whilst not preserving a narrative of the battle itself, do provide us with our main first-hand testimony concerning Marcus Crassus. His letters in particular are important evidence for the build-up to the campaign and its aftermath, in which he was involved. Unfortunately, his surviving letters have a number of gaps in them, and in particular we have no record of how the news of the defeat was broken and received. As a contemporary and sometimes friend, sometimes foe of Crassus, his comments are especially important. Furthermore, it appears that he wrote a secret memoir, only published after his death, in which he wrote what he truly thought about the people and events of his life.[349] Apparently Crassus came out of this rather badly, despite their supposed reconciliation.[350]

Caesar – *Civil Wars* (100–44 BC)

We have only one other contemporary of Crassus whose writings preserve a mention of the battle. Caesar in his commentary on the Second Civil War has the following brief mention:

> leaving in his rear the neighbouring Parthian enemy, who a little before had slain the commander, Marcus Crassus, and had kept Marcus Bibulus closely invested, he [one of Caesar's Pompeian adversaries] led the legions and cavalry out of Syria.[351]

This aside was hardly a glowing tribute to his former political sponsor and triumviral partner. Had he lived to conduct his own Parthian campaign then we may have had a more fulsome commentary on Crassus' campaign and its failure.

Velleius Paterculus – *History of Rome* (first century A.D.)

Paterculus was a Roman historian who wrote a short Roman history in two books, circa AD 30, which made mention of the Carrhae campaign. He deals with it briefly and has little detail, mistakenly claiming that it was King Orodes who faced Crassus at Carrhae. His brief account contains a number of the standard clichés that had grown around the campaign, namely Crassus' lust for money as a cause of the war and the tribunes casting curses on Crassus as he left. He also devotes a few words to the role of Cassius, and again portrays his actions in a positive light;

> Remnants of the legions were saved by Gaius Cassius, who not only retained Syria in its allegiance to the Roman people, but succeeded, by a fortunate turn of events, in defeating and putting to rout the Parthians when they crossed its borders[352]

Josephus, *Antiquities of the Jews* and *History of the Jewish War* (first century AD)

Josephus preserves a few important details concerning the overall campaign, particularly concerning Gabinius' and Crassus' activities in the East and gives us an invaluable non-Roman perspective to the details; one that is free from having to conform to the expected narrative. He was a Jewish commander during the great Jewish Revolt against Rome (AD 66–73), who changed sides and became a Roman ally.

Appian's histories of the Syrian War, Mithridatic Wars & Civil Wars – and the Parthian Wars? (second century AD)

Appian was a Greek from Alexandria who wrote extensively on the history of Rome, with an interlinking series of works on the various Roman wars. He wrote in the mid-second century AD and used a wide range of sources, which gives his work a good level of detail. His history of the Syrian wars provides us with details of the Roman expansion in the East, as does his work on the Mithridatic wars. His work on the civil wars preserves a great deal of information about Crassus and the build up to the Carrhae campaign. On several occasions throughout his works he states that he would write a history of the Parthian wars, but no trace of it remains, if indeed he ever got around to writing it.[353]

Lost Original Sources for the Battle

Having covered in brief the few surviving sources that provide us with details of the First Romano-Parthian War and the Battle of Carrhae, we can now turn our attention to the possible original sources, which the later writers used but now no longer survive.

Livy, *History of Rome* (late first century BC)

Of all the historians of Rome, Livy is generally considered to have been the greatest. Living under the reign of Augustus, he wrote a history of Rome from its foundation to 9 BC that encompassed some 142 books. Unfortunately for us, nothing after book forty-five, which stops at 167 BC, survives intact. Nevertheless many modern scholars insist that virtually every account on Roman history written after Livy was based upon him, including all the details we have for the Carrhae campaign. In truth we have no clear idea which of our later sources used him and to what degree. There are several compilations of the later Livy books still in existence, notably the *Periochae* and *Obsequens*, but they do nothing more than précis his work.

Nicolas of Damascus, *Universal History* (first century BC)

Nicholas of Damascus is the other great lost historian from whom many scholars believe that many of the later accounts of Carrhae derive. He was a Hellenised Syrian born in 64 BC and served at the court of Herod the Great. He wrote a universal history of the East in 144 books, but nothing remains aside from a few fragments. He certainly would have provided an authoritative account of the war and not purely from a Roman perspective, but the almost total absence of any surviving material makes any judgements over who used his material useless.

Quintus Dellius' history of the Parthian Wars (first century BC)

Quintus Dellius is widely considered to be the main source for the account of Carrhae, which we find in Plutarch.[354] During the Second Roman Civil War, he was a follower of Cassius. He then served under Mark Antony and accompanied him on his invasion of Parthia during the second Romano-Parthian War, of which he wrote an account.[355] We know that Plutarch used him as a source for his life of Mark Antony, but we do not know whether his history encompassed the first war, and it does not explain the seemingly first-hand account of Carrhae given by Plutarch. By the time Dellius came to write his history, Cassius was long dead.

Apollonius' history of the Carrhae campaign (first century BC)

Apollonius is introduced to us by Cicero (in a letter to Julius Caesar, in 45 BC):

> His [Publius Crassus'] freedman Apollonius I used to esteem highly and think well of, even when Crassus was alive; for he was devoted to Crassus, and adopted himself extremely well to his highest pursuits, and was therefore much beloved by him. After Crassus' death, however, he struck me as being all the more worthy of friendship, inasmuch as he considered it incumbent upon him to pay respect and attention to those whom Crassus had been fond of, and who won his affection.[356]

A little later in the same letter we have notice of Appollonius' credentials as a historian:

> At the present moment, however, fired with enthusiastic admiration of your [Caesar's] exploits, he desires to record them in the Greek language. I think he is competent to do so, he has great ability, he has the experience, he has been engaged for some time past in that kind of literary effort[357]

Here we have an ideal candidate for a history of the Carrhae campaign. He was a slave of Publius Crassus, which meant that he may have accompanied his master to the East, he was devoted to the memory of his master and the Crassi as a whole and he had just finished a work of history: 'that kind of literary effort'. Can we assume that this 'literary effort' was a work on the Carrhae campaign and one that vindicated and glorified both Crassus and his son Publius? Certainly this is the view some modern scholars have supported.[358] Thus in the period after Carrhae, there is a strong possibility that a pro-Crassus history of the Carrhae campaign was written, which most probably included eye-witness accounts of the battle itself, to show off Publius' bravery. This was written by a man who was either there personally or who would have interviewed survivors of the battle. Certainly the surviving son, Marcus Crassus junior, would have had an interest in exonerating the memories of both his father and younger brother. The only drawback of such an account is that it would not be pro-Cassius and would not have painted Crassus in such a poor light as the one in Plutarch does. Nevertheless it is likely that this history was written and would have been available to later writers.

Pro-Cassius source, history of the Carrhae campaign (first century BC)

There is enough evidence to speculate that there may have been more than just Apollonius' contemporary history of the Carrhae campaign published in the late Republic. In fact there are three reasons to suspect that a work was published on behalf of Gaius Cassius. Firstly, the account given in Plutarch combines what appears to be an eye-witness account of the battle along with a noticeable pro-Cassius bias. Secondly, Cassius himself would have wanted to distance himself from the disaster at Carrhae and exonerate himself for his actions (which may on occasions be viewed as cowardice), as well as promoting his subsequent defence of Syria. Thirdly, if there was a pro-Crassus version of the battle being published, then he would need to counter any negative coverage that he might receive from it. For all three of these reasons we can speculate that Cassius had commissioned a work on the Carrhae campaign on his return to Rome, which provided an eye-witness account with an anti-Crassus and pro-Cassius slant. It is probably this work that we can see as the basis for Plutarch's account, either directly, or transmitted through a third party. Several names have been suggested for the author of such a work, but this is taking the speculation too far.[359]

Testimony of Artavasdes, king of Armenia (first century BC)

It has been mentioned earlier (chapter seven) that King Artavasdes of Armenia, when he saw that Parthia's victory in the war was not going to be as clear cut as he had thought, began to feed information to the Romans, via a third party:

> The son of King Orodes of Parthia is in our province, and Deiotarus, whose son is to marry the daughter of Artavasdes, a good source of information, has no doubt that the King himself will cross the Euphrates with his whole power as soon as summer comes.[360]

This leads us to the possibility that, as well as telling the Romans what the Parthians were currently up to, he could have informed them of what occurred at Carrhae, as reported to him by the Parthians. He definitely could have informed them of how badly the Parthians treated the remains of Crassus and the whole misuse of the poor man's head as a theatrical prop. Although this would not have been published directly, there could have been official reports, as well as inclusion in some of Cicero's' works (though none of his surviving works indicate this). Nevertheless it is another possible source of information for the campaign.

Survivors' histories of the Carrhae campaign and later captivity (first century BC)

Taking our speculation to the extreme, it is possible that the return of the Roman prisoners of war in 20 BC sparked a renewed interest in their stories, especially given the general lack of knowledge about the Parthian east. Therefore it is possible that some works were written on the whole Carrhae campaign and its aftermath, using eye-witness accounts from some of the survivors.

Later histories of the Romano–Parthian wars

We know from later surviving sources that whenever there was a Romano–Parthian war, there was a flurry of historical works accompanying them. Lucian, in his work *On the Writing of History*, written in the second century AD, commented that the Fifth Romano–Parthian War (AD162–165), sparked off a flurry of histories of the Romano–Parthian conflict, all of which he considered to be second rate:

> Crepereius Calpurnius of Pompeiopolis wrote the history of the war between the Parthians and the Romans at its very outset . . . Another of them has compiled a bare record of the events and set it down on paper, completely prosaic and ordinary, such as a soldier or artisan or peddler following the army might have put together as a diary of daily events.[361]

This indicates that there was a whole genre of works on the Romano–Parthian wars, many of which could have used aspects of previous works as an introduction, but again this remains nothing more than informed speculation.

We can see, therefore, that the few surviving sources which detail the Battle of Carrhae and the whole Romano–Parthian War are but a poor reflection of the primary sources that were available in the Roman period. There were possibly two eyewitness accounts, if not more, and a whole number of accompanying works that would have utilised them, all produced when the battle was still in living memory. What we have today merely reminds us of how much knowledge has been lost since the fall of the ancient world.

The Battle in History

As well as ancient works detailing the battle or the campaign, there were a large number of works which utilised the Battle of Carrhae for other purposes, whether as an example to learn from, or for dramatic effect. In each case, the battle is used rather than detailed, but many of these references preserve fragments of information which we do not have in our main surviving sources.

The Battle of Carrhae as an exemplar

References to the Battle of Carrhae and the campaign as a whole can be found across a number of other Roman works, held up as an example of what not to do in certain circumstances. Cicero started this process in his work *De Divinatione* (On Divination), where he used the Carrhae campaign on three occasions to highlight the dangers of ignoring omens[362]. Similar themes occur during the histories of Dionysius of Halicarnassus and the Memorable Sayings of Valerius Maximus.[363] A second theme was for the battle to be used in works on military matters. Both Frontinus' *Stratagems* and Polyaenus' work of the same name refer to the defeat, as does Tacitus' *Germania*.[364] Various references can also be found in the geographical works of Pliny and Strabo, in connection with various places in the East.[365]

The Battle of Carrhae as drama

Crassus' death at Carrhae was a theme soon taken up in Roman drama, especially under the Augustan poets. We have already referred to Horace who made dramatic use of the fate of the Roman prisoners, but the other Augustan poets all made reference to the loss at Carrhae. This is from Ovid's *Fasti*:

> The pride of the nation had been fostered by the deaths of Crassus and his son, when soldiers general and standards perished together.[366]

and this from his *Ars Amatoria*:

> Parthian, thou shalt pay the penalty; rejoice you buried Crassi, and your standards that shamefully endured barbarian violence.[367]

From Propertius we have the following:

> No longer does the Euphrates allow Parthian horsemen to glance behind their backs, and regrets keeping possession of the Crassi.[368]

And finally:

> Rejoice, Crassus, if any consciousness be yours amid the grave's black sands: now we may cross the Euphrates to your tomb.[369]

Thus in death, Crassus became what he never managed to in his life: a Roman hero, albeit a tragic one. His death gave the Roman dramatists a wonderfully tragic story with which to work. However we are not aware of any specific drama's written about the Carrhae campaign.

The Battle of Carrhae as antiquated knowledge

Throughout the centuries that followed, knowledge of the defeat at Carrhae and Crassus' death became a staple in the works of Roman writers. Historians as varied as Justin, Ammianus Marcellinus, Zosimus, Eutropius, Orosius and Jerome all pass comment on the campaign.[370] The standards of the comments vary, with Jerome even claiming Crassus and his son were both captured alive by the Parthians.[371]

In the fifth century AD, the Romano-Gallic poet and writer Sidonius considered knowledge of the defeat at Carrhae to be important as the following make clear. The first is from the panygeric of Anthemius:

> yet that possession was bought by me with the blood of Crassus; at Carrhae I paid down the price; nor did I remain unavenged[372]

This from a letter to Felix, bishop of Ticinum:

> he takes no account of the ruinous attempt on the Euphrates and of Carrhae drenched with the blood of the Crassi[373]

And this from his panegyric of Avitus:

> insomuch as the Parthian Sapor freely restored my standards and laying aside his Royal tiara, wept for the deaths of the Crassi[374]

Thus, even five hundred years after Carrhae, educated men showed off their knowledge of the battle and its results, assuming, or should we say challenging, their audience to be aware of the battle. Even when the Western Empire had fallen (AD 476) the memory of Carrhae was kept alive by the Byzantine historians of the Eastern Roman Empire. As late as the ninth century, George Synkellos, a historical chronicler, had an entry as follows:

> At that time, Crassus succeeded Gabinius and acquired control of the Syrian government. In launching an invasion against the Parthians, he took it upon himself to loot all the furnishings of the Jewish temple, including the 2,000 talents that Pompey had left untouched. Now when he crossed the Euphrates River he was killed with the main body of his army, Crassus' quaestor Cassius rescuing the survivors and with great carnage driving out the Persians [Parthians] from the whole of Syria. Cassius then moved with haste against Judea, took 30,000 hostages, captured Tarichaiai, and killed Pisailos for collaborating with the partisans of Aristoboulos and his son in their insurrection against Hyrkanos and Antipatros.[375]

We can see that some eight hundred years later, the Battle of Carrhae was still resounding in the histories of Rome, long after the end of the seven hundred-year conflict that it had created. It is a testament to the importance of the battle and its consequences for the ancient world.

Appendix III

Sources for Parthian History

When dealing with the Parthians, we need to be fully aware of the extent of our ignorance on the subject. Despite the fact that the Parthian empire lasted for over 470 years, was one of the two great civilisations of the ancient world and spanned an area from Syria to India and Central Asia, we have a ridiculously small amount of surviving material about it. A brief survey of the sources will reveal how truly little we know about this fascinating civilisation.

Native Sources

The first and main point to note is the almost total absence of any surviving Parthian documents. Not only was the Parthian civilisation swept away by its successors, the Sassanid Persians, but they too were swept away by the Muslim invasions. This double blow has meant that virtually no literary material survives from Parthian sources. The only historical documents of any note from the Parthian period are the Babylonian astronomical records, which as well as recording astronomical data, record some of the historical actions of that particular year.[376] Even in fragmentary form they provide an invaluable record of the Parthian control of Mesopotamia in the period 141 to the 90s BC. They throw fresh light on Parthian command structures in the region, notably the use of four native generals mentioned in chapter two. Nevertheless despite these valuable insights, their narrow remit still leaves us in the dark about wider matters. This lack of native documents means that we are largely reliant upon non-Parthian sources, which leaves large gaps in Parthian internal history (such as their foundation) when these events do not impact upon the external world.

With a lack of written sources, our only remaining native sources come from coins and archaeology. As can be seen from the modern works on the subject, we have a considerable number of Parthian coins which survive and they can help us reconstruct the outline of a number of events, notably those surrounding the reigns of the various Parthian kings.[377] However, once again, they are limited in the scope of what they can tell us about the details of Parthian history. Other archaeological finds are another possible source of information, and notable digs have been carried out at Nisa and Dura-Europus.[378] However, given the relatively low awareness of the Parthian civilisation, especially in comparison to the earlier Achaemenid Persian empire, and the fact that a number of these sites are all in politically sensitive parts of the world (the former Soviet Union, Iran, Iraq and Afghanistan), then we can understand why work on Parthian sites is not as advanced as on those relating to other periods or peoples. Nevertheless, given the poor state of our other sources, archaeology remains the best hope we have for gaining more knowledge on the Parthians.

Surviving Graeco-Roman Sources on Parthian History

As noted above, we are largely reliant on non-Parthian sources for the history of Parthia. As with the previous section on sources for the Battle of Carrhae, we have to acknowledge the difference between those sources that survive and those that were in circulation in the ancient world. Throughout this analysis of the First Romano-Parthian War we have encountered a number of sources which contain sections on Parthian history. Although there were a number of works by Greeks or Romans devoted to Parthian history, none of them survive, which means that we are reliant on later works which incorporate some of their material.

Polybius, *Histories* (second century BC)

As well as being our earliest surviving source for Roman history, Polybius is our earliest source for Parthian history, with five chapters of book ten (numbers 27–31) devoted to the Eastern campaigns of Antiochus III against the Parthians, a campaign that resulted in the temporary loss of Parthian independence. These chapters are intact in themselves, but we do not have the conclusion of the campaign. Nevertheless, they were written less than seventy years after the events occurred and were likely to have been based on eye-witness accounts.[379] Not only does this shed light on the campaign itself, but shows that the Parthians were being dealt with by the Hellenistic historians (who again, unfortunately, do not survive). Furthermore, he shows us that they had entered the consciousness of Rome, well before the two empires eventually clashed, in which he is unique amongst our surviving sources.

Diodorus, *Library of History* (mid- to late first century BC)

Coming a century after Polybius, we have the history of Diodorus. He was a Greek Sicilian writing in the late Republic and composed a 'world' history, which covered a number of different ancient races, from the earliest times to around 60 BC. He made extensive use of a range of Hellenistic historians, all of which are now lost, and has a number of references to early Parthian history, notably their role in the wars of succession following the death of Alexander the Great. Had more of his work survived then we undoubtedly have more detail on Parthian history. By the time he wrote his histories, Rome and Parthia would have just clashed, though the ancient world would not have yet been partitioned between the two.

Isidore of Charax, *Parthian Stations* (late first century BC)

The 'Parthian Stations' of Isidore was a short geographical work which detailed the trade routes across the Parthian Empire. Starting in Syria, the work lists the various towns and cities along the way until it reaches the Parthian eastern borders of China and India. The work only survives in fragments, but is a fascinating account of the origins of the Silk Road.[380]

Strabo, *Geography* (early first century AD)

As we have seen throughout this work, the *Geography* of Strabo provides us with a number of sections on Parthian history, geography and society, especially in book eleven. It is unfortunate that Strabo's other works do not survive, as at one point he states:

But since I have said much about the Parthians in the sixth book of my historical Sketches and in the second book of my History of events after Polybius, I shall omit discussion of that subject there, lest I may seem to be repeating what I have already said.[381]

If Strabo had shown less consideration for his reader and actually repeated himself, we would know so much more about Parthia. For his Parthian sections, he referred to the works of Apollodorus and Poseidonius (see below).

Pliny, *Natural History* (first century AD)

The encyclopaedic *Natural History* of Pliny preserves a number of notes on aspects of Parthian history, geography and culture. He was a Roman senator who wrote a wide ranging work on various aspects of the ancient world. The sources of his Parthian references are unknown. He was killed whilst observing the famous eruption of Mount Vesuvius in AD 79.

Josephus, *Antiquities of the Jews* and *History of the Jewish War* (first century AD)

Whilst technically Josephus was Jewish, we can place his works in the Graeco-Roman category, as Judea was rarely independent in this period, but fell under either Seleucid or Roman suzerainty. Josephus has a few references to the Parthians in his work and in this respect he is part of a wider Jewish tradition. The cities of Mesopotamia contained a large Jewish population, who had been uprooted from Judea by the Seleucids, due to their various rebellions, and settled elsewhere. When the Parthians took Mesopotamia from the Seleucids, the various Jewish communities maintained their links with Judea, which on occasion were exploited by the Parthians, as we saw during the First Romano-Parthian war. Thus, many Jewish works in this period would have had access to information about the Parthians.

Appian, *Syrian Wars* (second century AD)

Appian's *Syrian Wars* provides us with a few snippets of early Parthian history, but has little detail. This is most probably due to his desire to keep them aside for his work on Parthian history (which, if ever written, does not survive).

Justin's epitome of Pompeius Trogus (third century AD)

Justin's epitome of the works of Pompeius Trogus (see below), though brief, provides us with our best source for Parthian history as a whole. His narrative covers the whole period from the foundation to the First Roman-Parthian War and beyond; his books on Parthian history (41 and 42) form an indispensable starting point for the subject.

Eusebius and Jerome, chronicles (fourth century AD)

The chronicles of Eusebius and Jerome, both of whom were fourth century AD Christian chroniclers, provide us with some interesting nuggets of information concerning Parthia (which by then no longer existed). Eusebius is especially good at detailing the clashes between the Parthians and the Seleucids over Mesopotamia in the second century BC, whilst Jerome confirms the date of the foundation of the Arsacid dynasty to be 248 BC.[382]

Byzantine Sources

As we have seen previously, there are a number of Byzantine histories and chronicles which preserve fragments of earlier works on Parthian history, notably Arrian's *Parthica*. The Byzantine histories are on the whole neglected by ancient historians, but as shown with Synkellos, they can preserve accounts which throw fresh light on the subject. Other goods works include those by Zosimus and Photius.

Lost Graeco-Roman Works on Parthian History

We know that there were a number of specialist histories written about Parthia, which now no longer exist, but were available to the later writers.

Hellenistic Historians

Though we have no clearly-attested fragments it is clear, given the role that Parthia played in eroding the power of the Seleucid empire (including the capture of two kings), that there must have been a significant amount of material written on the Parthians in late-third and second century BC histories. We can see this in Polybius' account of the Seleucid–Parthian War of c.210 BC, taken from an unnamed Hellenistic source.[383]

Apollodorus, *Parthica* (late second or early first century BC)

Apollodorus was a Greek historian who lived in the Mesopotamian city of Artemita. We are told that he wrote a history of the Parthians in four volumes.[384] Apart from one fragment the work is totally lost, although we believe that it is the source for virtually all of Strabo's passages on Parthia. His work would have been an invaluable source, given the fact that it was written by someone who lived under Parthian rule and would therefore have avoided any pro-Roman bias. It has also been suggested that his work informed the histories of Pompeius Trogus (see below), though this is disputed.[385]

Poseidonius, *Histories* (early first century BC)

Poseidonius was a philosopher, geographer and historian from Rhodes. He was ambassador to Rome in the late Republican period and counted a number of the leading Romans, such as Pompey and Cicero, amongst his friends. He wrote a history of Rome from 146–88 BC in fifty-two books, continuing from where Polybius left off, which heavily influenced Diodorus. Strabo quotes him on the composition of the Parthian Council of Elders, so we can assume that he had a detailed account of the Parthians in his work at some point.[386] Sadly, nothing of substance remains of his work.

Pompeius Trogus, *Historiae Philippicae* (late first century BC/early 1st century AD)

Pompeius Trogus was a contemporary of Livy who wrote a world history from the time of the Assyrians to AD 9, in forty-four books. The scope of his work complimented that of Livy and his focus was on the East and away from domestic Roman politics. Given that the epitome of this work made by Justin in the third century (see above) is our best source for Parthian history, we can only wonder what level of detail we would get from the original. His forty-first and forty-second books dealt with Parthian history and would have given us a detailed narrative from the foundation onwards.

Arrian, *Parthica* (second century AD)

Arrian was a Graeco-Roman writer most famous for his work on Alexander the Great (which is our best surviving source for him). He also composed a work on the Fourth Romano-Parthian War, under Emperor Trajan, in seventeen books.[387] Arrian's work digressed onto the subject of Parthian origins and was much used by Byzantine writers (Zosimus, Synkellos and Photius). We do not know what other earlier Parthian topics he touched on, but again little of this work survives.

Appian's history of the Parthian Wars (2nd century A.D.)

As we have seen, on several occasions throughout his other works Appian stated that he would write a history of the Parthian wars.[388] Unfortunately, no trace of it remains and many scholars have wondered, given the survival of his other material and the total absence of any of his Parthian fragments, whether it ever existed. We know that he certainly planned it, but whether he ever got around to writing it is another question.

Later histories of Romano-Parthian wars

As noted in appendix two, we know that every Romano-Parthian war was accompanied by a flurry of literary works (not unlike the situation today). Although we have no clear details, it is possible that a number of them touched on Parthian history, though it is likely that if they did, then they would have used one of the above works.

We can clearly see that we only possess a small percentage of the works that were written on Parthian history by Greek and Roman authors.

Histories from other regions

Given the size of the Parthian Empire, it is not surprising that they were written about by a number of the other great ancient civilisations. We have a few reports from Chinese sources referring to the Parthians which date from the late second and early first century BC, when the Parthian and Han Empires established the diplomatic and trade relations which led to the creation of the Silk Road.

This was written around 91 BC.

> When the first embassy was sent from China to An-his [Ar-sak or Parthia] the King
> of Parthia ordered 20,000 cavalry to meet them on the eastern frontier . . . After the
> Chinese embassy had returned they sent forth an embassy to follow the Chinese
> embassy, to come and see the extent and greatness of the Chinese empire. They
> offered to the Chinese court large birds' eggs and jugglers from Li-kan [Petra].[389]

These comments tell us a little about the extent and governance of Parthian territory.

> The king of the country of Parthia rules at the city of P'an-tu [Hecatompylus].
> The country is not subject to a tu-hu [Chinese governor].
> They also make coins of silver, which have the king's face on the obverse and the
> face of his consort on the reverse. When the king dies, they cast new coins.[390]

Finally, the following comments were written around AD 90:

> Several hundred small and large cities are subject to it, and the country is several
> thousand li in extent; this is a very large country.
> When the Emperor Wu-ti first sent an embassy to Parthia, the King ordered a
> general to meet him on the eastern front with 20,000 cavalry. The eastern frontier
> was several thousand li distant from the King's capital.[391].

Clearly the Chinese were greatly impressed by the size and might of the Parthian empire. On
the other hand, from the Chinese perspective the Parthians living to their west were naturally not as civilised as themselves. Nevertheless, the two powers traded and exchanged
diplomatic courtesies and had a common enemy in the barbarians from Central Asia (be they
Scythian, Saka or Hun), who periodically threatened to overrun the northern borders of both
empires.

As well Chinese sources, there are various Armenian, Indian and Arabic historical traditions that touch on Parthian history and that are generally ignored by modern Western
historians. We lack a comprehensive survey of this material, which shows, once again, the
problems faced with studying Parthian history. Whilst the empires of Rome, Persia, China
and India have modern inheritors all too willing to associate themselves with a glorious
past and thus explore the various historical sources to the full, Parthia stands alone in this
respect; civilisation without a clear inheritor. The extent of our ignorance concerning the
Parthians is quite alarming. What we do know shows us a magnificent Eastern civilisation,
which for over four hundred years was one of the ancient world's great powers, and was the
equal of the might of Rome.

Appendix IV

King Lists

Kings of Parthia (c.247– 50 BC)

Exact dates for the majority of the Parthian kings are impossible to determine. The names in brackets are their real names before assuming the throne and the name Arsaces.

Arsaces I		c.247–211 BC
Arsaces II		c.211–191 BC
Arsaces III	(Priapatius)	c.191–176 BC
Arsaces IV	(Phraates I)	c.176–171 BC
Arsaces V	(Mithradates I)	c.171–138 BC
Arsaces VI	(Phraates II)	c.138–128 BC
Arsaces VII	(Artabanus I)	c.128–124 BC
Arsaces VIII	(Mithradates II)	c.123–88 BC
Arsaces IX	(Gotarzes I)	c.91–81 BC
Arsaces X	(Orodes I)	c.80–76 BC
Arsaces XI	(Sinatruces)	75–70 BC
Arsaces XII	(Phraates III)	69–58 BC
Arsaces XIII	(Mithradates III)	c.57–54 BC
Arsaces XIV	(Orodes II)	c.57–37 BC
Arsaces*	(Pacorus I)	c.50–38 BC

* There is no consensus over whether Pacorus actually became king and assumed the name Arsaces (but see Chapter 7). He has not here been given the numeral XV to avoid confusion as some Parthian king lists include him and some don't. The ones that don't have his brother (Phraates IV) as Arsaces XV.

Kings of Macedon (359–167 BC)

From the period when Macedon gained dominance over the states of Greece.

Philip II	359–336 BC	Pyrrhus	287–285 BC
Alexander III (The Great)	336–323 BC	Lysimachus	287–281 BC
Alexander IV	323–310 BC	Seleucus I	281 BC
Philip III	323–317 BC	Ptolemy	281–279 BC
Olympias	317–316 BC	Antigonus II	276–239 BC
Cassander	315–297 BC	Demetrius II	239–229 BC
Philip IV	297 BC	Antigonus III	229–221 BC
Alexander V	297–294 BC	Philip V	221–179 BC
Antipater I	297–294 BC	Perseus	179–167 BC
Demetrius I	294–288 BC		

Kingdom of Macedonia
abolished by Rome 167 BC

Seleucid Kings (c.311–64 BC)

From the foundation of the Seleucid empire, following the death of Alexander the Great.

Seleucus I	c.311–281 BC	Demetrius II (again)	129–125 BC
Antiochus I	281–261 BC	Cleopatra	126–123 BC
Antiochus II	261–246 BC	Antiochus VIII	126–96 BC
Seleucus II	246–226 BC	Seleucus V	126 BC
Seleucus III	226–223 BC	Antiochus IX	114–95 BC
Antiochus III (The Great)	223–187 BC	Seleucus VI	95 BC
Seleucus IV	187–175 BC	Antiochus X	95 BC
Antiochus IV	175–164 BC	Demetrius III	95–88 BC
Antiochus V	164–162 BC	Antiochus XI	95 BC
Demetrius I	162–150 BC	Philip I	95–83 BC
Alexander I	150–145 BC	Antiochus XII	87 BC
Demetrius II	145–139 BC	Philip II	83 BC
Antiochus VI	145–142 BC	Tigranes (King of Armenia)	83–69 BC
Antiochus VII	138–129 BC	Antiochus XIII	69–64 BC

Seleucid empire annexed by Rome 64 BC

Notes and References

Chapter One

1 This is the traditional date, as used in the Varronian system, but the Romans themselves had a number of differing dates for their city's foundation, spread throughout the eighth century BC and beyond.

2 Books 2 –10 cover the Republic from its foundation down to 292 BC. Books 11–19 are lost.

3 A good introduction to the problems of early Roman history and its sources can be found in T Cornell, *The Beginnings of Rome: Italy and Rome from the Bronze Age to the Punic War* (London, 1995).

4 Books 20–45, which cover the period from 218 to 167 BC

5 His work principally covers the period from 220 –168 BC, but also encompasses the period 264–146 BC and is our finest first-hand account.

6 In particular, see the lives of Flamininus, Aemilius Paulus, Marius, Sulla, Sertorius, Lucullus, Pompey, Crassus and Caesar.

7 Again this date is open to question. There are numerous works on this subject, but again see Cornell, *Beginnings of Rome*.

8 There were several different assemblies, with differing functions and membership. The two main ones were the *Comitia Centuriata*, which was based on the centuries and the *Comitia Tributa*, based on the tribes. Again for a clear understanding of the differences, see T Cornell, *Beginnings of Rome*.

9 Notably at the Battle of Cannae in 216 BC. See G Daly, *Cannae* (London, 2002). This is also an excellent reference work on the Roman army.

10 For a fuller account of the Pyrrhic Wars, see P. Garoufalias, *Pyrrhus, King of Epirus* (London, 1979).

11 Plutarch wrote a biography of him, which still survives.

12 Plutarch, *Pyrrhus*, 21.9–10.

13 The battles of the Ticinus and Trebia rivers both took place in 218 BC, Lake Trasimene in 217 BC and Cannae in August 216 BC. Polybius (3.117.2–4) gives casualties of 70,000, though this is a high estimate. Livy (22.49.15) has just under 50,000 men killed.

14 Once again this date is open to question, see T Cornell, *Beginnings of Rome*.

15 It must be pointed out that this 'alliance' has been called into question by many modern scholars. See D Magie, 'The "Agreement" between Philip V and Antiochus III for the Partition of the Egyptian Empire', *Journal of Roman Studies*, 29 (1939), pp 32–44; and R Errington, 'The Alleged Syro-Macedonian Pact and the Origins of the Second Macedonian War', *Athenaeum*, 49 (1971), pp 336–354.

16 This concept was developed by a number of modern historians of the period. There are too many works to reference properly here (see the bibliography), but a good synthesis of their views can be found in E Gruen (ed.), *Imperialism in the Roman Republic* (New York, 1970). More recently this theory was been challenged by counter arguments that place greater emphasis on the economic and social imperatives. See W Harris, *War and*

Imperialism in Republican Rome (Oxford, 1979) and W Harris (ed.), *The Imperialism of Mid-Republican Rome* (Rome, 1984).

17 See S Mandell, 'The Isthmian Proclamation and the Early Stages of Roman Imperialism in the Near East', *Classical Bulletin*, 65 (1989), pp 89–94.

18 See E Badian, *Titus Quinctius Flamininus; Philhellenism and Realpolitik* (Cincinnati, 1970).

19 The Jugurthan War of 112 to 106 BC. Sallust wrote a history of this war, which still survives.

20 These barbarian invasions were not ended until the battles of Aquae Sextiae (102 BC) and Vercellae (101 BC), both won by the Roman general, Gaius Marius.

21 These being the turbulent tribunate's of Tiberius Gracchus in 133 BC and his brother Gaius Gracchus in 123 BC. See Plutarch's biographies of the two men.

22 For a more detailed explanation see E Gabba, *Republican Rome, The Army and the Allies* (Berkeley, 1976) and R Smith, *Service in the Post Marian Army* (Manchester, 1958).

23 Appian wrote a history of the Mithridatic Wars, which still survives. At the time of writing there is only one modern work on Mithridates in English: B McGing, *The Foreign Policy of Mithridates VI Eupator King of Pontus* (Leiden, 1986).

24 These being Lucius Magius and Lucius Fannius, former officers of Fimbria who joined Mithridates rather than ally with Sulla. They conducted negotiations between Sertorius and Mithridates, which resulted in another Roman officer (Marcus Marius) being sent by Sertorius to aid Mithridates in his fight against Rome (Plutarch, *Sertorius*, 23–24).

25 As reported by Appian, *Mithridatic Wars*, 102 and 109; Plutarch, *Pompey*, 41; Dio, 37.11.1; and Florus, 1.40.15.

Chapter Two

26 Though we can only estimate the empire's northern borders.

27 In the East they were know as the Askhanians or Asghanians. They themselves most commonly used the royal title of Arsacids.

28 It is estimated that the revolt took place in 521 BC and the rebels were crushed in battle. We are informed of this from an inscription from Behistun; see N Debeviose, *A Political History of Parthia* (Chicago, 1938), pp 4–5.

29 Herodotus (*Histories*,7.66) records the Parthians in his breakdown of the army of Xerxes, saying that they were commanded by an Artabazus, son of Pharnaces. Aeschylus (*Persians* 995) preserves the name of an Arsaces (the name of the first Parthian king) who was killed fighting in the Persian invasion of Greece (480–479 BC), though this is likely to have been a common name and does not infer a direct connection.

30 Arrian, *Anabasis*, 3.11.4; and Curtius, *History of Alexander*, 4.12.11.

31 Diodorus, 18.3.3; Justin, *Epitome*, 41.4, however, states that Parthia was given to a Macedonian ally named Stasanor.

32 Diodorus,18.39.6.

33 *Ibid*,., 19.14.1.

34 Diodorus, 19.29.2; Justin, 41.4, states that they were also in the opposing army of Eumenes.

35 See Appendix III for a fuller account of these sources and other minor ones which mention these events.

36 See J Wolski, 'The Decay of the Iranian Empire of the Seleuicids and the Chronology of the Parthian Beginnings', *Berytus*, 12 (1956/8), pp 35–52; and J Neusner, 'Parthian Political Ideology, *Iranica Antiqua*, 3 (1963), pp 40–59.

37 Strabo, *Geography*, 11.9.2 .The Ochus is the modern River Atrek, east of the Caspian Sea.

38 Strabo, *Geography*, 11.9.2.

39 Strabo, *Geography*, 11.9.3.

40 Justin, *Epitome of The Philippic History of Pompeius Trogus*, 41.1.

41 If you assume that Justin meant Gaius Regulus instead of Marcus. See T Broughton, *Magistrates of the Roman Republic: Volume 1* (1952) , p 213 and J Lerner, *The Impact of Seleucid Decline on theEastern Iranian Plateau* (Stuttgart, 1999), p 15 for a fuller explanation.

42 Justin, *Epitome*, 41.4.

43 Justin, *Epitome*, 41.4.

44 Justin, *Epitome*, 41.5.

45 Zosimus, *History*, Translated by Green and Chaplin (1814).

46 See W Adler & P Tuffin, *The Chronography of George Synkellos. A Byzantine Chronicle of Universal History from the Creation* (Oxford, 2002), p 412.

47 Translated by J H Freese (1920).

48 Quintus Curtius Rufus, *History of Alexander*, 4.12.11.

49 Appian, *Syrian Wars*, 65.

50 Dio Cassius, *History of Rome*, 40.14.3.

51 Herodian, *History of Rome*, 6.2.7.

52 For an example of this, see the surviving Babylonian astronomical charts in A Sachs & H Hunger, *Astronomical Diaries and Related Texts from Babylonia Volume III* (Vienna, 1996).

53 The most recent ones are J Wolski, 'The Decay of the Iranian Empire', pp 35–52 and J Lerner, *The Impact of Seleucid Decline*, ch 1.

54 J Lerner, *The Impact of Seleucid Decline*, p 17.

55 Pliny, *Natural History*, 6.49.

56 J Lerner, *The Impact of Seleucid Decline*, p 18.

57 Isidore of Charax, *Parthian Stations*,11.

58 J Neusner, *Parthian Political Ideology*, p 47, argues persuasively that this was a later adoption.

59 This has been challenged recently by A Invernizzi, 'Parthian Nisa, New Lines of Research', in J Wiesehöfer (ed.), *Das Partherreich und seine Zeugnisse* (Stuttgart, 1998), pp 45–59. He argues that the city was actually founded by Mithradates I.

60 Synkellos, *Chronography*.

61 Justin, *Epitome*, 41.5.

62 J Neusner, '*Parthian Political Ideology*', p 50.

63 Justin, *Epitome*, 41.4.8.

64 Strabo, *Geography*, 11.8.8.

65 Justin, *Epitome*, 41.4.9.

66 Athenaeus, *Deipnosophistae*, 83, referring to Poseidonius, *History*, 16. See J Lerner, *Impact of Seleucid Decline*, pp 35–37.

67 For a fuller account of this process see J Lerner, *Impact of Seleucid Decline*, ch 2.

68 Justin, *Epitome*, 41.5.

69 F Walbank, *A Historical Commentary on Polybius Volume II*, p 238, argues that Pliny (*Natural History*, 6.113) infers that the Parthians had annexed further Seleucid territories in the intervening period, namely the regions of Choarene and Comisene.

70. See J Wolski, 'L'Historicité D'Arsace Ier', *Historia*, 8 (1959), pp 22–238; and Walbank, *Historical Commentary on Polybius II*, pp 235–236.

71 Possibly caused by the murder of Diodotus II by a usurper, Euthydemus, circa 221 BC.

72 Justin, *Epitome*, 41.5.7.

73 Polybius, *Histories*, 10.27–31, covers the campaign in some detail.

74 For a more in depth analysis of this period, see J Lerner, *Seleucid Decline*, ch 3.
75 *Ibid*, pp 46–47; though we cannot find this view in Justin, who merely states that Priapatius succeeded Arsaces II and ruled for 15 years.
76 These events are recorded in contemporary Babylonian astronomical records, fragments of which survive today. See Sachs & Hunger, *Astronomical Diaries, Volume III*.
77 All taken from the Babylonian astronomical records, see Sachs & Hunger, *Astronomical Diaries Volume III*.
78 Diodorus, 34.19.
79 See Sachs & Hunger, *Astronomical Diaries Volume III*; also see R Van der Spek, 'New Evidence from the Babylonian Astronomical Diaries Concerning Seleucid and Arsacid History', *Archiv für Orientforschung*, 44–45 (1997–8), p 171.
80 Justin, *Epitome*, 38.10.
81 Josephus, *Antiquities of the Jews*, 13. 251–252, quoting Nicholas of Damascus, fragment 92.
82 Diodorus, 34.19.
83 Justin, *Epitome*, 42.1.1–2.
84 Justin, *Epitome*, 42.2.2.
85 Diodorus, 34.21; Justin, *Epitome*, 42.1.3.
86 The evidence for this is both numismatic, see E Newell, *Mithradates of Parthia and Hypaosines of Characene* (New York, 1925), and from the Babylonian texts, see Sachs & Hunger, *Astronomical Diaries Volume III*.
87 Justin, *Epitome*, 42.2.4–5.
88 Strabo, *Geography*, 11.14.15.
89 Plutarch, *Sulla*, 5.5.
90 Joesphus. *Antiquities*, 13.384–386.
91 Isidore of Charax. *Parthian Stations*, 6.

Chapter Three

92 In 205, 171, 168, 131, 97 and 95 BC.
93 See R Syme, 'The Sons of Crassus', *Latomus*, 39 (1980), pp 403–408.
94 Plutarch, *Crassus*, 3.2.
95 *Ibid*, 4.2.
96 This modern name is from the Latin for allies: *socii*. Hence the war against the *socii* or the Social War.
97 Plutarch, *Crassus*, 4.1.
98 *Ibid*, 5.1–4.
99 *Ibid*, 6.1.
100 For a fuller account, see Plutarch, *Pompey*, 16–20; and Appian, *Civil Wars*, 107–115.
101 His traditional date of birth was 115 whilst Pompey was born in 106 BC.
102 Plutarch, *Crassus*, 7.9.
103 *Ibid*, 9.3.
104 Plutarch, *Crassus*, 9.2, states that he was Claudius Glaber, whilst Appian, *Civil Wars*, 1.116, names him as Varinius. For a full discussion, see T Broughton, *Magistrates* II, p 109 and 115.
105 *Ibid*.
106 When the prestigious office of censor was re-launched during Crassus' consulship of 70 BC, both men were given the job, despite the shame of their defeat to Spartacus.

107 Plutarch, *Crassus*, 10.1.
108 Appian, *Civil Wars*, 1.121.
109 Velleius, 2.30.6.
110 This can be found throughout the ancient sources, especially Plutarch, *Crassus*, 12.2–3, and *Pompey*, 23.1–2.
111 *Ibid*.
112 For a fuller discussion see A Ward, 'Cicero's Fight Against Crassus and Caesar in 65 and 63 BC', *Historia*, 21 (1972), pp 244–258.
113 Sallust produced a work on the Catilinarian Conspiracy which still survives. There are a number of modern works on it also; a good one being E Hardy, 'The Catilinarian Conspiracy in its Context; a Re-Study of the Evidence', *Journal of Roman Studies*, 7 (1917), pp153–228.
114 Suetonius, *Julius Caesar*, 9.
115 Though a number of later sources such as Plutarch, *Crassus*, 13, and Dio, 39.10.3, claim to have made use of it. Primarily it accused both Crassus and Caesar of being behind the Catilinarian Conspiracies.
116 See Plutarch, *Pompey*, 43.2, for Crassus leaving Rome; and Cicero, *Pro Flacco*, 32, which records him turning up in the East.
117 Appian, *Civil Wars*, 2.9; also see Plutarch, *Crassus*, 14.1, and *Pompey*, 47.1.
118 Cicero, *Letters to Atticus*, 2.25.1.
119 *Ibid*, 2.22.5.
120 Cicero, *Letters to Friends*, 14.2.2.
121 Cicero, *Letters to Quintus*, 2.3.3–4.
122 Cicero, *Letters to Friends*, 1.9.9.
123 Appian, *Civil Wars*, 2.17; Plutarch, *Pompey*, 51.3 and *Caesar*, 21.2. Also see See E Gruen, 'Pompey, the Roman Aristocracy and the Conference at Luca', *Historia*, 18 (1969), pp 71–108; and C Luibheid, 'The Luca Conference', *Classical Philology*, 65 (1970), pp 88–94.

Chapter Four

124 Valerius Maximus, *Memorable Sayings*, 1.6.11; Florus 1.46.2
125 This can be seen by Polybius' inclusion of the Seleucid-Parthian War in his *Histories* (10.27–31).
126 Strabo, *Geography*, 11.14.15.
127 An excellent example of this is A Keaveney, 'Roman Treaties with Parthia circa 95–64 BC', *American Journal of Philology*, 102 (1981), pp 195–212. He argues from a wholly Romano-centric view that there was a treaty between Rome and Parthia, negotiated by Sulla.
128 This being the so-called Parthian 'Dark Age' between c. 91–70 BC when we lose any clear narrative of events in Parthia, but know that there were a number of overlapping royal reigns.
129 The Second Mithridatic War being a minor affair between Mithridates and the Roman general Lucius Licinius Murena (83–81 BC), which ended in a stalemate.
130 Sallust, *Histories*, 4.67, preserves what he claims is a letter from Mithridates VI to Sinatruces, concerning the formation of an anti-Roman alliance against Rome.
131 Plutarch, *Lucullus*, 30.1.
132 *Ibid*, 30.2.

133 See Plutarch, *Pompey*, 33.6; Dio, 36.45.3; *Periochae of Livy*, 100. Also see A Keaveney, 'Roman Treaties with Parthia', pp 202–212, though again he makes long-term conclusions from what was only a short-term alliance.
134 *Ibid.*
135 *Ibid.*
136 Dio, 37.5.4.
137 Dio, 37.5.5.
138 Dio, 37.6.4–7.2; Plutarch, *Pompey*, 28.2.
139 Cicero, *De Domo sua*, 23 and 55; *Periochae of Livy*, 105; Appian, *Syrian Wars*, 51.
140 Dio, 39.56.2–3.
141 Strabo, *Geography*, 12.3.34, states that the war was opposed by the Senate.
142 For a more machiavellian interpretation of this division, see chapter eight.

Chapter Five

143 Plutarch, *Crassus*, 16.2.
144 See A Keaveney, 'The King and the War-Lords: Romano-Parthian Relations Circa 64–53 BC', *American Journal of Philology*, 103 (1982), pp 412–428.
145 *Ibid.*
146 Pliny, *Natural History*, 2.147; Horace, *Odes*, 3.5.10.
147 Plutarch, *Crassus*, 21.2.
148 Cicero, *Letters to Friends*, 1.9.20.
149 Plutarch, *Crassus*, 16.5–6.
150 Cicero, *De Divinatione*, 1.29.
151 Cicero, *De Domo Sua*, 123.
152 Plutarch, *Comparison of Nicias and Crassus*, 2.5.
153 Cicero, *De Divinatione*, 2.84.
154 Cicero. *Letters to Friends*, 1.9.20.
155 *Ibid*, 5.8.1.
156 Plutarch, *Crassus*, 17.1–2.
157 Dio, 39.60.4.
158 Plutarch, *Crassus*, 17.4.
159 Plutarch, *Crassus*, 17.4 ; Dio.40.13.4.
160 Josephus, *Jewish War* 8.8 and *Jewish Antiquities*, 7.1.
161 Plutarch, *Crassus*, 17.5.
162 We only know the name of one other family, the Karen.
163 This has led some scholars to talk of there being two Parthian Kingdoms, one in the west ruled by the Arsacids and one in the east ruled by the Suren. See W Tarn, *The Greeks in Bactria and India* (Cambridge, 1938), pp 204, 224 and 344–345.
164 Plutarch, *Crassus*, 21.6.
165 Plutarch, *Crassus*, 21.7.
166 It has also been argued that this occurred in 55 BC, see A Keaveney, 'The King and the Warlords', p 412. The exact chronology is impossible to determine.
167 Plutarch, *Crassus*, 21.7.
168 Plutarch. *Crassus*, 28.1–2; Dio 40.16.1–3.
169 Plutarch, *Crassus*,18.2.
170 *Ibid*, 19.3.

171 *Ibid*, 22.2–3.
172 Dio, 17.3.
173 See D Kennedy, 'Ancient Sources for Zeugma', in *The Twin Towns of Zeugma on the Euphrates* (Michigan, 1998), pp 139–162.
174 See Isidore of Charax, *Parthian Stations*, 1.
175 M Brosius, *The Persians* (London, 2006), p 95.
176 Festus, 9.17.1, a fourth-century compilation, introduces a new element, and has Crassus being guided across the Euphrates at Zeugma, by a Parthian deserter named Mazzarus.
177 Plutarch, *Crassus*, 19.3–6.
178 Dio, 40.18.1–19.4.
179 Plutarch, *Crassus*, 20.1.
180 *Ibid*, 21.1–3 & 22.4–6.
181 *Ibid*; and Dio, 40.20.1. Also see Florus, 1.46.6, which tells us that he was a Syrian named Mazaras.
182 Plutarch, *Crassus*, 22.4–6.
183 *Ibid*, 22.1–2.
184 *Ibid*, 22.6. Dio has him with the Roman army until the Battle.
185 Plutarch, *Crassus*, 18.3.
186 This was the plan whereby Germany, faced with two enemies on opposite borders (France and Russia), intended to attack France first, knocking them out of the war before turning east to face the Russian army.

Chapter Six

187 Appian, *Civil Wars*, 2.18.
188 Plutarch, *Crassus*, 20.1.
189 For the late Republic, numbers of soldiers in a legion could vary. The only hard and fast rule was that a legion should be composed of ten cohorts. A cohort should have been composed of six centuries, and a century (despite the name) was usually around eighty men. However these guidelines could vary depending upon circumstance.
190 Florus, who compiled a second century epitome of Roman history, puts the total figure at eleven legions, some 55,000 men, but makes no mention of any auxiliary forces (1.46.2). His source is unknown, but he did use the now-lost works of Livy for much of his own work.
191 Plutarch, *Crassus*, 25.2.
192 *Ibid*, 25.7.
193 Cicero, *Letters to Friends*, 13.16.
194 Cicero, *Brutus*, 282.
195 Caesar, *Gallic War*, 3.7–9, 3.11 & 3.20–27.
196 For his career and arguments arising out of it, see G. Sumner, *The Orators in Cicero's Brutus* (Toronto, 1973), pp 149–150.
197 Dio, 40.15.
198 Justin, 41.2.
199 Justin, 41.2.
200 Justin, 41.2.
201 Lucian, *On the Writing of History*, 29.
202 Plutarch, *Crassus*, 25.1.

203 N Debeviose, *Political History of Parthia*, p 83, takes this line. A Sherwin-White, *Roman Foreign Policy in the East 168 BC –AD 1* (London, 1984), p 287 mentions this, but takes it no further.

204 Plutarch, *Crassus*, 18.3.

205 *Ibid*, 22.6.

206 Dio, 40.22.1.

207 *Ibid*, 40.22.3.

208 Dio, 30.23.1.

209 Dio, 40.24.1–2.

210 Dio, 40.21.2, uses the phrase 'uneven grounds and wooded' (ἡ γάρ χώρα ἀνώμαλός τέ πηι ἥν).

211 Plutarch. *Crassus*, 23.2.

212 Plutarch, *Crassus*, 23.6.

213 *Ibid*, 23.5.

214 *Ibid*, 23.3–4.

215 Each cohort consisted of six centuries of men. Each century, despite the name, consisted on average of eighty men. Thus a cohort would be 480 men, if the army was at full strength.

216 *Plutarch, Crassus*, 23.3–4.

217 *Ibid*, 23.4.

218 *Ibid*, 23.6–7.

219 *Ibid*, 24.5.

220 *Ibid*, 25.2.

221 *Ibid*, 25.3.

222 *Ibid*, 25.2.

223 *Ibid*, 25.7–8.

224 *Ibid*, 25.11.

225 *Ibid*, 25.12.

226 Those taken prisoner would have been able to report these events, if they survived their period of incarceration in Parthia to be returned to Rome in 20 BC (see appendix I).

227 Plutarch, *Crassus*, 26.1–3.

228 *Ibid*, 26.4–5.

229 *Ibid*, 26.5–6. Plutarch has Crassus make reference to the Roman victory over Tigranes at Tigranocerta in 69 BC and the defeat of Antiochus at Magnesia in 190 BC. 1000 ships is an overly pessimistic view of Roman naval losses in the First Punic War.

230 Plutarch, *Crassus*. 27.2.

231 *Ibid*, 21.1.

232 *Ibid*, 22.5–6.

233 *Ibid*, 27.5

234 Dio, 40. 25.1.

235 *Crassus*, 27.5–6.

236 The estimate of 4,000 is from Plutarch, *Crassus*, 28.1.

237 *Ibid*, 27.6–8

238 The story can be found in Plutarch *Crassus*, 28.1–2, and was repeated in Orosius, 6.13.3, in the fifth century AD.

239 Plutarch, *Crassus*, 28.2.

240 *Ibid*, 28.3–4.

241 *Ibid*, 29.3–6.

242 *Ibid*, 29.4–5.

243 Dio, 40.25.4–5.

244 *Ibid*.

245 Plutarch, *Crassus*, 30.2.

246 Dio, 41.26.2.

247 Plutarch, *Crassus*, 30.3.

248 Plutarch, *Crassus*, 30.4–5; Polyaenus, another second-century writer, also reports that Crassus did not believe the offer to be genuine, but was persuaded by his soldiers, in *Stratagems*, 7.41.

249 Plutarch, *Crassus*, 30.5.

250 *Ibid*, 31.2.

251 Plutarch, *Crassus*, 31.5, favours the first, whilst Polyaenus, *Stratagems*, 7.41, favours the second.

252 Plutarch, *Crassus*. 31.7, Dio. 40.27.4

253 Dio, 40.27.3, is often quoted as being the sole source for this, though the Florus epitome, 1.46.10, does also contain this story and dates to the second century AD (a century earlier). This story was actually used by Sigmund Freud, in his work *The Interpretation of Dreams*, ch 7, section C, 'Wish Fulfilment'. Unfortunately he made an error and believed that this was done by a Parthian queen. You can draw your own conclusions about Freud's patterns of thought here.

254 Valerius Maximus, *Memorable Sayings*, 1.6.11.

255 This led some later historians to state that Crassus had been captured after the Battle of Carrhae. For example: Jerome, *Chronicle*, 2nd Year of the 181st Olympiad.

256 Horace, *Epistles*, 1.18.56–57 and *Odes*, 4.15.6–8. They remained there until 20 BC when Augustus negotiated for their return.

257 Plutarch, *Crassus*, 33.3; and Polyaenus, *Stratagems*, 7.41.

258 For a fuller discussion of this episode, see D Braund, 'Dionysiac Tragedy in Plutarch's Crassus', *Classical Quarterly*, 43 (1993), pp. 468–474. He takes a negative view of the whole incident.

259 Plutarch, *Crassus*, 31.7; and Appian, *Civil Wars*, 2.18, though Appian believed that this was out of a total force of 100,000.

260 Appian, *Civil Wars*, 2.110, where he states that Caesar assembled a force of 16 legions and 10,000 cavalry.

Chapter Seven

261 Plutarch, *Cicero*, 36.1.

262 Josephus, *Jewish War*, 180.

263 See E Fantham, 'The Trials of Gabinius', *Historia*, 24 (1975), pp 425–443.

264 Though he did nominate his new father in law, Q Caecilius Metellus Pius Scipio Nasica, as his colleague for the final few months of the year.

265 Plutarch, *Pompey*, 55.1.

266 Cicero, *Letters to Friends*, 3.3.1.

267 The Cassii Longinii have recorded consulships in 171, 164, 127, 124, 107, 96 and 73 BC.

268 He was quaestor in 54 BC (the minimum age for this post being 29). He was later praetor in 44 and consul designate for 41 BC. Given that the minimum age for a praetorship was 39 and 42 for a consul, this would give us a date of birth of c. 83 BC.

269 Josephus, *Antiquities*, 1.119 and *Jewish War*, 1.180; Dio, 40.28.1, states 'the Parthians at this time did not advance beyond the Euphrates'.

270 Egnatius fled with 300 cavalry (Plutarch, *Crassus*, 27.6) and Cassius had at least 500 with him (Plutarch. *Crassus*, 29.5).

271 See Josephus, *Antiquities*, 1.119–122, and *Jewish War*, 1.1180–182, for the campaigns of 52 BC.

272 Cicero, *Letters to Atticus*, 5.9.1.

273 Dio, 40.28.3; Cicero *Letters to Atticus*, 5.20.3.

274 Cicero, *Letters to Atticus*, 5.11.4.

275 *Ibid*, 5.14.1.

276 *Ibid*, 5.15.1.

277 Cicero, *Letters to Friends*, 3.2.1.

278 Cicero, *Letters to Atticus*, 5.13.3.

279 *Ibid*, 5.15.1.

280 *Ibid*, 5.16.4.

281 Cicero, *Letters to Friends*, 15.3.1.

282 Cicero, *Letters to Atticus*, 5.18.1–2.

283 *Ibid*.

284 *Ibid*.

285 Cicero, *Letters to Friends*, 15.1.2–3. Tarcondimotus was a Cilician prince and a Roman ally, put on his throne by Pompey.

286 N Debeviose, *Political History of Parthia*, p 100.

287 Cicero, *Letters to Friends*, 15.1.2.

288 *Ibid*, 15.4.7.

289 *Ibid*, 15.1.3.

290 Cicero, *Letters to Atticus*, 5.20.3.

291 Dio, 40.29.1.

292 Dio, 40.29.3; Cicero, *Letters to Atticus*, 5.20.4. It is also recorded in the *Epitome of Livy*, 108.

293 This encounter is also briefly referred to by Velleius Paterculus, 2.46.4.

294 Cicero, *Letters to Friends*, 2.10.2.

295 *Ibid*, 8.10.1.

296 Cicero, *Letters to Atticus*, 5.21.2.

297 *Ibid*, 6.1.14.

298 Cicero, *Letters to Atticus*, 6.1.14.

299 If Artavasdes was feeding the Romans information by 50 BC then he could, and most probably would, have told them how Orodes had further humiliated Rome by using Crassus' head in a Greek play. This intimate source of information would validate the story as used by Plutarch and invalidate theories such as Braund's, which claim that the story was nothing more than a literary construct.

300 Cicero, *Letters to Atticus*, 5.21.2 and 6.1.14.

301 *Ibid*, 6.2.6.

302 *Ibid*, 6.3.2.

303 *Ibid*, 6.4.1.

304 *Ibid*, 6.6.3.

305 *Ibid*, 6.9.5.

306 Caesar, *Civil War*, 3.3.31.

307 *Epitome of Livy*, 108.

308 Cicero, *Letters to Atticus*, 7.2.8.

309 Justin, *Epitome*, 42.4.

310 Dio, 40.30.2.

311 Though it can be argued that in the first century Parthian monarchy, some heirs had coins minted whilst their fathers were still ruling; see A Nitkin, 'Early Parthian Coins from Margiana', in V Curtis (ed), *The Art and Archaeology of Ancient Persia (London, 1998), pp 14–18.*

312 There is an interesting section in a recent article that agrees with this view: M Gray-Fow, 'The Mental Breakdown of a Roman Senator: M. Calpurnius Bibulus', *Greece and Rome*, 37 (1990), pp 182–184. He further postulates that Egyptian authorities had Bibulus' sons murdered when they were there, possibly recruiting fresh troops. The indication is that Egypt was looking to ingratiate themselves with new Parthian over-lords in this period.

313 Cicero, *Letters to Atticus*, 6.1.14.

314 Despite the similarity in ages, Caesar's career placed him in a different political genera-tion to that of Crassus and Pompey.

Chapter Eight

315 By contrast, Rome only lost three legions in the Varus disaster in Germany in AD 9, with Carrhae therefore being twice the scale.

316 See F Romer, 'Gaius Caesar's Military Diplomacy in the East', *Transactions of the American Philological Association*, 109 (1979), pp 199–214.

317 Pompey was born in 106 BC, Caesar in 102 or 100 BC.

318 Plutarch, *Caesar*, 32.6 and *Pompey*, 60.4.

319 All of Plutarch's biographies were paired (one figure from Roman history with one from Greek). Naturally Caesar was paired with Alexander the Great. Nicias died in 413 BC, executed after leading a disastrous Athenian attempt to conquer the city of Syracuse in Sicily.

320 Plutarch, *Comparison of the Lives of Nicias and Crassus*, 4.4.

321 *Ibid*, 4.5.

322 He was quaestor in 53 BC, giving him a birth date of c. 82 BC given that the minimum age for the office was twenty-nine.

323 Justin, *Epitome*, 42.4.6, states that the Parthians were worried that Marcus Crassus would use his position with Caesar to seek revenge on the Parthians and it may be the case that he would have played a significant role during Caesar's abortive Parthian War.

324 Syme argues that he died at some point after 49 BC, but we are not told this at any point; he simply disappears off the record. See R Syme, 'The Sons of Crassus', p.407 and *Augustan Aristocracy* (Oxford, 1986), p 273.

325 Dio, 51.4.3.

326 Dio, 51.23.2–27.1.

327 His full name was Marcus Licinius Crass Frugi which indicated that he had been adopted from the Pisones Frugi family. See R Syme, 'Piso Frugi and Crassus Frugi', *Journal of Roman Studies*, 50 (1960), pp 12–20.

328 See Syme, *Augustan Aristocracy*, ch 20.

329 See O Bopearachchi, 'Indo-Parthians', in J Wiesehöfer (ed), *Das Partherreich und seine Zeugnisse* (Stuttgart, 1998), pp 389–495.

330 In all fairness the title of this work should really be *The Victory of Parthia*, rather than *The Defeat of Rome*.

331 Tacitus, *Annals*, 6.42.

332 *Cambridge History of Iran 2*, p 683.

333 This decision was a crucial one for the history of the region and meant that Mesopotamia

would never have the same heritage as the rest of the Mediterranean. It also kept Rome centred on the Mediterranean rather than looking out to the wider world, which might have happened if the Roman Empire had an outlet into the Indian Ocean from the Persian Gulf.

Appendix I

334 A recent article by K Harl, 'The Roman Experience in Iraq', *Journal of the Historical Society*, 7 (2007), pp 213–227, reviews this whole conflict.

335 Pliny, *Natural History*, 6.18.47.

336 Plutarch, *Life of Antony*, 37.2 and 40.4.

337 Horace, *Odes*, 3.5.5–12.

338 Florus, 2.20.4.

339 Plutarch, *Antony*, 46.2–47.2.

340 An interesting question is how many standards were lost during the Carrhae campaign. Although it might seem there should be seven, as there were seven legions, it has been noted that no source actually records either how many eagles Crassus lost (some may have made it back with the survivors) or exactly how many were returned to Augustus. In the 1880s a legionary eagle turned up in America, with its owner claiming that it was one of Crassus' lost eagles, though there is no evidence whatsoever to back up this bold assertion. See C Hoeing, 'A Roman Eagle in Rochester', *American Journal of Archaeology*, 29 (1925), pp 172–179.

341 The triumphal arch, which was in the Roman Forum, no longer exists, but there is also confusion between this arch and the one that Augustus had erected to celebrate his triumph at the Battle of Actium in 31 BC. It is possible that there was only one arch and that it was rebuilt or later added to in order to commemorate this event. For a full discussion of this subject, see J Rich, 'Augustus' Parthian Honours', *Papers of the British School of Rome*, 66 (1998), pp 71–128; and C Rose, 'The Parthians in Augustan Rome', *American Journal of Archaeology*, 109 (2005), pp 21–75.

342 Augustus, *Res Gestae*, 29.

343 He began his theory in two early articles: H Dubs, 'An Ancient Military Contact between Romans and the Chinese', *American Journal of Philology*, 62 (1941), pp 322–330; and 'A Roman Influence upon Chinese Painting', *Classical Philology*, 38 (1943), pp 13–19. His most detailed explanation of his theory came in a 1957 lecture which came out as a book: *A Roman City in Ancient China* (London, 1957); and was repeated in an article: 'A Roman City in Ancient China', *Greece and Rome*, 4 (1957), pp 139–148.

344 H Dubs, *A Roman City in Ancient China*, pp 1–3. It is interesting that he ended his first article by stating that there was no evidence of these men having been settled in China; Dubs, 'An Ancient Military Contact', p 329.

345 *History of the Former Han Dynasty*, translated by H Dubs, p 10.

346 W Tarn, *The Greeks in Bactria and India* (Cambridge, 1938).

347 *The Daily Telegraph*, 2 February 2007.

Appendix II

348 D Braund, 'Dionysiac Tragedy in Plutarch's Crassus', *Classical Quarterly*, 43 (1993), pp 468–474.

349 Dio, 39.10.3.
350 It is believed that Sallust made use of this source. It remained available to scholars for several centuries.
351 Caesar, *Civil Wars*, III. 31.3.
352 Velleius Paterculus, *History of Rome*, 2.46.4.
353 Notably in Appian, *Syrian Wars*, 9.1.
354 See F Adcock, *Marcus Crassus, millionaire* (Cambridge, 1966), p 59.
355 Strabo, *Geography*, 11.13.3.
356 Cicero, *Letters to Friends*, 13.16.1–2.
357 *Ibid*, 13.16.4.
358 See A Lintott, 'A Historian in Cicero *ad familiares* – P. Licinius(?) Apollonius', *Rheinisches Museum fur Philologie*, 119 (1976), p 368; and E Rawson, 'Crassorum Funera', *Latomus*, 41 (1982), p 548.
359 Rawson, 'Crassorum Funera'.
360 Cicero, *Letters to Atticus*, 5.21.2.
361 Lucian, *On the Writing of History*, 15 & 16.
362 Cicero, *De Divinatione*, 1.29, 2.22 and 2.84.
363 Dionysius of Halicarnassus, 2.6.4; Valerius Maximus, *Memorable Sayings*, 1.6.11.
364 Frontinus, *Stratagems*,1.1.13; Polyaenus, *Stratagems*, 7.41; Tacitus, *Germania*, 37.
365 Pliny, *Natural History*, 2.147, 5.86 and 6.47; Strabo, *Geography*, 12.3.34, 16.1.23 and 16.1.28.
366 Ovid, *Fasti*, 5.583–585.
367 Ovid, *Ars Amatoria*, 1.179–180.
368 Propertius, 2.10.13–14.
369 Propertius, 4.7.83–85.
370 Justin, *Epitome*, 42.4.4; Ammianus Marcellinus, 23.3.1; Zosimus, 3.23.3; Eutropius, 6.18.1; Orosius, 6.13.2–5; Jerome, *Chronology*, 181st Olympiad.
371 Jerome, *Chronology*, 181.2.
372 Sidonius, *Panegyric of Anthemus*, 454–456.
373 Sidonius, *To Felix*, 250–251.
374 Sidonius, *Panegyric of Avitus*, 98–100.
375 George Synkellos, *Chronography*. Interestingly, Crassus' plundering of the Temple treasure is is a fact which survives in no other source except Josephus.

Appendix III

376 In this respect they resemble the now-lost Roman pontifical annals, see B Frier, *Libri Annales Pontificum Maximorum: the Origins of the Annalistic Tradition* (Michigan, 1999).
377 See P Garner, *The Coinage of Parthia* (Chicago, 1968); and D Sellwood, *An Introduction to the Coinage of Parthia*, 2nd edition (London, 1980).
378 See A Invernizzi, 'Parthian Nisa, New Lines of Research' and F Miller, 'Dura-Europos under Parthian Rule', both in Wiesehöfer (ed), *Das Partherreich*, pp 45–59 and 473–492 respectively.
379 Walbank, *Historical Commentary on Polybius II*, p 232.
380 W Schoff, *The Parthian Stations of Isidore of Charax* (Philadelphia, 1914).
381 Strabo, *Geography*, 11.9.3.
382 Eusebius, in the entries for the 160th, 162nd and 171st olympiads; Jerome places the foundation of Arsacid rule in the first year of the 133rd olympiad.
383 Polybius, *Histories*, 10.27–31.

384 Athenaeus, *The Deipnosophists* 15.29; and Strabo, *Geography* 11.7.3.
385 See W Tarn, *Greeks in Bactria and India*, p 45.
386 Strabo, *Geography*, 11.9.3.
387 See Photius, *Bibliotheca*.
388 Notably in *Syrian Wars*, 9.1.
389 See F Hirth, *China and the Roman Orient*, 2nd edition (New York, 1966), p 35.
390 *Ibid*, p 139.
391 *Ibid*, p 36.

Bibliography

The Roman Conquest of the East

The books listed below are by no means a comprehensive list on what is a massive topic. They are merely a guide to the best works on the subject, and the ones used in this work. They have been limited to those from the mid-twentieth century or later and published in English.

1. The Roman Conquest of the East

Badian, E, *Foreign Clientelae* (264–70 B.C.) (Oxford, 1958).

―――, *Roman Imperialism in the Late Republic* (Ithaca, 1968).

―――, *Titus Quinctius Flamininus; Philhellenism and Realpolitik* (Cincinnati, 1970).

Ball, W, *Rome in the East* (London, 2000).

Broughton, T, *Magistrates of the Roman Republic, Volumes 1 & 2* (New York, 1952).

Champion, C, (ed.) *Roman Imperialism* (Oxford, 2004).

Champion, G, *Pyrrhus of Epirus* (Barnsley, 2009).

Cornell, T, *The Beginnings of Rome: Italy and Rome from the Bronze Age to the Punic War* (London, 1995).

Daly, G, *Cannae* (London, 2002).

Derow, P, 'The Arrival of Rome; From the Illyrian Wars to the Fall of the Macedon', in A. Erskine (ed.) *A Companion to the Hellenistic World* (London, 2003).

Eckstein, A, Senate *and General: Individual Decision Making and Roman Foreign Relations 264-194 B.C.* (Berkeley, 1987).

―――, *Mediterranean Anarchy, Interstate War and the Rise of Rome* (Berkeley, 2006).

―――, *Rome Enters the Greek East. From Anarchy to Hierarchy in the Hellenistic Mediterranean, 230-170 BC* (London, 2008).

Edkamp, P, (ed.), *A Companion to the Roman Army* (London, 2010).

Errington, R, 'The Alleged Syro-Macedonian Pact and the Origins of the Second Macedonian War' *Athenaeum* 49 (1971), 336-354.

―――, *Dawn of Empire: Rome's Rise to World Power* (London, 1972).

Evans, R, *Roman Conquests: Asia Minor, Syria and Armenia* (Barnsley, 2011).

Gabba, E, *Republican Rome, The Army and the Allies* (Berkeley, 1976).

Garoufalias, P, *Pyrrhus, King of Epirus* (London, 1979).

Graham, D, *Rome and Parthia: Power, Politics and Profit* (North Charleston, 2013).

Grainger, J, *The Roman War of Antiochus the Great* (Leiden, 2002).

―――, *Roman Conquests: Egypt and Judaea* (Barnsley, 2013).

―――, *Rome, Parthia and India: The Violent Emergence of a New World Order 150-140 BC* (Barnsley, 2013).

Green, P, *From Alexander to Actium* (Berkeley, 1990).

Grimal, P, (ed,) *Hellenism and the Rise of Rome* (London, 1968).

Greenhalgh, P, *Pompey, the Roman Alexander* (London, 1980).

Gruen, E, (ed.) *Imperialism in the Roman Republic* (New York, 1970).

_____, *The Hellenistic World and the Coming of Rome, Volumes I & 2* (Berkeley, 1984).

_____, *Studies in Greek Culture and Roman Policy* (Berkeley, 1996)

Harl, K, 'The Roman Experience in Iraq', *Journal of the Historical Society* 7 (2007), 213-227.

Hammond, N, 'Illyria, Rome and Macedon in 229-205 B.C.' *Journal of Roman Studies* 58 (1968), 1-21.

Harris, W, *War and Imperialism in Republican Rome 327-70 B.C.* (Oxford, 1979).

_____, (ed.) *The Imperialism of Mid-Republican Rome* (Rome, 1984).

Jashemski, W, *The Origins and History of the Proconsular and the Propraetorian Imperium to 27 B.C.* (Chicago, 1950).

Kallet-Marx, R, *Hegemony to Empire; The Development of the Roman Empire in the East from 148 to 62 B.C.* (Berkeley, 1995).

Keaveney, A, 'Roman Treaties with Parthia circa 95 – circa 64 B.C.', *American Journal of Philology* 102 (1981), 195-212.

_____, 'The King and the War-Lords: Romano-Parthian Relations Circa 64-53 B.C.', *American Journal of Philology* 103 (1982), 412-428.

Kennedy, D, 'Parthia and Rome; Eastern perspectives', in D. Kennedy (ed.) *The Roman Army in the East* (Michigan, 1996), 67-90.

Keppie, L, *The Making of the Roman Army* (London, 1984).

Magie, D, 'The 'Agreement' between Philip V and Antiochus III for the Partition of the Egyptian Empire', *Journal of Roman Studies* 29 (1939), 32-44.

_____, *Roman Rule in Asia Minor, Volumes I & II* (Princeton, 1950).

Mandell, S, 'The Isthmian Proclamation and the Early Stages of Roman Imperialism in the Near East', *Classical Bulletin* 65 (1989), 89-94.

Matyszak, P. *Mithridates the Great: Rome's Indomitable Enemy* (Barnsley, 2008).

_____, *Roman Conquests: Macedonia and Greece* (Barnsley, 2009).

Mayor, A, *The Poison King: The Life and Legend of Mithradates, Rome's Deadliest Enemy* (Princeton, 2011).

McGing, B, *The Foreign Policy of Mithridates VI Eupator King of Pontus* (Leiden, 1986).

Millar, F, *The Greek World, the Jews and the East* (Chapel Hill, 2006).

Raaflaub, K & Rosenstein, N, (eds.) *War and Society in the Ancient and Medieval Worlds* (Cambridge, 1999).

Raaflaub, K, (ed.) *War and Peace in the Ancient World* (London, 2007).

Rea, C, *Leviathan vs. Behemoth: The Roman-Parthian Wars 66 BC–217AD* (Milton Keynes, 2014)

Rich. J & Shipley, G, *War and Society in the Roman World* (London, 1993).

Rosenstein, N & Morstein-Marx, R, (eds.) *A Companion to the Roman Republic* (London, 2006).

Sartre, M, *The Middle East under Rome* (London, 2005).

Sheldon, M, *Rome's Wars in Parthia: Blood in the Sand* (London, 2010).

Sherk, R, (ed.) *Roman Documents from the Greek East* (Baltimore, 1969).

Sherwin-White, A, *Roman Foreign Policy in the East 168 B.C. – A.D. 1* (London, 1984)

Shotter, D, *Rome and Her Empire* (London, 2003).

Smith, R, *Service in the Post Marian Army* (Manchester, 1958).

Stark, F, *Rome on the Euphrates* (London, 1966).

Taylor, M, *Antiochus The Great* (Barnsley, 2013).

Toynbee, A, *Hannibal's Legacy: the Hannibalic War's Effects on Roman Life Volumes 1 & 2* (Oxford, 1965).

Traina, G, *Carrhes, 9 juin 53 av. J.-C. Anatomie d'une défaite* (Paris, 2010)

Wallace, R & Harris, E, *Transitions to Empire* (Oklahoma, 1996).

Walbank, F, *A Historical Commentary on Polybius, Volume II* (Oxford, 1967).

Waterfield, R, *Taken at the Flood: The Roman Conquest of Greece* (Oxford, 2014).

2. The Rise of Parthia

Arnaud, P, 'Les Guerres Parthiques de Gabinius et de Crassus et la politique occidentale des Parthes Arsacides entre 70 et 53 av. J.-C.', in E. Dabrowa (ed.) *Ancient Iran and the Mediterranean World* (Krakow, 1998), 13-34.

Assar, G, 'Recent Studies in Parthian History I', *The Celator 14.12* (2000), 6-22.

_____, 'Recent Studies in Parthian History II', *The Celator 15.1* (2001), 17-27 & 41.

_____, 'Recent Studies in Parthian History III', *The Celator 15.2* (2001), 17-22.

_____, 'Genealogy and Coinage of the Early Parthian Rulers I', *Parthica* 6 (2004), 69-93.

_____, 'Genealogy and Coinage of the Early Parthian Rulers II. A Revised Stemma', *Parthica* 7 (2005), 29-63.

_____, 'A Revised Parthian Chronology of the Period 165-91 BC', *Electrum* 11 (2006), 87-158.

_____, A Revised Parthian Chronology of the Period 91-55 BC', *Parthica* 8 (2006), 55-104

Bellinger, A. (1949). 'The End of the Seleucids', *Connecticut Academy of Arts and Sciences* 38, 51-102.

Bickermann, E, 'Notes on Seleucid and Parthian Chronology', *Berytus* 8 (1944), 73-83.

Bivar, A, 'The Political History of Iran under the Arsacids', in E. Yarshater (ed.) *The Cambridge History of Iran, Volume 3.1; The Seleucid, Parthian and Sasanian Periods* (Cambridge, 1983), 21-99.

Brodersen, K, 'The Date of the Secession of Parthia from the Seleucid Kingdom', *Historia* 35 (1986), 378-381.

Colledge, M, *The Parthians* (London, 1967).

_____, *Parthian Art* (London, 1977).

Curtis, J, *Mesopotamia and Iran in the Parthian and Sasanian Periods: Rejection and Revival c.238 BC- AD642* (London, 2000).

Dabrowa, E, 'The Political Propaganda of the First Arsacids and its Targets (From Arsaces I to Mithradates II)', *Parthica* 10 (2008), 25-31.

_____, *Studia Graeco-Parthica: Political and Cultural Relations Between Greeks and Parthians* (Wiesbaden, 2011).

Debeviose, N, 'Parthian Problems', *American Journal of Semitic Languages and Literatures* 47 (1931), 73-82.

_____, *A Political History of Parthia* (Chicago, 1938).

Dobbins, K, 'Mithradates II and his Successors ; A Study of the Parthian Crisis 90-70 BC', *Antichthon* 5 (1975), 63-79.

_____, 'The Successors of Mithradates II of Parthia', *Numismatic Chronicle* 15 (1975), 19-45

Dobiás, J, Les premiers rapports des romains avec les parthes et l'ocuptaion de la syria', *Archiv Orientalni* 3 (1931), 215-256.

Drijvers, J, 'Strabo on Parthia and the Parthians' in J. Wiesehöfer (ed.) *Das Partherreich und seine Zeugnisse* (Stuttgart, 1998), 279-293.

Fyre, R, 'Parthian and Sasanian History of Iran', in J. Curtis (ed.) *Mesopotamia and Iran in the Parthian and Sasanian Periods; Rejection and Revival c. 238 B.C.–A.D. 642* (London, 2000), 17-22.

Garner, P, *The Coinage of Parthia* (Chicago, 1968).

Grajetzki, W, *Greeks and Parthians in Mesopotamia and Beyond 331 BC – 224 AD* (London, 2011).

Invernizzi, A, 'Parthian Nisa, New Lines of Research', in J. Wiesehöfer (ed.) *Das Partherreich und seine Zeugnisse* (Stuttgart, 1998), 45-59.

Koselenko, G, 'Les Cavaliers Parthes', *Dialogues d'histoire ancienne* 6 (1980), 177-199.

Kuhrt, A & Sherwin-White, S, *Hellenism in the East* (London, 1987).

_____, *From Samarkhand to Sardis* (London, 1993).

Lerner, J, 'Seleucid Decline on the Eastern Iranian Plateau', *Berytus* 42 (1995/96), 103-112.

_____, *The Impact of Seleucid Decline on the Eastern Iranian Plateau* (Stuttgart, 1999).

Lewis, T, *The history of the Parthian Empire, from the foundation of the monarchy by Arsaces, to its final overthrow by Artaxerxes the Persian; contained in a succession of twenty nine kings* (London, 1728).

Lozinski, B, *The Original Homeland of the Parthians* (Hague, 1959).

Mielczarek, M, *Cataphracti and Clibanarii; Studies on the Heavy Armoured Cavalry of the Ancient World* (Lodz, 1993).

Newell, E, *Mithradates of Parthia and Hypaosines of Characene* (New York, 1925).

Neusner, J, 'Parthian Political Ideology', *Iranica antique* 3 (1963), 40-59.

Rawlinson, G, *The Sixth Great Oriental Monarchy; or the Geography, History & Antiquities of Parthia* (London, 1873).

Rea, C, *The Rise of Parthia in the East. From the Seleucid Empire to the Arrival of Rome* (Milton Keynes, 2013).

Sarkhosh-Curtsi, V, & Stewart, S (eds.) *The Age of the Parthians. The Idea of Iran, Volume II* (London, 2007).

Schippman, K, *Grundzüge der Parthischen Geschichte* (Darmstadt, 1980).

Schoff, W, *The Parthian Stations of Isidore of Charax* (Philadelphia, 1914).

Sellwood, D, *An Introduction to the Coinage of Parthia, 2nd edition,* (London, 1980).

Shayegan, M, *Arsacids and Sasanians: Political Ideology in Post-Hellenistic and Late Antique Persia* (Cambridge, 2011).

Tarn, W, 'Seleucid–Parthian Studies', *Proceedings of the British Academy* 16 (1930), 105-135.

_____, *The Greeks in Bactria and India* (Cambridge, 1938).

Van der Spek, R, 'New Evidence from the Babylonian Astronomical Diaries Concerning Seleucid and Arsacid History', *Archiv für Orientforschung* 44-45 (1997-8), 167-175.

Wiesehöfer, J., 'Kings of Kings and Philhellen; Kingship in Arsacid Iran', in P. Bilde, (ed.) *Aspects of Hellenistic Kingship* (Aarhus, 1996), 55-66.

_____, (ed.) *Das Partherreich und seine Zeugnisse* (Stuttgart, 1998).

_____, 'Iran from Arsaces I to Artabanus IV; the Parthian Reign', in *Ancient Persia* (London, 2006), 115-149.

Wolski, J, 'The Decay of the Iranian Empire of the Seleucids and the Chronology of the Parthian Beginnings', *Berytus* 12 (1956/8), 35-52.

_____, *L'Empire des Arsacides* (Lovanii, 1993).

_____, *The Seleucids, The Decline and Fall of Their Empire* (Krakow, 1999).

_____, *Seleucid and Arsacid Studies: A Progress Report on Developments in Source Research* (Krakow, 2003).

Ziegler, KH, *Die Beziehungen Zwischen Rom und dem Partherreich* (Wiesbaden, 1964).

3. Marcus Licinius Crassus

Unfortunately none of the three substantial biographies of Crassus are currently in print:

Adcock, F, *Marcus Crassus, Millionnaire* (Cambridge, 1966)

Marshall, B, *Crassus: A political Biography* (Amsterdam, 1976).

Ward, A, *Marcus Crassus and the Late Roman Republic* (Columbia, 1977).

There are however a number of articles which deal with aspects of Crassus' career.

Cadoux, T, 'Marcus Crassus; A Revaluation', *Greece and Rome* 3 (1956), 153-161.

Gray, D, *In the Shadow of Caesar: Marcus Licinius Crassus and the True Power Behind Caesar* (Milton Keynes, 2013)

Gruen, E, 'Pompey, the Roman Aristocracy and the Conference at Luca', *Historia* 18 (1969), 71-108.

Hillard, T, 'Crassus in 61', *Liverpool Classical Monthly* 6 (1981), 127-130.

Hillman, T, 'Plutarch and the First Consulship of Pompeius and Crassus', *Phoenix* 46 (1992), 124-137.

Linderski, J, 'Were Pompey and Crassus Elected in Absentia to their First Consulship?', *Mélanges offerts à Kazimierz michalowski* (Warsaw, 1966), 523-526.

Luibheid, C, 'The Luca Conference', *Classical Philology* 65 (1970), 88-94.

Marshall, B, 'Crassus' Ovation in 71 B.C.', *Historia* 21 (1972), 669-673.

_____, 'Crassus and the Command against Spartacus', *Athenaeum* 51 (1973), 109-121.

_____, 'Crassus and the Cognomen Dives', *Historia* 22 (1973), 459-467.

_____, 'Problems in the Career of Crassus', *Liverpool Classical Monthly* 3 (1978), 159-164.

Mattern-Parkes, S, 'The Defeat of Crassus and the Just War', *Classical World* 96 (2003), 387-396.

Parrish, E, 'Crassus' New Friends and Pompey's Return', *Phoenix* 27 (1973), 357-380.

Rawson, E, 'Crassourm Funera', *Latomus* 41 (1982), 540-549.

Regling, K, 'Crassus' Partherkrieg', *Klio* 7 (1907), 357-394.

Rowland, R, 'Crassus, Clodius, and Curio in the Year 59 B.C.', *Historia* 15 (1960), 217-223.

Rubinsohn, Z, 'A Note on Plutarch, Crassus X.1', *Historia* 19 91970), 624-627.

Salmon, E, 'Catiline, Crassus, and Caesar', *American Journal of Philology* 56 (1935), 302-316.

Sanders, H, 'The So-Called First Triumvirate', *Memoirs of the American Academy in Rome* 10 (1932), 55-68.

Simpson, A, 'The Departure of Crassus for Parthia', *Transactions and Proceedings of the American Philological Association* 69 (1938), 532-541.

Stanton, G, & Marshall, B, 'The Coalition between Pompeius and Crassus 60-59 B.C.', *Historia* 24 (1975) 205-219.

Syme, R, 'Piso Frugi and Crassus Frugi', *Journal of Roman Studies* 50 (1960), 12-20.

_____, 'The Sons of Crassus', *Latomus* 39 (1980), 403-408.

Timpe, D, 'Die Bedeutung der Schlact von Carrhae', *Museum Helveticum* 19 (1962), 104-129.

Ward, A, 'Cicero's Fight Against Crassus and Caesar in 65 and 63 B.C.', *Historia* 21 (1972), 244-258.

_____, 'Problems in the Career of Crassus', *Liverpool Classical Monthly* 3 (1978), 147-157.

4. Other Works Cited

Adler, W & Tuffin, P, *The Chronography of George Synkellos. A Byzantine Chronicle of Universal History from the Creation* (Oxford, 2002).

Braund, D, 'Dionysiac Tragedy in Plutarch's Crassus', *Classical Quarterly* 43 (1993), 468-474.

Dubs, H, 'An Ancient Military Contact between Romans and the Chinese', *American Journal of Philology* 62 (1941), 322-330.

_____, 'A Roman Influence upon Chinese Painting', *Classical Philology* 38 (1943), 13-19.

_____, *A Roman City in Ancient China* (London, 1957).

_____, 'A Roman City in Ancient China', *Greece and Rome* 4 (1957), 139-148.

Hoeing, C, 'A Roman Eagle in Rochester', *American Journal of Archaeology* 29 (1925), 172-179.

Hirth, F, *China and the Roman Orient: Researches Into Their Ancient and Mediaeval Relations as Represented in Old Chinese Records* (New York, 1966).

Holt, F, *Thundering Zeus: The Making of Hellenistic Bactria* (Berkeley, 1999).

Kennedy, D, 'Ancient Sources for Zeugma', *The Twin Towns of Zeugma on the Euphrates* (Michigan, 1998), 139-162.

Lintott, A, 'A Historian in Cicero *ad familiares* – P. Licinius (?) Apollonius', *Rheinisches Museum fur Philologie* 119 (1976), 368.

Moore, P, 'Two Notes on Pliny's Natural History', *Classical Review* 23 (1973), 13-14.

Rich, J, 'Augustus' Parthian Honours' *Papers of the British School of Rome* 66 (1998), 71-128.

Rose, C, 'The Parthians in Augustan Rome', *American Journal of Archaeology* 109 (2005), 21-75.

Sachs, A & Hunger, H, *Astronomical Diaries and Related Texts from Babylonia, Volume III* (Vienna, 1996).

Schoff, W, 'Some Aspects of the Overland Oriental Trade at the Christian Era',
Journal of the American Oriental Society 35 (1915), 31-41.

Sumner, G, *The Orators in Cicero's Brutus* (Toronto, 1973).

Syme, R, *The Augustan Aristocracy* (Oxford, 1986).

Index